The Mysterious Murder of Martha Moxley:

Did the Political and Financial Power of the Kennedy/Skakel Families Trump the Truth?

By Joe Bruno

Knickerbocker Publishing Company

© 2016, Joe Bruno
(jbruno999@aol.com)
ALL RIGHTS RESERVED. This book contains material protected under International and Federal Copyright Laws and Treaties. Any unauthorized reprint or use of this material is prohibited. No part of this book may be reproduced or transmitted in any form or by any means, electronic or mechanical, including photocopying, recording, or by any information storage and retrieval system without express written permission from the author / publisher.

*"Only the good die young.
And the evil seems to live forever."
- Iron Maiden*

Chapter One

"I Think She's Dead!"

It was Halloween morning 1975 in the Belle Haven section of the tony town of Greenwich, Connecticut, and 15-year-old Shelia McGuire set out to find her best friend, the blond and beautiful, Martha Moxley, who had mysteriously disappeared the night before.

The previous night was "Mischief" or "Hell Night" in Greenwich; a night in which the neighborhood youths, bored from experiencing the extravagances of the filthy rich, go on a yearly rampage to cause as much damage as possible. Armed with toilet paper, eggs, shaving cream, baseball bats, golf clubs, and M-80 explosives, the youths plotted to wreak havoc on the neighborhood's houses, mailboxes, traffic signs, and even the three two-man booths the guards use as command stations to protect the self-absorbed people of the neighborhood.

Shelia knew that Martha had made tentative plans the night before to unite with a gang of youthful revelers. But instead of joining the unruly crowd herself, Shelia attended a pre-Halloween party at the friend's house with a boy named David; a first date that Martha had arranged. Shelia had returned home at around midnight, not satisfied about how the date had gone and intent on telling Martha how miserably she had failed in wooing a boy she had a desperate crush on.

Warm in her bed, Shelia drifted off into a troubled sleep, and at 2 am she was awaken by her mother.

"Shelia, Dorthy Moxley is on the phone," her mother said. "She said her daughter Martha's not home yet, and she's wondering if she attended the same Halloween party as you did."

Shelia told her mother, that as far as she knew, Martha had gone to her boyfriend Jeffrey Grey's house to rustle him up some dinner. Shelia didn't mention that Martha's after-dinner activities included plans to decorate the town with eggs, toilet paper, and shaving cream, and any other goo they could get their hands on.

At 4 am, Dorthy Moxley again phoned Shelia's residence, and this time the extreme stress was evident in her voice.

"No, we still haven't seen or heard from Martha," Mrs. McGuire told Martha's mother.

After Mrs. McGuire hung up the phone, Shelia told her mother, "It's Mischief Night. Kids all over town are drinking, and who knows what else. Martha will be okay."

Thinking Martha was probably someplace sleeping off too much booze, or pot, or maybe both, Shelia dropped back into an uneasy sleep.

When Shelia woke up around 11 am, she discovered that Martha had still not returned home, and that the town was in a frenzy looking for the missing girl. Shelia decided to join the search.

After making the rounds of known make-out spots, Shelia soon found herself on a deserted patch of grass and trees on the northwest side of the Moxley property, just yards from Walsh Lane, which divided the Moxley's home from that of Rushton Skakel. Ethel Skakel Kennedy was Rushton Skakel's younger sister. Ethel was the wife of the late Robert F. Kennedy, the former Attorney General of the United States and the brother of John F. Kennedy, the assassinated President.

After crossing Walsh Lane, Shelia became fixated on a large, dreary, silvery-blue pine, which, even though its base was down a steep slope, still towered over the Moxley house, which was about 200 yards southeast of the tree. Suddenly, Shelia spotted something down the slope that looked like a blue mattress with a pink sleeping bag sitting on top of it. As

Shelia slowly stepped down the slope, the mattress and the sleeping bag started to take a different and unimaginable shape.

Shelia later said, "All of a sudden the picture I was seeing was not what I was telling myself it was, but rather this incredible horrific sight of this child that I knew so well. And there was no escaping what was before me now.

"Martha was lying on her stomach. Her feet were pointed toward the slope and her head was pointed toward her house. She was wearing navy-blue pinwale corduroy jeans, and they were pushed down and bunched up around her ankles. She was naked from the waist down. On her torso she had a navy L.L. Bean-style down jacket that had those Michelin Man puffs around them. I think her arms were up around her head. Her face was down.

"She had what I thought were scratches and gouges in her right hip. They were covered in blood and pine needles and debris. I was standing above her, so I had some view of her other side. On that side, too, she'd been scratched from her hips down to the thighs. And there was blood in her hair."

Shelia, tears streaming down both sides of her face, sprinted towards the Moxley house. When she got there, she banged frantically on the front door.

"Let me in, let me in!" she screamed.

Finally, the door was answered by Jean Walker, the wife of celebrated Beetle Bailey cartoonist, Mort Walker. Dorthy Moxley was right behind her.

"I found Martha," Shelia said.

"Where?" Dorthy said.

"Under the pine tree."

"Is she okay?"

"No, but she will be," Shelia said. "I think she was either raped, or attacked by dogs. We better call 911."

"I think we better go look," Walker said. She turned to Dorthy Moxley. "It would be better if you stood here."

Walker took Shelia's hand, and they hurried towards the slope where the tree was located. When they reached the top of the slope, Walker continued downward, while Shelia stood transfixed at the top of the slope.

"At first, I thought it was some kind of prank," Walker said.

As she inched forward towards the tree, Walker spotted Martha's body, partially hidden by the low, overhanging limbs of the tree that crouched down only inches from the ground. Fearing the worse, she bent down and touched the exposed small of Martha's back.

It was colder than the frost on a champagne glass.

Walker trudged up the slope, grabbed Shelia's hand again, and they headed back to the Moxley house.

Dorthy Moxley met them at the front door.

"Is Martha okay?" she asked.

"No, I'm afraid not," Walker said. "I think she's dead."

Chapter Two

The Funeral

On November 4, 1975, Martha Elizabeth Moxley was eulogized in a brief ceremony at the First Lutheran Church of Greenwich, before she was buried in nearby Putnam Cemetery. The ceremony was attended by more than 500 mourners, and the Greenwich Police Department, closing the barn door after the horse had escaped, was 15-strong, and they had surrounded the church as if they expected the murderer to suddenly appear and kill again. Their unofficial statement was that they were there "as much to see who did not attend and who did attend."

To add the bizarre to the ridiculous, Captain Thomas Keegan was hidden behind a row of cars, using a camera equipped with a long telephoto lens, to discreetly take pictures of the mourners for possible later use as evidence.

Evidence of what, Keegan did not fully explain.

The presses appearance at the church was not greatly appreciated by the locals. Students at Greenwich High School had been instructed, either by the school or by their parents, not to talk to the press. A handful of them even pelted a network television camera with stones, which caused the assembled media to scatter to safety.

The eulogy was written by Martha's classmates, who said Martha had once said while reflecting about death and dying, "I want everyone to be happy at my funeral and remember all the good times we had."

During the funeral ceremony at the church, Reverend Richard McManus offered the Moxley family his sympathy. "On behalf of the community of Greenwich, especially the Christian Community. You have experienced something which probably none of us has ever experienced and probably never will."

Reading from the eulogy written by the students, Reverend McManus said, "Martha was a happy girl who made friends easily and brightened the lives of everyone she met. Martha Moxley loved life. Every day was something special. She made more friends in only a short time in Greenwich (her family had moved from California in 1973) than most people made in a lifetime.

"She was always the first to come around, and she was fun to be around. It was an education to be with her. The Moxley family was the perfect foursome. They enjoyed tennis, skiing and dinner together. Martha loved her family, as well as her $100 cat and her collection of frogs."

After the church ceremony, a number of teenagers collapsed in tears as the coffin was lifted onto a hearse and then driven to Putnam Cemetery.

Chapter Three

The Skakels

Ethel Skakel Kennedy was born into an exceedingly rich family, even richer than the Kennedy family, whom she married into by tying the knot with Robert "Bobby" Kennedy on Saturday, June 17, 1950. At the time Ethel married RFK, the Skakels were reported to be the second richest family in America; second only to the family of Henry Ford. The Skakel's were of English descent, and they were died-in-the-wool Anglo-Saxon Protestants, unlike the Irish Kennedys, who, on the surface, were fervent Catholics.

On November 25, 1917, George Skakel, against his mother's wishes, married Ann "Big Ann" Brannack, whose parents were born dirt-poor in Liverpool, England and were devout Catholics. After his father James, died in 1916 from alcoholism, Skakel grew up in a household where to his mother, Grace, Catholicism was a dirty word. However, when his older brother Bill shocked his mother and married a Catholic girl a few months earlier, George told his mother, the former Mary Grace Jordan, that he, too, was intent on marrying a Catholic. His mother, already having lost one son to the Holy Catholic Church, became apoplectic when George slapped her with the bad news.

Big Ann, an extremely attractive woman, was over six feet tall and very persuasive. She saw George, who was 5 feet 4 inches and barely 140 pounds, as a good man, but more importantly, as a go-getter, who could improve her living conditions, which presently consisted of residing in a poor Irish Ghetto in Chicago.

Florence Kumpfer was a lifelong friend of Big Ann's.

Kumpfer said, "Ann was required to go to Church every day by her mother, Margaret, who was an Episcopalian who had converted to Catholicism. The nuns were very strict, but Ann was a Catholic's Catholic. Her mother had installed that strong, strong religion in her.

"Ann was a strong woman. She told George that if he wanted to marry her, he had no choice but to make a Catholic priest in a Catholic Church perform the service."

George was not a religious man, and he felt his mother's convictions were based on faulty beliefs. Even though his mother attended his wedding at St. Mary's Catholic Church, she was not too happy. She was even less happy when George and Big Ann moved into one of Chicago's densest Catholic neighborhoods, two blocks from a Catholic school and a Catholic church. It did not please Grace Skakel one bit when she learned that Big Ann's mother had moved in with George and Big Ann; living and breathing her Catholic way of life.

The six children born to George and Ann Skakel, due to their mother's Catholic fanaticism, were brought up, to different degrees, in the Catholic faith (George Sr. really didn't care one way or another). This led to their estrangement from Grace Skakel. Grace and her son, Bob, eventually moved to California.

"There was not a lot of closeness with grandmother Grace and Big Ann," said Bob Skakel. "The division between Big Ann's Catholicism and the Skakel's Protestantism was too strong."

The animosity was so great that Grace Skakel refused to visit her son George's family in Chicago. To try a reconciliation with his mother, George took his wife, his daughter, Ethel, and son, Jim, to California to meet his mother.

That turned out to be a disaster.

"George really loved those family get-togethers," Doris Skakel, his sister-in-law said. "But the bad blood and hostility between his wife and mother, two strong-willed, sharped tongued, and opinionated women was so overt that George finally dropped any hope for a reconciliation.

"During that visit, Big Ann grabbed Gracie, a tiny and frail-looking woman, as she walked out of the kitchen. Ann plunked Gracie on her knee and then proceeded to bounce her up and down like a little child. Gracie tried desperately to squirm free, but she was helpless in Big Ann's grip. Big Ann laughed so uproariously, you could hear her a block away. Gracie was horribly embarrassed. I was really shocked. If George had been there, he would have been very upset."

That was Big Ann's and her children's last visit to California.

When George wanted to see his mother, he told Big Ann that he was going on a "business trip." Big Ann saw through his charade, but she was so busy with her social endeavors, she hardly realized George was absent from her home.

By the late 1920s, George was the sole support of his mother, and he rained her with gifts, including a brand new model Ford.

Grace Skakel died of a heart attack on January 4, 1936. George flew to California for his mother's burial services, which was held in a small Episcopalian church. But Big Ann and her brood of six stayed put in Chicago.

Chapter Four

The Start of an Empire

In 1919, George Skakel and his two chums, Walter Gramm and Rushton Fordyce, started the Great Lakes Coal & Coke Company. Their offices were in the swank Standard Oil Building at 910 South Michigan Avenue, in Chicago, Illinois.

"George Skakel was a man of vision," said Walter Gramm's son, Patrick. "He was a man of inexhaustible energy and smarts. He was good with figures. He was a leader with savvy who wouldn't let anything stand in his way. Most importantly, he could smell a profit when he saw one."

From its inception, Skakel decided his company would be a maverick; they would only sell large quantities of high-quality coal, a risk his competitors wouldn't take for fear of getting stuck with unsold coal when sales were sluggish.

His son, George Jr., who was Ethel's older brother, later said of his father, "When my father got into the coal business, he said there was no use selling tons of coal or a carload of coal. Sell freight-rates and that's it! That was his mentality; just go for the big orders."

The main problem was that there were thousands of coal mines in the United States, and each had their own peculiar characteristics. George visited these mines, and by asking questions, he learned the differences.

Even though George had never gone beyond grade school, he was a voracious reader. He devoured books on chemistry, geology, and metallurgy, and he absorbed as much information as he could from the business journals.

Armed with this knowledge obtained by hard work and diligence, George concentrated on selling the coal that was more salable; meaning of higher quality. He also made side deals with the mine owners to buy large quantities at lower-than market prices. By selling better quality coal at cheaper prices, his best customers, like Standard Oil, flocked to buy their coal from Great Lakes Coal & Coke Co. Using this strategy, George drove his competitors into the ground, and like pressured water from a fireman's hose, the profits gushed in.

When George and his partners decided to build their own coal refining plant, the profits grew exponentially. They built their plant in Port Arthur, Texas, with a fifty-thousand-dollar loan from Continental of Chicago Bank. Large aluminum companies, like Alcoa, used refined coal to produce their aluminum, and George propelled his coal-processing company to the head of the line of those selling coal to the aluminum companies. His biggest coup was getting long-term contracts with Alcoa's competitors, Reynolds Aluminum and Kaiser Aluminum.

"My father and his partners bragged between them that they used to pay out that Port Arthur Plant every six weeks," said Jim Skakel, George's eldest son. "The plant cost fifty thousand dollars, and every six weeks they made fifty thousand dollars. After the first six weeks, they paid off their loan, and it was all pure profit from there on in.

"In theory, there was no reason for their company to exist. The oil companies and the aluminum companies could have easily dealt directly with each other. They didn't need Great Lakes. But they didn't want to bother; they had bigger fish to fry. Anyone could have done what George Skakel and his partners did. They were very lucky, and the money started rolling in."

Despite their different nationalities and religions, years later, part of the animosity between the Skakels and the Kennedys was that George Skakel made this fortune legitimately. While, on the other hand, Kennedy patriarch, Joseph A. Kennedy, made the bulk of his early wealth during Prohibition in the illegal bootlegging business, with Mafia partners like Frank Costello and Al Capone.

Unlike his mother and wife, George was very open-minded about religion. He once fired his plant's personnel manager because the man boasted to George that he would never hire a Catholic.

According to his son, Rushton, who later fathered Tommy and Michael Skakel, his father "held no prejudices pertaining to race, color, or creed."

"Everyone was equal in my father's eyes," Rushton said. "My father got the first 'Jew' as a member of the exclusive Greenwich Country Club in the 1940s. Me and my family were allowed to swim at the Jewish Community Center pool when we still lived in Chicago. The Jews were the only ones who could afford a good pool.

"My father was not a Catholic, but he was really godly-good. During my entire life, he only told me one joke that was not nice. He said, 'I know a lady who sleeps with cats [Katz]. And sometimes with Mr. Nussbaum, too.'"

Great Lakes Coal and Coke became a booming business, and uncultured Big Ann, poor from birth, spent her husband's money with gusto.

"George Skakel made money, and Ann Skakel showed him how to spend it," Florence Kumpfer said. "Ann felt that if anybody suddenly got a lot of money handed to them, they'd be stupid not to know how to spend it. And Big Ann wasn't stupid.

"She could buy anything she wanted because George was very generous. She aspired to have beautiful things, and if you had enough money like Big Ann did, you could have everything beautiful."

As much as Big Ann enjoyed spending money, she yearned for the Skakels to be considered philanthropists. She joined the Miserecordia Board, founded by Chicago's Cardinal Mundelein, in order to raise money for a home for unwed mothers, run by the Sisters of the Poor. Because of her outward nature and intimidating figure, Big Ann became one of the biggest fund-raisers on the board. Ann was further driven by the fact that the husbands of all the other woman fund-raisers were Catholic, unlike her husband, George, who was tepid to any religion, including the Catholic Church.

"Ann became active in everything," Florence Kumpfer said. "She was a church woman, joining church boards and frequently running church functions, such as bridge and sewing parties. She also got involved in political organizations, mostly for the socializing."

But no matter how hard she tried, Big Ann's money didn't buy her the respect she coveted from her contemporaries.

"Despite all of Ann's efforts to reinvent herself, she still wasn't very sophisticated or cosmopolitan," said Patrick Gramm, whose mother was a member of Chicago's WASP society. "Ann Skakel was part of the Irish enclave on the South Side, a very fine lace-curtain group. She was a woman who found her greatest satisfaction within the confines of her church as a devout Catholic. There were always a few priests around the Skakel house."

For his part, George exalted in his new-found wealth, and he played the part of a successful businessman to the hilt. He joined the posh Chicago Athletic Club, and he became one of the few non-Catholic members of the Catholic South Shore Country Club. It was on the links of the latter that George hobnobbed with the swells, and he boasted to his mother that he had played golf with the general manager of the Illinois Central Railroad and the Lieutenant Governor of Ohio.

But both George and Big Ann Skakel had a dirty little secret that was not a secret at all to those who closely observed their behavior. George and Big Ann had addictive personalities, and they both drank too much in their respective activities. George did his imbibing on the golf courses, in country clubs, and at power lunches. Big Ann did her drinking mostly at dinner parties.

"Neither of them could drink," Florence Kumpfer said. "They just couldn't hold their liquor."

Whereas George's alcoholism was hereditary (his father drank himself to death), Big Ann got caught up in the gleeful whirlwind of her luxurious affairs.

For most of his life, George was a functional alcoholic, offset by long periods of going on the wagon, only to fall off much harder than before. Big Ann was a borderline alcoholic, struggling to attend dinner parties, while nursing a short beer, or a long scotch.

As we shall see, this curse of alcoholism would trickle down to haunt future generations.

Chapter Five

Ethel Skakel

On April 26, 1928, Ethel Skakel was born kicking and screaming in Chicago's Lying-In Hospital. Although tiny Ethel was underweight for a newborn, she screamed louder and longer than any of the other babies born at the maternity hospital on that same day. For Big Ann, now 36 years old and pushing 200 pounds pre-pregnancy, it would be her next-to-last child.

The Skakel child born right before Ethel was Patricia. She was born with a club foot, and she needed more than a dozen operations by the time Ethel was born. So, it concerned Big Ann that Ethel seemed to be overly frail.

"The doctors told George and Ann that Ethel was perfectly healthy and not to worry about her small size." Florence Kumpfer said. "They also pointed out that Ethel's sisters, Georgeann, now nine, and Pat, were also petite, perhaps taking after her father."

With George's money, Big Ann was able to hire the help she needed to take care of the children so that she could continue with her social activities. With George being a workaholic, the Skakel children were often under the care and supervision of hired help, and subsequently, they saw very little of their parents.

"At the core, George Skakel was a businessman," Patrick Graham said. "He didn't have time for his family."

Jim Skakel, the eldest Skakel son, was even unkinder to his father.

Jim Skakel said, "If all his kids had been born without legs, that would have been the luck of the draw. Dad would still be out doing business."

As George Skakel's Great Lakes Coal & Coke Co grew to immense proportions, he often took long trips around the country to promote his business. And Big Ann was right there at his side to bask in the glow of his achievements.

"Mrs. Brannack, Ann's mother, actually helped raise those children," Florence Kumpfer said.

Rushton Skakel, the future father of Thomas and Michael Skakel, admitted his generation of Skakel children were psychologically harmed by the continued absence of both parents.

"They were gone for three months at a time," Rushton Skakel said. "We always missed them."

Jim Skakel was named after his alcoholic grandfather. Because of his constant erratic and sometimes violent behavior, Jim demanded most of his parent's attention.

"Jimmy was a wild one, a terror, a little villain," Florence Kumpfer said. "He was into everything, so he demanded more attention. He was the oldest boy, his mother's favorite, and Ann had the most problems with him. I remember he came to visit us one night for dinner and we all had to go to church. When we returned, we discovered that he had entered the basement of the apartment house behind us and had stolen the toys of the children who lived there."

As a result of Jim's wild behavior, combined with Patricia's handicap, Ethel got the short end of the attention stick from her parents.

Big Ann, without her husband's consent or permission, decided to raise all her children as Catholics. This did not go over well with George, who, by nature, was calm and thoughtful, unlike Big Ann, who was the life of every party. Still, George said nothing to Big Ann about his misgivings about raising his children as Catholics.

But he did open up to his brother Curt's second wife, Doris.

"I remember we were talking about our families," Doris said. "And George said 'Sometimes my children don't seem to belong to me.' My mouth dropped because I knew George loved his children. He gave me the strong feeling that he felt alienated from them because Ann was such a strong Catholic. He never felt a part of any of that. The whole Catholic issue put a strain on their marriage."

Chapter Six

The Stock Market Crash of 1929 and the Great Depression

On October 29, 1929, Black Tuesday pummeled Wall Street into the state of chaos, fear, and hopelessness. Billions of dollars flowed down the drain (it was reported that there were $50 billion of losses in the first week alone), and thousands of investors were left penniless. By the end of the first day, the Wall Street area of Downtown Manhattan was filled with mindless investors, who, like zombies, aimlessly shuffled down the street in the state of shock.

During the 1920s, the U.S. stock market underwent rapid expansion, reaching its peak in August 1929, after a period of wild speculation. By then, production had already declined and unemployment had risen, leaving stocks in great excess of their real value. Among the other causes of the eventual market collapse were low wages, the proliferation of debt, a struggling agricultural sector, and an excess of large bank loans that could not be liquidated.

Stock prices began to decline in September, and they continued their descent into October. On October 18, the collapse began.

Panic set in, and on October 24, Black Thursday, a record 12,894,650 shares were traded. Investment companies and leading bankers attempted to stabilize the market by buying up great blocks of stock, producing a moderate rally on Friday.

On Monday, however, the tempest started again, and the market went into a total free-fall. Black Monday was followed by Black Tuesday, in which stock prices collapsed completely, and 16,410,030 shares were traded on the New York Stock Exchange in that single day. Billions of dollars were lost, wiping out thousands of investors, and stock tickers ran hours behind because the machinery could not handle the tremendous volume of trading.

After October 29, stock prices rebounded and there was a considerable recovery during the following weeks. But that was only a temporary reprieve.

In 1930, stock prices continued to drop as the United States slumped into the Great Depression, and by 1932 stocks were worth only about 20 percent of their value in the summer of 1929.

The stock market crash of 1929 was not the sole cause of the Great Depression, but it did accelerate the global economic collapse of which it was also a symptom. By 1933, nearly half of America's banks had failed, and unemployment was approaching 15 million people, or 30 percent of the workforce.

While the above is all too true, the story of desperate investors jumping out of windows to their deaths was a myth accidentally perpetrated by Will Rodgers, the famed American cowboy, stage and motion picture actor, and humorist, who wrote a nationally syndicated newspaper column.

A few weeks after the crash, Rogers wrote, in what was supposed to be a comedic piece, "When Wall Street took that tail spin, you had to stand in line to get a window to jump out of, and spectators were selling space for bodies in the East River."

Yet, newspapers around the country ran this article as factual, and the suicide myth grew exponentially.

The truth is, as a result of the stock market crash, there was only one reported jumping suicide, and it happened on the day after the crash and could have been for any reason, including accidental loss of balance, or temporary insanity.

Winston Churchill, the great British statesman, was visiting New York City during the crash. He witnessed the lone window-jumper.

Churchill later wrote: "Under my very window a gentleman cast himself down fifteen stories and was dashed to pieces, causing a wild commotion and the arrival of the fire brigade. But we don't know why the man committed suicide. It could have been because of the crash, or it could have been because of any number of other reasons that people kill themselves over."

The second reported stock market crash-related suicide didn't happened until November 8, and this victim used a gunshot wound to the side of his head to end his life.

After the crash, financier, Wellington Lytle, had only four cents left to his name. Before he blew his brains against the far wall, he left a suicide note that said, in part, "My body should go to science, my soul to Andrew W. Mellon, and my sympathy to my creditors."

The fact is, after the stock market crash, sticking ones head into a gas oven was the most popular form of self-destruction.

The Stock Market Crash of 1929 ruined most businessmen, and while it put a severe dent in George Skakel's bank account, it didn't wipe him out.

George Skakel was heavy into the stock market. But unlike most others, he bought stocks with ready cash, and not on margin, where an investor buys a stock with a small percentage down, and a loan from his broker for the balance, paying full interest on the loan. When a stock goes down precipitously, as it did on Black Tuesday, the broker can activate the dreaded "margin call" (in other words pay off the balance now, or else), erasing fortunes in a matter of seconds.

Since he had no margin calls to worry about, George lost only the money he actually had invested in the stock market.

"Dad didn't go broke," Jim Skakel said. "But he didn't have the money that he had before. One minute we had a big house near the University of Chicago. When the bottom fell out, we were back in an apartment on Drexel Boulevard."

What helped George Skakel survive during the Great Depression was that instead of a three-way partner split of the profits from Great Lakes Coal and Coke, it suddenly became a two-way split, 80% in his favor.

Rushton Fordyce was a drunkard, and it cost him his percentage of the business.

"Fordyce was a drinking man, and one day he turned in an order for a couple of truckloads of coal to be shipped to Standard Oil," Jim Skakel said. "My father got the coal and had it delivered. A few days later, the head of the refinery, Fordyce's father-in-law, called and said, "What the hell is this?' My father said, 'It's the coal your ordered.' The head of the refinery said, 'George, I know you well. You wouldn't do anything like this. We'll take the coal, but we didn't order it.'

"Fordyce was drinking, and he just made up the order out of thin air."

George Skakel was an honorable man, and he expected his partners to act in the same manner. As a result, when the partnership was formed, George insisted that the following clause be part of the contract:

"If any of the participants to this contract flagrantly and clearly violate any of the terms, the partnership may be dissolved by any of the partners who have not violated the terms."

With Fordyce in clear violation of maintaining the integrity of Great Lakes Coal and Coke, George threw him out on his ear, without as much as a "fare-thee-well."

Soon, the fifty-fifty split between George and his remaining partner, Walter Gramm, became an eighty-twenty split, the big piece of the pie going to George Skakel.

One day, it came to George's attention that Gramm was playing the stock market on margin with company funds. This was another clear violation of the original partnership agreement. But instead of giving Gramm the old heave-ho like he did with Fordyce, because Gramm was such a value to the company, George kept him on as a twenty-percent partner.

During the Depression, George and Gramm sometimes needed ready cash to keep the company from going under. Since their reputation in the business was so pristine, creditors mostly gave them what they needed. But one time, with money short all around, it was Big Ann, herself, who bailed out Great Lakes Coal and Coke, and she did it with her own husband's cash.

"Aunt Ann was a resourceful woman," said Betty Skakel Medaille, William Skakel's (George's older brother's) daughter. "Over the years, Uncle George would ask her how much she needed to run the house. She would tell him a figure that was twice as much as she actually needed. He would fork it over, without a word, and she would bank half of it. And then in the middle of the month, she'd come to George again. So she had a healthy little account. When the Crash came, and George found his private parts in the proverbial sling, Aunt Ann said, 'Here, dear, let me help you out.'"

But it was the Great Lakes Coal and Coke's relationship with oil companies, like Standard Oil, that kept them thriving during the Depression while other companies bit the dust.

"Those people were willing to carry the company for a while," Patrick Gramm said. "George and my father had marvelous relationships with their suppliers, the oil companies, who had deep pockets. The oil companies saw Great Lakes Coal as doing a great service for them – making a market for the petroleum coke. The oil companies didn't want to see them go under, so they said, 'Well, don't worry about paying the bills for a while.'

"I remember in the thirties, when everyone else was doing badly, we were living a very good life."

By the mid-1930s, when most companies were failing, Great Lakes Coal and Coke was thriving. The reason was aluminum.

Aluminum was used to manufacture airplanes, and Great Lakes Coal and Coke had a virtual monopoly on the metal. With the airplane industry in accelerated ascent, aluminum became almost as valuable as gold. Very quietly, George Skakel, with his 80% of Great Lakes Coal and Coke, became one of the richest men in America. If not quite in the same monetary stratosphere as John D. Rockefeller, Henry Ford, and Andrew Mellon, George became a legitimate multimillionaire and reportedly one of the 20 richest men in the United States.

Jim Skakel said, "In judging other men, my father's standard was when those men made their fortune, not how big it was. He was always proud he made his money in the Depression; the worst of the Depression."

One of the keys to George's success was his firm belief that no publicity was good publicity. All the major newspapers in the country tried to get interviews with George to find the secret of his success, but George would have none of that.

"You can't quote silence," was George's motto.

"We always tried to keep a low profile," Patrick Gramm said. "We never sought public relations, because we were one of the largest private companies and had a monopolistic position in certain areas, and we just didn't want to attract attention to ourselves. We just stayed quiet and made money."

After Robert Kennedy married Ethel Skakel, there was an internal strife between the two rich and powerful families; one being Irish-Catholic with big national ambitions, the other being a mixed bag, with Big Ann firmly in the Pope's corner, and George Skakel, of English descent, decidedly unreligious and with a "mum's the word," outlook on life.

A Skakel confidant later said, "The difference between George Skakel and Joe Kennedy was that old man Skakel paid to keep his name out of the newspapers, and old man Kennedy paid to put his name in the newspapers."

Chapter Seven

The Skakels Move East

Big Ann Skakel was nothing if not full of surprises.

With six kids already in the bank, Ethel being the youngest, in May of 1932, long-and-large-bodied Big Ann Skakel told jockey-sized George Skakel that he had done it again. At age 40, Big Ann was pregnant.

One Skakel confidant jokingly told another, "Jesus, seven kids with that Amazon! I don't know who puts him up to it!"

The joyous day was February 14, Valentine's Day, when blond and blue-eyed "Little Ann" Skakel burst into this world.

"Little Ann looked like her mother more than any of the others," Florence Kumpfer said. "She was their only blond child."

Because his business was divided between Chicago and New York City, the Big Apple now getting most of Great Lakes Coal and Coke's play, George Skakel decided to move his brood to the Northeast. Since it was late spring, he settled on a rented house in Monmouth Beach, New Jersey, nearly 60 miles from New York City, where he had his office in the two-year-old Empire State Building. Because all her friends, family, and social activities were in Chicago, this wasn't exactly great news for Big Ann. But, as always, she made the best of a bad situation.

While George toiled in Manhattan (a two-hour commute, including a ferry ride each way), Big Ann hit the beach daily with her seven children, aided by two nannies and the ever-present Florence Kumpfer. This is when Big Ann first got an inkling that maybe little Ethel was somewhat of a tomboy.

"Ethel was a cute and talkative and agreeable little girl who played with the boys all the time," Kumpfer said. "But there was nothing exceptional about her. She toddled along with the rest of them."

In September, the summer season being over and the beach no longer a lure, George moved his family to a rented mansion in Larchmont, New York, twenty-five miles northeast of Manhattan. The house, which came fully furnished, was set on a dozen acres, and there were so many rooms, no one in the family had actually visited all of them.

"It was a fabulous place," said Rushton Skakel. "It was so big, none of us could believe it, and it was mind-boggling beautiful."

Since there was a Catholic church and school directly across the road, the mansion was especially appealing to Big Ann, who immediately enrolled six of her children in the Dominican Day School, a privately-funded school, ruled with an iron ruler by Sister Alma Rose, a disciplinarian of the highest order.

A parent of one of the students said, "Sister Alma Rose was in her mid-thirties, and she had something of a masculine nature and mentality – direct and hard."

Big Ann knew her children had been spoiled from birth, and now it was time for a little discipline. Big Ann figured Sister Alma Rose was just what her bratty Skakel kids needed to set them on the straight and narrow.

Sadly, even the stern Sister Alma could do nothing to change the continued troubling behavior of the Skakel children.

Chapter Eight

Family Alcoholism

While the Skakel children continued to struggle in school, George and Big Ann Skakel began banging the bottle on a daily basis.

Playing "Lord of the Manor" to the hilt, George held parties almost every day of the week. Most were "business meetings," where George's colleagues and customers were motored in by limousine from New York City. George had the limos stocked with the finest booze money could buy, so when the guests arrived, they were more than a little gassed and ready to blast into full-party mode.

Dozens of servants attended to the guests, bestowing on them the primest cuts of beef, pork and veal, in addition the most pricy pearls of the sea, including Scottish Lobster, Coffin Bay King Oysters, Black King Kong Shrimp, and of course, Beluga Caviar – all of which were not easy to come by in the depths of the Depression. Besides having almost unlimited cash, George also had the connections to get whatever commodity he wanted, legally, or if necessary, illegally (Prohibition ended on December 5, 1933, which made top-shelf booze easier and much cheaper to obtain).

To impress his guests, George planned the spectacular surprise of serving the Japanese fish delicacy "Fugu." But he was talked out of it by his supplier, who told George that "Fugu is one of the most deadly fish in the world, and if not prepared properly, one drop of Fugu poison can instantly kill a human being."

"In that case, let's go with the Bluefin Tuna," George said.

Wanting to give his guests the impression that the Skakels and their children were a wholesome All-American family, all seven of the Skakel children, even the toddler, Annie, became part of George Skakel's elaborate presentation to his guests.

It was like a Tom Tierney 1920s Paper Dolls full color book come to life.

Rushton Skakel, who like his father, lived life as an alcoholic, later said, "I was ten years old when I moved into the house in Larchmont. That house, like all of our houses, was used mainly for business. It was the way for Dad to get together with his customers. Dad was establishing his business in New York City, so my parents had party after party. There were parties literally every day.

"That's when Dad started drinking. Dad's alcoholism hit him when we were in Larchmont because of all the parties and all of the drinking that took place. My mother drank, but I never considered her an alcoholic. At least, I never saw her snookered like Dad was every day.

"And that's when we children started drinking. As little tots, my sisters, and brothers, and I would take glasses with a little liquor, or a little wine left in them into the kitchen. And instead of emptying the alcohol into the sink, we drank it. My sister, Georgeann, who was 15 when we got to Larchmont, was already an alcoholic. Alcohol ran through our family. That's how we grew up."

Mary Begley was a friend of the Skakel family, and she witnessed the Skakel kids boozing it up first hand.

"Georgeann Skakel wasn't the only one of the Skakel children who had a drinking problem," Begley said. "Jimmy Skakel had a horrible reputation as an alcoholic. We would hear about those 'crazy Skakels' and people would say, 'Oh, can you imagine the Skakels? They have a son who's an alcoholic at the age of sixteen."

Maybe George Skakel got tired of waking up hung-over every morning, or maybe Big Ann saw the month's food and booze bills, and said "enough is enough!" But after two years of bedlam and booze in the mansion in Larchmont, the Skakels moved into a white, Colonial-style house in Rye, New York, five miles northeast of Larchmont. The whispered reason for the move was that Sister Rose Lima had given up on correcting the Skakel kid's bad behavior, so Big Ann was forced to decide on a different tactic.

Instead of educating her sons, Jim, 14, George Jr., 13, and Rushton, 12, in a school at Rye, Big Ann sent them to Canterbury in New Milford, Connecticut, a Roman Catholic school known for its monastic discipline. Canterbury was run by a no-nonsense disciplinarian, Dr. Nelson Hume, who opened the school in 1915 with only 15 students on board. 101 years later, Canterbury is still going strong, and in 2016, it had 350 boarding and day students.

Dr. Hume's original staff consisted of his brother, Alec, who concentrated on the boys in the lower grades of grammar school. Also on the staff was Phil Brodie, who taught Latin and was the Director of Athletics. He was called "The Czar of the Dining Room," for his no-nonsense insistence of perfect decorum while the students dined.

The days were filled with classes on boring subjects like math and science, in addition to a daily two-hour spiel on the essential doctrines and the vagaries of the Catholic religion. Canterbury had a strict set of rules, and if a student wouldn't or couldn't properly adjust to the tasks at hand, they were immediately expelled. Several years before the Skakels attended Canterbury, one of the students who couldn't cut it, and quit before he was tossed, was John Fitzgerald Kennedy.

The Skakel boys had been coddled since birth, and any form of discipline to them, especially the type insisted on at Canterbury, was a foreign concept.

"It was a strict school in the English tradition, with tea time in the morning, noon tea, and tea again at night," the underachieving Jim Skakel said. "All the students had to wear blazers, and the highest grade you could get, if you were lucky, was a 65, which was passing. The reason our grades were so low was because they'd lower your score for signing your name or the date improperly, or they'd dock you if you didn't perform your tasks fast enough. The discipline was just too tough for most of us."

Not surprisingly, Jim Skakel was given the gate from Canterbury, after just one year in attendance, because he threw a tantrum at a member of the Canterbury staff.

Jim tried to explain his expulsion thusly: "I caught the headmistress of the house I was living in going through my bureau drawers and my clothes and other stuff. She was just one of those nosy broads, but that was my personal property and nobody touched that. I told her off and that was that."

In May of 1935, after Dr. Hume expelled Jim, he contacted Big Ann and explained to her that maybe Canterbury was not the ideal institution for all three of her boys.

As a result, Big Ann decided to send a distress signal to Sister Rose Alma at the Dominican Day School, where Pat, 9, and Ethel, 7, were still students.

Big Ann phoned Sister Alma, and said, "You have to help me do something with my boys. I can't control them anymore."

"I think I have an idea," Sister Rose Alma said.

"Please Sister, I'll try anything," Big Ann said.

"Today is Saturday," Sister Rose Alma said. "Meet me in my study at noon on Monday. I have someone I think you'll want to meet."

When Big Ann arrived at Sister Rose Alma's study, she was greeted by the good sister, who introduced her to 21-year-old Martin Boswell McKneally, a pre-law major at Holy Cross. Decades later, McKneally, after serving in the Army in the Second World War, became the National Commander of the American Legion. He was then elected to Congress, and he served for two years, from January 3, 1969, until January 3, 1971.

But in 1935, he was just an ambitious young man who saw the cash-cow potential of the Skakels.

"I think you should consider Mr. McKneally as a companion for your children and a tutor for the boys," Sister Rose Alma told Big Ann.

The problem for Big Ann, besides the obvious, was that she was planning a three-month summer vacation in Europe with her husband, George, and getting her three out-of-control teenagers out of her graying hair was of paramount importance.

The first thing Big Ann noticed about McKneally was that he was exceedingly handsome, if a little on the effeminate side. Even though he was from Newburgh, New York, McKneally spoke with an affected stage-oriented accent, as if he were imitating the famed English actor, Lawrence Olivier.

But this was no time to quibble. So, Big Ann, after just a cursory interview, hired McKneally on the spot to be a companion for her children for the summer.

"If he's good enough for Sister Rose Alma, he's good enough for us," Big Ann told her husband.

"Well, I'd like to see for myself," George said.

McKneally, on the other hand, seemed to be more impressed with Big Ann than she was with him, at least at the beginning of their relationship.

"She was a woman of great largesse, a woman of enormous personality, charm and vigor," McKneally said. "She had great style and the money to back it up."

Just days after his meeting with Big Ann, McKneally arrived at the Skakel house for the Easter holidays so that George Skakel could give him the once-over. George liked what he saw, and was so impressed with McKneally, that besides giving him the task of watching his children for the summer, he told McKneally that if he met expectations he would find a place for him at Great Lakes Coal and Coke.

"He liked the way I presented myself," McKneally later said. "He seemed desperately anxious to have someone in his company with whom he could be close; a confident, so to speak. He needed someone whose loyalty and commitment would be beyond reproach."

As for the boys, McKneally seemed overly enraptured with them, which, years later, would make sense to everyone, when McKneally came out of the closet as a gay man, not a fashionable thing to do at the time.

"From the beginning I was highly attracted to the boys," McKneally said. "They were extraordinarily handsome and could have been movie actors. They enjoyed wit, humor, and laughs. I went upstairs with them to the third floor where they had their bedrooms, and soon we all became great friends."

McKneally had a totally different take on Ethel.

"Ethel was a mere child at the time," McKneally said. "She loved the wildness of her brothers, and she followed them around like a puppy dog. She seemed always lost and not very bright. She had to find her own identity, which was riding horses and athletics. But she was a most charming girl who gave her father much pleasure, when he was home, which wasn't often. She liked to entertain him by clowning around to get his attention. She was a real funny girl, relating to him in a special way."

McKneally also pointed out the correlation between Big Ann's relationship with her husband and Ethel's relationship with the man she would later marry.

"Big Ann always felt she had to be with her husband, just as later Ethel felt she had to always be with Bobby (Kennedy)," McKneally said.

With the summer drawing to a close, and her girls firmly ensconced at the Dominican Day School, it was Big Ann's task to find edifices of education for her sons. She decided the best thing to do was to separate them, so they could sink or swim on their own.

Using a little arm-bending – Big Ann was real good at that – she was able to convince Dr. Nelson Hume to take Rushton, the calmest of the Skakel boys, back at Canterbury.

In addition, Big Ann deposited Jim at the non-Catholic boarding school, Raymond Riordan in Highland, New York. There, Jim leaned how to fly planes and play football, and little else. The school was so lax in its rules, it was right up Jim Skakel's alley.

As for George Jr., he took up residence at the Portsmouth Priory, located on Narragansett Bay on Portsmouth; a Canterbury clone run by Benedictine monks, one of whom had only one eye, and it was always bloodshot. That lone orb was particularly foreboding to young George, who, during his stay at Portsmouth Priority, diligently minded his P's and Q's – of vodka.

One of George's classmates was the physically tiny and scholastically unimpressive, Robert Francis Kennedy, who George told his brothers was "a little dick with ears."

Years later "Little Dick" Kennedy would marry George's sister, Ethel, bringing together two privileged families with more skeletons in their closets than Vincent Price.

Chapter Nine

The Skakels Move to Greenwich, Connecticut

In 1935, the Skakels made a financially strategic move to a 30-room country manor on Lake Avenue in Greenwich, Connecticut, a bastion of blue-blooded Anglo-Saxton Protestants. There was no sign at the Greenwich border that said, "Catholics Need Not Apply," but there might as well have been.

But Big Ann knew what she wanted, and she would not let well-healed wannabe aristocrats stand in her way. Her only friend was the perpetually perplexed and aptly named, Dodo Jacobs, the wife of an executive at AT&T, whose daughter, Anita, chummed with Big Ann's daughter, Ethel, at the storied Greenwich Academy.

Dodo once asked Big Ann, "Why in God's name did you move to Greenwich, of all places?"

Prior to 1991, there was no state income tax in Connecticut and that fact wasn't lost on George Skakel.

"Why? Because of the taxes," Big Ann said. "My George is making so much money, and with all the stupid taxes in New York City and New York State, combined with the federal taxes, we were absolutely up to our necks in taxes."

But then Big Ann's shoulder slumped, and she told Dodo, "The truth is I am miserable here. I'd be willing to crawl the length of Michigan Avenue on my hands and knees if only my husband would take me back to Chicago."

When it came to making money George Skakel was a genius, but he was also no slouch when it came to saving money.

After her husband, Zalmon Simmons Jr., heir to the Simmons Bedding Company fortune, passed away in 1934, Frances Simmons was living all alone in a 30-room Greenwich mansion. Since her sons were living in mansions on either side of her, it would have been foolish for Frances to continue in her present living conditions. Minutes after her husband was comfortably six feet under, Frances put the mansion up for sale. But alas, due to the Depression, not many people had enough money for a down payment, let alone the ability to buy it in cash.

Enter George "Deep Pockets" Skakel.

"Dad paid only $100,000 for the house," said Rushton Skakel. "In those days that was a fortune to most people, but to my father it was pocket money."

For his hundred grand, George Skakel not only bought the house of Big Ann's dreams, but Mrs. Simmons threw in all her furniture for free; including, reportedly, several king-sized Simmons mattresses. The truth was that Frances Simmons knew it was impossible to get rid of her clunky furniture at any price, and it would cost her big bucks to have the furniture carted away.

Pat Grant Mudge was a classmate of Ethel's at the Greenwich Academy. She had the pleasure of being a house guest of the Skakels on numerous occasions.

"The furniture was big and heavy and dark," Pat Mudge said. "It had great big tables and sideboards and other ornate things. They were almost like church pieces. You couldn't use those pieces in any other house because they were so monstrously large."

The Greenwich residents, to George Skakel's dismay, looked at the Skakels like they were dog excrement on the soles of their shoes.

One of the nicest things said about the Skakels was that they were, "a little bizarre."

Another old-time Greenwich male resident was a little more precise.

"Rowdy, Irish pricks," is how he defined them.

One young lass, friendly with Ethel, and whose family had lived in Greenwich since the Pilgrims landed at Plymouth Rock, said, "My parents and Ethel's just wouldn't have been congenial together. Their backgrounds were so different. They just didn't have anything in common."

Pam Jacobs, another one of Dodo's daughters, was more than a little insulted when Ethel once told her, "My family loved Larchmont so much better because the people in Larchmont are not as snobbish as those in Greenwich, and there are more Catholics there.

"Despite all their money, the Skakels were not in the Greenwich Social Register, and that was a very sad problem for them," Pam Jacobs said. "I felt the Skakels were sort of pathetic, moving in the same place with this incredible powerhouse of people – the WASP culture of the world – and they did it only because of taxes. They were too naïve to know what they were getting into. They were totally ignored, shunned.

"It was hurtful for Ethel, too. But her way of dealing with it was to joke about herself."

Rushton Skakel hung around Greenwich until 1993; 18 years after the murder of Martha Moxley cast suspicion on his sons, Michael and Tommy.

About his introduction to Greenwich, Rushton said, "We weren't accepted for a long time; maybe never. We hadn't been brought up in a Greenwich type of world. We'd been brought up in the Chicago way, where you were innocent until proven guilty. In Greenwich, you were guilty until proven innocent.

"In Chicago, everyone was effusive, outgoing, and talkative. There was no braggadocio. In Greenwich it was very stuffy. People would ask questions like, 'What club do you belong to? Where do you vacation?'"

Greenwich folk were so overwrought with prejudice, when department store magnate, Bernard Gimbel, moved into Greenwich, he was allowed into the private country clubs, but his wife, Alva, had to stay home because she was Jewish.

The Skakel's Catholicism was treated in almost a medieval manner by some of their neighbors.

One Greenwich crone said, "I didn't know any Catholics, except for our Irish maids, and they smelled so different. That's how I identified Catholics – by their smell."

What pissed off George Skakel Sr. more than anything else was that he, himself, was not a Catholic, so why should he be treated like a leper by the citizens of Greenwich? As a result, George stuck out his tiny chest, and he decided to do something about it.

He lied.

In the Greenwich Directory, George said his main church was Episcopalian, even though the closest he ever came to an Episcopalian Church was the spelling of its name. Then, he said he received his education at the Kent Preparatory School in Kent, Connecticut, a school name he picked out of the phone directory.

Finally, George decided to stand up to Big Ann, and he begged her to send their girls to the nondenominational Greenwich Academy, so that for the first time they could sit in a classroom and not be suffocated by Catholics.

Big Ann caved in, but only a little.

"Alright, I'll agree to that," Big Ann said. "But when it's time for them to go to college, it must be Catholic."

Big Ann's concession to the girl's high school education made George happier than a woodpecker in a lumber yard. Still, the Greenwich Protestant populace continued to treat George like he had trench mouth. George withstood that indignity by diving deep into the bottle.

Although the Skakels were ostracized by their Puritan neighbors in Greenwich, they were pretty good themselves when it came to dishing out the sanctimony.

One summer, Bob Skakel, the son of George Skakel's younger brother, James Curtis Skakel, and his mother, Doris, came to visit the Skakels in Greenwich. Unfortunately for little Bob, his father's income as a U.S. border patrolman on the Texas/Mexican border was barely enough to make ends meet. Bob Skakel spent the early part of his life living in a three-room house that would fit in the corner of the Skakel's Greenwich living room.

When he first entered the Skakel compound, Bob had the wondrous look of a child upon entering Disneyland.

"Thirty rooms and a swimming pool, I must say I was a little green-eyed," Bob later said. "My father was nothing like my Uncle George. Dad couldn't sell a dollar bill for fifty cents if he tried."

But after just a month in Greenwich, Bob began seeing things in a different light.

"What I finally saw was too much money, too much everything, and no closeness," Bob said. "I felt sorry for the boys having to go away to camp when they had just come home from school. I felt I wouldn't trade places with them for anything in the world. And I've felt the same way as an adult."

Bob's father, Jim, was a virulent anti-Catholic, having learned this lesson from his parents. So, it came as culture shock when Bob came into contact with a family, thanks to Big Ann, who lived in a house that was a virtual monument to the Catholic Church.

"On Sunday after Mass, the nuns and the priests came for cocktails and conversations," Bob said. "It was a Sunday-afternoon ritual. I'd never seen anything like it. Aunt Ann was always the center of attention. On Sunday afternoons, she glorified in her surroundings. I always thought that was a little odd."

It was common knowledge that Ethel was the one child who was most like her mother. Ethel was unabashedly Catholic, and she made no bones about it. And woe to them who felt differently.

"From the time Ethel was a child, she helped Big Ann carry the cross," Martin McKneally said. "There were only two things important in Ethel's life. Jesus Christ came first, and then came Bobby Kennedy."

And, it was Ethel, because of the pro-Catholic and anti-every other religion tutelage of her mother, who was downright mean to young Bob.

One day, Bob was playing with Ethel and her younger sister, Pat, in Ethel's bedroom, which was also a shrine to the Catholic religion.

"We were smiling and playing, when all of a sudden she got a mean look on her face," Bob said. "She said to me, 'Bob Skakel, you're not going to heaven when you die. Do you know that?' I didn't know what to say so I just blurted out 'Why not?' She was all too happy to tell me.

"She said, 'You're not going to heaven because you are not a Catholic. That means when you die, you're going to hell.'"

Bob rushed to his mother, Doris, crying and his body shaking like a leaf in a windstorm.

Between gulps of air, Bob told his mother what Ethel had said: that because he was a Catholic, when he died he was going to hell and not to heaven.

Not too pleased that Ethel had terrorized her little boy, Doris just hugged him and said, "Oh, Ethel was just teasing you. Don't pay attention to that nonsense."

But as Doris later related, it was not the only time her family's lack of a Catholic faith was thrown in her face. One day, it was Big Ann who said something to Doris that almost knocked her on her butt.

"Doris, if you and your husband became Catholics, there's nothing I wouldn't do for you," Big Ann said. "It would be very beneficial for you. Things for you could be much better. We could do a lot for you and your husband."

"I took what she said to me as a bribe," Doris said. "I didn't like what she said, but I didn't answer her back. And I never told my husband because I knew it would make him angry."

On one sunny Sunday afternoon, after Big Ann and her Catholic crew had returned from Mass, a gaggle of Big Ann's Catholic cronies sat on the porch with Big Ann, banging down more than a few of the 1921 French alcoholic invention: the "Bloody Mary."

Doris Skakel was sitting on the porch reading the Sunday Times, downwind from Big Ann and her pals, who, the more they belted down the Bloody Marys, the louder their rants became.

A waiter approached one of the ladies and said, "Another Bloody Mary, ma'am?"

The lady sniffed, and said, "Yes, I would like another one."

"Would you like it mild or hot?

She literally screamed, "I'd like it hotter than hell, where God is going to send all those damned heretics."

The other ladies caught the comment, and they readily agreed; shrieking loudly, as they pointed their fingers to the sky and then down to the floor.

"All of a sudden I hear this shouting back and forth, and the words that were clearly being repeated were 'damn heretic,'" Doris said. "Because of their glances back and forth towards me, I could see it was me they were talking about. I could see it was the Bloody Marys talking, too, but that was no excuse for their demeanor. They were supposed to be good Catholic ladies. Not bar tramps.

"Then it dawned on me, 'Is that the way they really feel if we're not Catholic?'

"Then, one of the men who was with them came down and sat next to me. He smiled and said, 'Hello, aren't you one of the Skakels from out West?' I was so angry, so I said, 'Yes, I'm one of the goddamn heretics!' He looked shocked and embarrassed, and he just got up and walked away. I never mentioned this to George Skakel, because I know how upset it would have made him."

Big Ann was not averse to perpetrating a little shenanigans when it came to enhancing her position in Catholic circles. But she needed a chump, someone, who by her associating with him, would elevate Big Ann into a clique of Catholic devotees far above those of mere Catholic mortals.

She found this man in the person of Thomas Merton, a Roman Catholic Trappist Monk. Merton had propelled himself into the public consciousness by writing his autobiographical Seven Story Mountain, in which he reflected on his early life and on his quest for a faith in God that led to his conversion to Roman Catholicism at the age of twenty-three (The title refers to the mountain of Purgatory in Dante's The Devine Comedy).

After his conversion, Merton quit his job as a teacher of English literature at St. Bonaventure's College, and he entered The Abbey of Our Lady of Gethsemane near Bardstown, Kentucky.

Flashing her husband George's money, Big Ann traveled to Bardstown, with several secretaries secretly in tow. Using an introduction from Daniel Walsh, Ethel's philosophy teacher in college, she proceeded to bamboozle Merton and the head monks at The Abbey into appointing her as Merton's personal secretary.

Of course, Big Ann, whose alleged secretarial work included opening Merton's fan mail, would do no direct secretarial work herself. And that's where the several secretaries that Big Ann had hired came into play.

"The Skakel's were our earliest benefactors," Brother Patrick Hart of The Abbey said. "By financing the monastery, the Skakels were allowing a monk to sit at a typewriter and write."

As Merton's "secretary," Big Ann was allowed to keep the original drafts of Merton's writings, which, at a later date, would be worth a substantial amount of money. Big Ann obtained the original drafts of such famed Merton's works like Silence of Heaven, Last of the Father's, and Sign of Jonas. Merton was so nice and accommodating, he signed several first editions of his books for Big Ann.

Then, using her clout as Merton's secretary, Big Ann convinced several other Monk authors to also give her original drafts of their work.

"Ann was interested in authors and wanted to get their manuscripts," Brother Patrick said. "She was considered a great collector. I thought that Merton was the only one, but Ann said she got manuscripts from other writers, whom she did not identify. She'd tell them, 'I'd love to do your secretarial work.'

"She would get the manuscripts that were annotated by the author, and then she would have her aides type clean copies. But Big Ann kept the original, which had all of the author's markings. Then, she'd have them elegantly bound in leather, the best leather money can buy, and she'd put them on elegant shelves in her home library, which was quite an impressive homage to the Catholic Church."

Due to Big Ann's altruistic and financial contributions, Dom James Fox, the sixth abbot of The Abbey of Our Lady of Gethsemane, who was a frequent visitor at the Skakel mansion in Greenwich, christened the Skakel house, Regina Laudis – In Praise of the Virgin. Big Ann, never one to miss an opportunity to enhance her credibility within the Catholic Church, used Regina Laudis on all her personal stationary. As a result, within a few years, the Monks at The Abbey dedicated a chapel in honor of the Skakels at The Abbey of Our Lady of Gethsemane.

George Skakel, who was still trying to fit in with the Greenwich society swells, was not enamored with is wife's activities concerning the Monks, and especially her sacred library, a room in which George refused to enter.

Jay Mayhew was the chief geologist for Great Lakes Coal and Coke. On his first visit to the Skakel mansion, George took Mayhew, a practicing Mormon, on the side, and said, "My wife has a home library totally dedicated to the Catholic Church. It's an obsession with her. Don't go into that room. Believe me, you don't want to see it. It might make you very uncomfortable."

Mayhew said, "George told me he just didn't like the room. He surprised me because he never indicated in any way at any time that he and his wife had points of disagreement."

One afternoon, while George was still in the city, Big Ann literally dragged Mayhew into the library, saying, "Come on, George is not home. I'm taking you into my library. He won't know a thing, but you absolutely have to see my library. It's breathtaking."

"Well, who was I to argue?" Mayhew said. "She was the boss's wife and an exceedingly large and strong woman. I don't think I could have resisted her, even if I wanted to.

"The room looked like the Mormon Tabernacle, with amphitheater seating; only on a smaller scale. There were religious statues and busts, and figures with wings like angels. There were also floor-to-ceiling books. I was very impressed."

Chapter Ten

Ethel and Her Wild Brothers

From the time she was eight years old, Ethel Skakel was a horse enthusiast. The walls of her bedroom in Greenwich were adorned with a montage of photos of her on horseback. While she was a student at Greenwich Academy she owned not one, but two horses. She named one Smoky Joe and the other Beau Mischief.

Billy Steinkraus, who later became a member of the United States Olympic Riding Team and was a friend of the Skakel family, said, "Ethel took to riding like she took to touch football with the Kennedy family. The first show horse she had ever rode was owned by Janet Lee Bouvier, years before Ethel had met her daughter, and Ethel's future sister-in-law, Jacqueline Bouvier Kennedy.

As a child, Ethel rode her horses everywhere. She once raced her horse through the front door of the Skakel mansion and right out the back door.

"She was galloping like mad," said a witness to the spectacle. "We all just sat in the living room with our mouths agape. It was a hell of a thing to do."

When Ethel was in college, she was scheduled to ride in a horse show at Madison Square Garden, then located on 50th Street and Eighth Avenue. Running late and still heading south on the Upper East Side, Ethel made a sharp right turn into Central Park. She continued west on the roadway meant for cars, until she came out on the west side of the park.

"She knew she could have been arrested for riding a horse across Central Park; the New York City police were just not as compliant as the Greenwich police," a friend said. "But Ethel just didn't care. She was not going to be late for that show."

While Ethel Skakel immersed herself in Equestrian activities, her brothers, Jim and George Skakel, became the scourge of Greenwich.

Whether they were swinging like Tarzan from the trees on their estate, or were playing "King of the Castle," their Greenwich neighbors were unimpressed and more than a little pissed off (In "King of the Castle," one of the Skakel boys stood on the roof of their Bentley, while the car, driven by another Skakel boy, careened through the wooded areas of Greenwich, trying to find a branch to knock the King off his castle).

The Skakel boys also had an old station wagon, which they used to give guests a tour of their estate; a tour which invariably ended with the station wagon zigzagging like a roller coaster down a hill and into the Skakel pond.

The Skakel boys also played with pistols; the kind that shot real bullets.

One of their neighbors later said, "These Skakel kids would get their cars up to ninety miles an hour in nothing flat. They would tear all over town, shooting large caliber pistols out the windows, like Clyde Barrow and Pretty Boy Floyd. Good thing they didn't kill anybody."

Another neighbor, while not giving the boys a pass, blamed a lot of what they did on lack of parental concern.

"The Skakel kids weren't spoiled as much as they were deprived," he said. "They had money, but they didn't have anything else. There was no family structure. Most families have a way of doing things, a pattern of behavior. There was no pattern at Lake Avenue. It was an abstract painting as opposed to a formal painting; more surreal than Rembrandt; a Jackson Pollock world where everything was exploding, where there was no cohesiveness.

"The Skakel house had a sadness about it. It didn't have a core. The family had no established roots. We all felt secure. I don't think they did. In fact, they were a mass of insecurity."

As soon as a Skakel was old enough to drive, their parents bought them a brand new car, which they then proceeded to drive around town in a totally reckless manner. It got so bad that the Greenwich police stationed a police car at the end of the Skakel's driveway, hoping to catch them in the act of breaking the law, either by speeding or reckless driving.

One neighborhood resident recalled, "Every cop in Greenwich was waiting for a Skakel car. They were all stopped at one time or another. But it was no big deal. The police never gave them more than a slap on the wrist, so what was stopping them from doing it over and over again? Nothing."

Both Jim and George Skakel Jr. were considered such dangerous drivers that Ethel's female friends were grounded by their parents if they ever hopped into a Skakel car, even for a ride to the church.

One day, George Jr. was invited to a friend's house to go swimming in their pool. But instead of parking in the driveway, like normal people are wont to do, George Jr. sped his car straight at the patio, as startled residents scurried for safety. He screeched on the brakes, and caused only minimal damage when his car hit the patio, but he did rip up 100 feet of expensive grass turf.

Neither George Skakel Sr. nor Big Ann were immune from car-related pranks by their sons.

One night, George Sr. returned home with a brand new Lincoln Zephyr, which he proudly showed to his sons. After their father had retired for the night, Jim and George Jr., along with two friends, slipped into the family garage. They pushed the new Zephyr to the top of a hill, jumped in and released the brake. The car glided down the hill and right into a ditch that was muddy with rainwater.

Another time, George Sr. returned with a brand-new Bentley for Big Ann, who was not home at the time. Again, after George

Sr. hit the rack, George Jr. and two of his pals got into the Bentley. They swiped the car, on the sides and in the back, against every tree in sight. Then they jumped from the speeding car just before it collided head-on with an oak tree; rendering the Bentley a total wreck.

"The car wasn't twelve hours old, and Mom never did see the car," Jim Skakel said, smiling.

Another time, the Skakel brothers decided that they wanted to build a bridge on a lake near their property. Again, with the help of their friends and their father's unlimited expense account, they purchased six brand-new Buicks. Then, one at a time, they drove the Buicks into the lake, hood to trunk, until the bridge was complete and they could go from one side of the lake to the other just by climbing across the top of the cars.

"All these cars ended up accordion-pleated in the water," Greenwich resident Pam Jacobs said. "And that was considered lots and lots of fun. No one in the Skakel house said, 'What a horrible thing to do.' It was like, 'Oh, isn't that funny? Isn't that amusing? What naughty boys!'

"They got no punishment whatsoever."

Not even the start of World War II, and the subsequent gas rationing, could stop the young Skakels from terrorizing Greenwich.

"Money talks, and the Skakels sure knew how to throw it around to their advantage," Pam Jacobs said. "They had a way of getting anything they wanted, including extra gasoline from a local garage."

Ethel Skakel was just as guilty of dangerous driving as were her brothers. Her first car was a sleek red Duesenberg convertible.

Her pal, Fanny Hawes, said, "We'd cruise around Greenwich because there wasn't much of anything else to do. Ethel used to go cruising down Merritt Parkway with the top down and waving at everybody. Ethel would yell to the driver of the car next to her, 'Hey buddy, your right rear jocelyn is loose.' Of course, there's no such thing as a jocelyn, but the driver would invariably pull over and rush to the back of his car to see what was wrong, as we drove away laughing hysterically.

"Ethel also drove at night at high speeds with her lights off, sometimes pulling off the paved road and hightailing it through the woods as a shortcut to get back to the Skakel mansion."

The Skakel sons' love for firearms was also problematical. While they were still in their teens, they became, what the Greenwich neighbors called, "gun nuts." Their father, George Sr., was also a gun fanatic, but he went on hunting trips to shoot game, while, to his sons, everything and anything was a potential target.

With the permission of their father, all three Skakel sons had a standing order with Abercrombie and Finch to deliver to the boys all the latest rage in rifles; the more firepower the better.

"They used to shoot up mailboxes and street lamps," said childhood buddy, Ken McDonnell. "There were forty-five caliber bullet holes in some of those mailboxes. They were using big stuff, and there was some retaliation. Some people went up to the Skakel home and put a few holes in their mailboxes.

"They were a crazy bunch. They were aiming for trouble. Even as a youngster you could feel it."

Their dangerous antics with guns frightened one of their neighbors to the point that he was almost ready to report them to the police.

"I couldn't believe what I was seeing," the neighbor said. "One time, I saw them repeatedly firing rifles from a second-story window of their home. At first, I didn't realize what they were firing at. But then I later found out that they were firing at a Grecian marble statue near their swimming pool. They were having a contest. The last one to shoot an ear off was a 'nigger baby.' The statue was totally destroyed."

One time, the Skakel's gunplay almost cost them a friend.

Greg Reilly was a close pal of the Skakels, and one day he accompanied the boys on one of their shooting rampages in the woods. Their intended targets were squirrels, and after hitting some and missing some, the Skakels decided to open fire on several large rocks in the area. Fortified by their daily ration of alcohol, the Skakel boys never thought about the possibility of the bullets ricocheting off the rocks and maybe hitting one of them. Or maybe they did and just didn't care.

Sure enough, in an instant, Reilly was on the ground, writhing in pain and bleeding from, luckily for him, a superficial shoulder wound. Although, Reilly was bleeding profusely, the Skakels decided to protect themselves.

Instead of driving Reilly to the Greenwich Hospital, where Reilly's bleeding would have been curtailed more quickly, they instead drove him to the hospital in Port Chester, New York, ten miles south. The reason for the change of venue was that every cop in Greenwich knew the Skakels were gun-happy, and they would likely be arrested for the incident. Reilly was treated and released in Port Chester, and nothing happened to the Skakels.

However, Greg Reilly's parents were pissed.

After their son was home safe in bed, the senior Reillys rushed to the Skakel mansion looking for some sort of retribution. Since George Sr. was away on a business trip, they confronted Big Ann.

"Ann Skakel totally stonewalled the Reillys," a neighbor said. "She had them bulldozed and buffaloed. When the Reillys threatened to go to the police, Big Ann told them, 'And to arrest who? Four people were firing guns; including your son. Who's to say which person fired the bullet that hit off the rocks and injured your son?' People said Big Ann agreed to pick up the Reilly's medical expenses and that was that."

George Skakel Sr. owned the Skakel Ranch in Moab, Utah, 235 miles south of Salt Lake City. The reason for the purchase was

Skakel's hope that ace geologist, Jay Mayhew, would find valuable minerals on the property.

One summer, George Skakel Sr. decided to send George Jr. and Jim to the ranch to work on the drilling rigs, under the supervision of Mayhew.

Right off the bat, Mayhew thought this was a crazy idea. But George Sr. was his boss, and Mayhew didn't want to anger him.

"George Jr. and Jim were wild and wacky young broncos," Mayhew said. "How the hell could I handle them if their own father couldn't? George just said that I would be the boss and tell them what to do, and if they didn't obey me, let him know, and he'd send them back home."

The Skakel boys flew in on a company-owned jet and settled into the Moab Hotel, the swankiest hotel in the area. Right off the bat, their arrival gave Mayhew a bad case of indigestion.

"They flew in on the company plane bringing automatic rifles, which were illegal for non-army persons to have at the time," Mayhew said. "They also had 45-caliber pistols and cases of ammunition. The purpose of all the artillery was just to have fun when they were down there.

"Instead of working on the ranch on the drilling rigs, like they were supposed to, they'd race around town in their cars shooting through the windows. By the time they left town, half the signs in Moab were cut off at ground level. I finally got an understanding from them that they wouldn't carry guns when they were in the car with me."

One afternoon, after the Skakels actually did an honest day's work, they returned to their hotel room with Mayhew.

"Jim was laying on the bed relaxing," Mayhew said. "George asked Jimmy something and Jimmy didn't answer, and George said, 'By God, when I ask you a question you better answer.' With that George pulled out a loaded and cocked forty-five, aimed it at his brother and pulled the trigger. The exploding of the gun going off in that room was enormous. I smelled the gunpowder, and when I opened my eyes I expected to see Jimmy dead on the bed."

But it seemed that George, considering all his gun slinging in the past, had become a crack shot, and he just grazed his brother on purpose.

"What happened was that the bullet had just put a crease just above Jim's stomach," Mayhew said. "It wasn't that bad, just enough to make a red line. George asked Jimmy, 'Does it hurt?' And Jim said, 'Well, I felt it!' We didn't even go to the hospital. But Jim could have been killed."

Chapter Eleven

George Skakel Sr. Uses World War II to Make Another Fortune

The Japanese bombing of Pearl Harbor turned out to be a big boon for the Skakel Family.

On December 7, 1941, at about 5 pm Greenwich, Connecticut time, Big Ann Skakel was told about the bombing after her normal Sunday ritual of church, brunch, and Bloody Marys, with her coterie of friends. The only emotion Big Ann showed was one of deep disappointment that her usual favorite Sunday radio serial show was preempted by the coverage of the destruction at Pearl Harbor.

"No one was gathered about the radio," Jim Skakel said. "Nobody got excited. Pearl Harbor just didn't ring a bell with us."

But it did ring a bell with George Skakel Sr., and that ring enlightened George that he was about to make enormous amounts of money, but not in the way he first expected.

Before the war was weeks old, George had a "spy" inside the United States Government, who told him the United States was working on a bomb of such magnitude it would be a game-changer when deployed. George also discovered that this bomb needed uranium as its main ingredient.

Seeing dollar signs flickering before his eyes, George quickly dispatched his crack geologist, Jay Mayhew, to the Skakel Ranch in Utah, with the directive, "Find me some damn uranium!"

Try as he could, Mayhew could find no uranium on the Skakel ranch. But he did strike oil, which made George as happy as a monkey with a peanut machine.

With his oil well pumping twelve hundred barrels a day, George immediately set up separate oil and gas subdivisions for Great Lakes Coal and Coke, and he put Mayhew in charge of both new subdivisions.

Mayhew said, "It was big money and George rubbed his hands together and said, 'Eureka!' Where have I been? This is the business for me.'"

While women all over America banded together to help the war effort, Ethel Skakel was a no-show. Ethel's older sister, Georgeann, did volunteer work at Fort Bragg in South Carolina. Ethel's pal, Pam Jacobs, worked as a nurse's assistant at Greenwich Hospital, and Pixie Meeks knitted mittens and scarf for the servicemen overseas. Many other Greenwich girls and women pitched in and did their part in the war effort, but nobody could recall Ethel doing even one minute of volunteer work.

One Greenwich female resident said, "All Ethel did was ride her horses. She never lifted a finger to do anything like us other girls did. It was like all this stuff was beneath her."

To be fair, due to her expert riding abilities, Ethel did perform in riding competitions, the proceeds of which went to the Red Cross and the British Relief Fund.

As for the Skakel boys, they all spent time in the military service with varying degrees of success.

Rushton, the quietest of the Skakel boys, was drafted into the Navy, where he was discharged after less than two weeks in the service. The cause of Rushton's discharge was bleeding duodenal ulcers, which were not detected when he passed his Navy physical. Rushton went home to Big Ann, and with the help of the best doctors money could buy, and a diet that consisted mostly of milk, he was able to pass the physical for the Army Air Corps, in which he served until the end of the war.

Jim Skakel was also drafted into the Army Air Corps, and he too was quickly discharged, the reasons for which were never made public.

George Skakel Jr. dropped out of Amherst College, and with his father's money pulling the strings, he was admitted into Naval Flight Training School at Pensacola, Florida. He passed with flying colors, and he received his commission as an Ensign in the Navy Reserve.

But instead of receiving combat orders, the Navy brass assigned George Jr. to flight instructor's school. Not only did George Skakel Jr. refuse this order, a direct violation of the Code of Military Justice, but he stole a Navy plane out of Pensacola and flew it all the way home to a small airport in Greenwich.

Jim Skakel later said of his brother, George, "My brother took on the entire Navy because he was determined not to be an instructor."

With the Skakel money most likely playing some part in the Navy's decision, even though George Jr. had committed serious crimes, where the punishment ranged from severe brig time to death for desertion, George was merely stripped of his wings as an officer and shipped off to the Island of Truk, part of the Carolina Island chain and northeast of New Guinea. Truk was a major Japanese logistical base and the home base for the Imperial Japanese Navy's Combined Fleet. Military experts said Island of Truk was the equivalent of the U.S. Navy's Pearl Harbor.

From the time he was a child, George Skakel Jr. liked the concept of "war," and on February 17, 1944, on the Island of Truk, he got exactly what he wanted.

Using submarines, battleships, and planes, the United States did to The Island of Truk what the Japanese had done to Pearl Harbor. When the smoke cleared, 250 Japanese planes had been destroyed, and the United States had gained control of the key airstrip.

After the war, George bragged to his friends back home that he had "machine gunned, like ducks, a bunch of Japanese soldiers taking baths on the Island."

As for George Skakel Sr., as a result of the war, the money kept flowing in. With the help of Colonel Alfred Parry, George got in real tight with the big shots in Washington who ran the newly created Army Transportation Corps.

After the bombing of Pearl Harbor, the Department of War recognized the need for a single manager of Army transportation, and they created a new branch, the Transportation Corps. Since the Revolutionary War, Army transportation had evolved into two branches, the Quartermaster Corps and the Corps of Engineers. The demands of World War I made the Army first realize its need for a single manager for military transportation. Thus, began an evolution over the next quarter century that culminated in the birth of the Transportation Corps during the opening months of World War II.

In March of 1942, the Army created a Transportation Division under Colonel (later Major General) Charles P. Gross in the Services of Supply. On July 31 1942, The Quartermaster Corps retained the trucks and the newly-created amphibious truck units, and the Engineers retained the assault landing craft in the engineer special brigades to conduct the Army's amphibious landings.

During the war, the Transportation Corps was responsible for moving soldiers from their training bases to the front, and managing the ports of embarkation and debarkation in between. Because the Axis Powers knew the importance of denying the Allies the use of deep-draft ports, the Transportation Corps had to rely on landing craft and amphibious vehicles to deliver men and material across bare beaches until the ports were secure.

This is where George Skakel Sr. used his business ingenuity to make huge amounts of cash.

One of his business associates said, "George Skakel could squeeze a coconut and fifty-dollar bills would fall to the floor."

With the help of Colonel Parry, George was able to buy three "tramp steamers." A tramp steamer is called a "contract carrier." Unlike an ocean liner, often called a "common carrier," which has a fixed schedule and a published tariff, a tramp steamer can carry anything to anywhere, and the freight rates are influenced by supply and demand.

George named his three steamers after his three daughters: the Ethel Skakel, the Patricia Skakel and the Ann Skakel. Then, George formed another subdivision of Great Lakes Coal and Coke, and, again with the help of Colonel Parry, he was able to sign lucrative contracts with the War Shipping Administration, a World War II emergency war agency of the United States government tasked to purchase and operate the civilian shipping tonnage the United States needed for fighting the war.

George kept 75% of the money from the business venture, and he awarded Colonel Parry the other 25%. Of course, Colonel Parry ran the business for George, and George did nothing more than count the money as it came gushing in.

"It was a good time for us, and my father made a lot of money," Jim Skakel said.

During the war, one of George's steamers was sunk by a German U boat. But when the war ended, George made additional cash by selling the remaining two steamers for scrap metal; a hot commodity at the time.

Still, with all George's money, his family still lived like a gun-happy version of the television program The Adams Family. Just like Gomez Adams indulged his lovely wife Morticia's every whim, George did the same for Big Ann. But what he couldn't do, no matter how much money he threw at the problem, was to give her and his brood class, or even a milligram of sophistication.

For instance, consider the Skakel's 30-room mansion on Lake Avenue in Greenwich. With all his cash, George couldn't even keep the two ground-floor toilets in working order.

Hope Larkin, a childhood pal of Ethel Skakel's, said, "God knows what those kids threw down the toilets. But Mrs.

Pulaski, the Polish day worker, was always mopping up the ladies room and the men's room, which were on opposite sides of the house from each other. Because both toilets were constantly overflowing, the whole ground floor smelled like an outhouse. And the lady of the house, she didn't seem to care."

An anonymous neighbor, was not as kind to Big Ann.

The neighbor said, "She wanted to give the impression she was a 'Lace Curtain Irish,' but she was nothing more than 'Shanty Irish' at heart. And that's all there was to it. The truth is, you can't polish a turd."

One possible reason Big Ann didn't give the toilet situation the attention it required was because she was too busy trying to control the numerous stray dogs her husband repeatedly brought home with him. Although they didn't damage the downstairs toilets, the dogs, again to the dismay of Mrs. Pulaski, did their business on the downstairs rugs. Besides the excrement stains and the stench that accompanied them, the dogs used the downstairs rugs as "scratching boards," forcing Big Ann to spend a small fortune to repeatedly replace the rugs.

"Dad must have been unusual, because any dog that ever saw him left their house and followed him home," his son Rushton said. "One time we had fifteen or more dogs. In those days, dogs that were worth five hundred dollars would follow Dad and stay with us. The owners would find out where the dogs were and demand that mother paid them five hundred dollars. They were justifiably angry.

"Mother would say fine, and then she would actually send them a dog-food bill that was higher than the price they wanted for the dog."

"That was typical Ann Skakel," the anonymous neighbor said. "She was as big as a house, and she was a bully. People were afraid of her; even her husband."

The Skakel dogs repeatedly charged at visitors, especially the mailman, so much so, the local United States Post Office designated the Skakel properly as a "war zone."

"I don't think we had the same mailman for two weeks in a row," Rushton Skakel said.

If it wasn't bad enough that the Skakel dogs caroused outside the front door, across the lawn, and constantly jumped in and out of the swimming pool, Big Ann had assembled a crew of assorted animals which made the Skakel front lawn their home.

"Ethel and her family had their whims with animals," said Greenwich resident Anne Morningstar Huberth. "Besides all their mutts running around, on the grounds they had a billy goat, a few sheep, about a dozen pigs, and dozens of chickens and bunny rabbits. Instead of a manicured lawn of the rich in Greenwich, it looked more like the backyard of a farmer in the Midwest."

With all the Skakel money, you'd think the Greenwich merchants would welcome their business with open arms. But that was far from the truth. Big Ann would run up big tabs at local merchants, food and otherwise, and when the time came to pay the bill, Big Ann suddenly had alligator arms. Some merchants never got paid a cent for the goods and services ordered by Big Ann.

Joe Buck, a Greenwich merchant said, "The Skakels were great as long as they paid their bills. When they came into the shop there would be this big flurry of activity because they bought in quantity. But the only thing that was exciting was whether we were going to get paid, or not. Fortunately, we never got stuck for any great amount, but other stores were not quite as lucky. The word around town about the Skakels was 'watch out.'"

Big Ann was so frugal with her money, she even counted the eggs after a delivery to make sure the servants were not stealing them.

The one merchant Big Ann did pay was her furrier. She owned several full-length mink coats and dozens of other coats made with assorted expensive animal furs.

One day on the train to New York City, she bragged to a friend, "Do you realize, dear, that I have on three mink coats."

The friend later said, "I had no idea what she was talking about. But then she explained to me that because of her size, the number of pelts needed to make her coat would make three mink coats for a normal-sized woman.

"She didn't have much culture, that's for sure. But she was one damn character."

Chapter Twelve

George Skakel Sr. Dives Deeply into the Bottle

By 1943, with the war raging in two continents, Big Ann Skakel finally accepted the fact that she would never be accepted as one of Greenwich's societal bluebloods.

"She was never able to make a life for herself here in Greenwich," Pixie Weeks said. "The kids did, but no matter how hard they tried to fit in, Mr. and Mrs. Skakel just didn't."

Even her husband's business associates found Big Ann crude, uncouth, and over-the-top aggressive. The mild-manner geologist, Jay Mayhew, found it best to try to avoid her, even though he worked for her husband.

"Mrs. Skakel was overbearing," Mayhew said. "She had a lot of money, and she lorded it over anyone who she felt was beneath her. She constantly picked on little people, like waiters and waitresses. She would yell, 'Take it back! Warm it up!' and 'Do this and do that.'

"George, who was a gentle man, watched her, and he obviously was offended and embarrassed by her actions. He never said anything, but I saw the look on his face. He was quite expressive, and his eyes would get wide, and he'd look away.

"It was clear that Mrs. Skakel felt that her money gave her power, something she didn't have when she was growing up. So, she wielded it. Otherwise, her repertoire was not very broad. She was a very shallow person."

Big Ann wore the best clothes money could buy, and she flashed diamonds on her hands, wrists, and around her bulky neck, that cost as much as most Americans could make in a lifetime. But try as she may to transform herself into a suburban lady of elegance, the women of Greenwich found Big Ann to be an obnoxious and obese vulgarian.

"She might have been a beautiful woman if she hadn't been so heavy and hadn't deported herself as a plain and shabby woman," a Greenwich socialite said. "She wore a bluish tint of eyeliner around her eyes, wore her blond hair cropped with no styling, and her stout figure had no contours, so she looked like a big block of granite. Had she been smaller and thinner, she would have been pretty. Still, she never would have fitted in."

Knowing he would never be accepted into Greenwich's high society, George Sr. decided to strut around town flashing the demeanor of a movie tough guy. Because George had previously been such a sweetheart, it shocked people when he walked into a merchant's place of business acting curt, mean, and cocky. And when he paid, it was always from a roll of hundred dollar bills, secured by rubber bands, and big enough to choke King Kong.

"My father always idolized the movie tough guys like Bogart and Cagney," Rushton said. "And he admired the baseball player, Leo Durocher, called Leo the Lip, because he acted tough too; on the field and off the field, where he got into many barroom brawls. My father liked to quote Durocher's pet statement, 'Nice guys finish last.'"

Sam Robbins owned a gun shop in Greenwich, and George was a frequent customer, buying firearms and ammunition. On several occasions, they went trap shooting together, so Robbins got to know George fairly well.

"George was not a simple, lovable guy," Robbins said. "He was short and abrupt and somewhat of an introvert. He didn't like to get cozy with anyone. I think his wife had something to do with that, because when she was around, George hardly said anything. As a rule, he never said a lot anyway, but whatever he said, he meant every syllable.

"In that sense he wasn't a gentle man. He was a tough guy, a ruffian. No doubt about it. He was the tower of strength that made Great Lakes Coal and Coke what it was. He thought big, and he was right most of the time. All his children inherited that same sense of thinking in awfully big terms."

In late 1943, George Skakel Sr. and his brood started vacationing for the winter in Varadero, Cuba, ninety miles east of Havana. He rented a large mansion filled with servants to satisfy Big Ann's every whim.

As for George, he mostly drank.

One of George's drinking buddies was his next-door neighbor, Cuban dictator Fulgencio Batista, who was not adverse from accepting money from anyone willing to pay for political favors.

"As little kids we used to go up and bang on Batista's door, yelling 'come to our party,'" Rushton Skakel said. "Batista's guards would just laugh, but sure enough, an hour later Batista, accompanied by his bodyguards, would knock on our door, all smiles.

"Dad would spend his days, sometimes with Batista, either golfing, fishing, or quail hunting. But every night he drank, and he drank heavily. It was in Cuba that he became a serious alcoholic, and mother was very concerned."

Another friend who George Skakel partied with was the writer, Ernest Hemingway, who lived in Cuba at the time.

"I remember me and my brother going to Hemingway's house, because he had called us and said, 'You have to come here to pick up your father. He's so drunk he can hardly walk,'" Rushton said. "When my father was sober, he was just a delightful individual. He was gentle and kind, but he could be tough, too. If he talked mean to a statue, the statue would say, 'Yes sir, no sir. No excuse, sir.'"

George Sr. also frequented, in the company of his strapping son, Jim, many of Varadero's copious saloons. When he accompanied his diminutive father bar-hopping, Jim, six feet two inches and a big drinker himself, toned his drinking down a bit so he would be ready when his father got into an argument with someone for no other reason except that he was drunk.

"My father would get himself into a jam with someone, and then he would introduce me to the other guy," Jim Skakel said. "So, then I had to be a quick negotiator for him. I'd usually say, 'Oh, don't worry, we're just leaving. My father is drunk. Don't pay any attention to him.' After we left the bar, I'd tell Dad, 'Please don't get into those things again. We don't need this.' But it kept on happening. When my father got drunk, he thought he was six feet tall."

For George Skakel Sr., the end of the war only gave him more reason to bang the bottle, and bang it good. During the week, when he had to keep up appearances at his office at the Great Lakes Coal & Coke Co. in New York City, George might have a martini or two at lunch. Then, after work at home, he was very careful not to imbibe too much booze, which would affect his following day's performance.

But on weekends, it was "party time."

"It was no secret that George Skakel used to get filthy drunk on the weekends," said Hope Johnston, one of the few Greenwich women who was on speaking terms with Big Ann Skakel.

"He'd get drunk on Friday night, and then he'd drink all day Saturday," Hope said. "His wife would try to sober him up on Sundays, and he'd be back to work on Monday. She'd always have priests in the house on weekends, and I'd see them helping her take Mr. Skakel up the stairs to his bedroom. It was quite sad, really."

One of the few times George broke his rule about getting drunk during working hours happened at the Men's Bar at the Waldorf, which in those days, was as swanky an establishment as there was in New York City.

It was early afternoon and whatever set off George Skakel was never uncovered. As he was sitting at the bar, he had a few heated words with the bartender. Then, without any warning, he stood up, like John Wayne did in Westerns, and he flung his glass at the expensive mirror behind the bar, causing it to shatter into little pieces, some of which made contact with the bartender's scalp. As the bartender used a rag to stop the bleeding on top of his head, George stormed out of the bar and staggered back to his office.

When he found out what his boss had done, George's assistant, Henry Walker, hurried to the Waldorf, spewing apologies from Mr. Skakel and waving a Great Lakes Coal & Coke Co. checkbook.

"The hotel management accepted our apologies gracefully because George was such a good customer and had never done anything like this before," said Walker. "They didn't want to hurt that relationship."

George spent the rest of his life either drunk, or just sober enough to continue to add to the Skakel's great fortune. The money, through various ventures, kept pouring into the coffers of the Great Lakes Coal & Coke Co.

Big Ann couldn't have been happier.

Chapter Thirteen

Ethel Skakel Obeyed Few Rules as She Sped Through Two Years of Catholic High School

In September 1943, Big Ann Skakel finally got her way concerning the Catholic education of her daughters; specifically Ethel.

Because George was intent on portraying his family as wealthy WASPS in order to gain entry into the Greenwich societal circles, Big Ann had agreed to send Ethel to Greenwich Academy High School. But by 1943, it was obvious to both George and Big Ann that the ruse wasn't working. The school Big Ann chose for Ethel's eleventh grade education was the Convent of the Sacred Heart – Maplehurst, a five-day-a-week all-girls school located at 174 Street and University Avenue in the Bronx, only a 30-minute train ride from Greenwich. Two of the Kennedy clan, Pat and Jean, had gone to Maplehurst, as did their mother, Rose.

Even though the Bronx area around Maplehurst had begun its steep decline, Maplehurst, located on the grounds of a Revolutionary War estate (George Washington slept there) was a plush area with acres of tall maples trees intertwined with luxurious rose gardens.

It was so idyllic, a visiting priest once said, "It was like an oasis in the middle of the Bronx. (In 1945, after Ethel graduated, the Convent of the Sacred Heart–Maplehurst moved to Greenwich, Connecticut).

The nuns at Maplehurst were strict disciplinarians, and Ethel was not used to discipline of any kind. But before Ethel spent a day at Maplehurst, Big Ann approached the right people to make sure Ethel was treated with kid's gloves, compared to the way the good nuns treated the other students.

At Maplehurst, Ethel's "rabbis" were none other than Mother Helen Bourke, the Dean of Students, and Mother Marian Duffy, the Dean of Discipline.

"Mrs. Skakel anticipated that Ethel might have trouble adhering to the strict rules at Maplehurst," a family friend said. "So, starting months before Ethel was admitted, Mrs. Skakel gained the admiration of the school administration by donating funds for the nuns to build a new chapel. As a result, the nuns were much more lenient with the daughter of a rich benefactor than they would have been with any of the other students."

Ethel certainly knew that her mother had greased the right palms at Maplehurst, and, on her very first night at Maplehurst, she decided to test her theory that she would be allowed special privileges.

After the lights were out and everyone else in the building was fast asleep, Ethel jumped out of bed and slid into the closet. There, she started banging her suitcases repeatedly into the wall, while yelling at the top of her lungs, "Dammit to hell!!"

While Ethel was making enough noise to wake up the dead, her roommate Eleanor Conroy said in a loud whisper, "Hurry, I hear one of the nuns coming!"

Ethel sped out of the closet and jumped into her bed, and she pulled the covers up to her chin.

The nun, rage spread across her wrinkled face, pushed open the door, and said, "What's going on in here?"

Ethel, pretending to have just awoken, said in her best good-little-girl voice, "I don't know what you mean, sister. I was sleeping. I didn't hear anything."

The nun contorted her face into a tight fist.

"You heard something," she said. "The whole world heard the racket coming from inside this room."

Ethel just closed her eyes and pretended to go back to sleep.

Five minutes after the nun had exited the room, Ethel jumped out of bed, ran into the closet again, and the banging and screaming commenced for the second time.

This time, the old nun, obviously aware of Big Ann's largess with the school, stood in her own bed until Ethel decided to end her annoying antics.

After Ethel was long gone from Maplehurst and Big Ann's money was no longer a factor, Mother Duffy admitted, "We didn't think she would last two weeks here because of all the discipline. In her own home she did not have a lot of discipline, if any. She was a free spirit, and extrovert of the first order. She didn't care about fitting in. We figured she'd go home one day and never come back."

The day after her first-night's mischief, Ethel was startled, and more than a little annoyed, when she discovered she would have to share a bathroom with the other girls. Still in her nightgown, the nuns directed Ethel to stand in line in a frigid hallway in order to get a pitcher of water to wash her face and brush her teeth.

"Life at Maplehurst was pretty Spartan," said Ethel's day-student classmate, Alice Meadows, who slept in her own bed at night because she lived across the street from Maplehurst. "For girls like Ethel, who were used to the finer things in life, having to share a bathroom was extreme. There were no luxuries, and she wasn't used to roughing it."

The thing that annoyed Ethel the most about Maplehurst was the fact that none of the girls were permitted to speak a word of English, starting with breakfast and continuing all day long during their classes, unless they were spoken to in class by one of the nuns. The girls were allowed to speak French at breakfast, but Ethel's French sounded like butchered Greek. So, rather than risk getting caught whispering at breakfast, she just pointed to anything she wanted in the chow line.

"No one was allowed to speak a word," Mother Duffy said. "It was a calamity if they did."

Still, Ethel was repeatedly caught talking when she shouldn't have, which one time exasperated Mother Duffy so much, she yelled at Ethel, "You are a detriment to society."

Not only did Ethel disregard the "no-talking" rule, but she was caught repeatedly using curse words, which caused the good nuns to shudder and make a quick sign-of-the-cross. Ethel also thought it was cute to squirt ink at her classmates when the teacher wasn't looking. She'd repeatedly, against the rules, grabbed a smoke in the bathroom during breaks, and after going home for the weekends, Ethel was constantly late for Monday morning assembly. And even if she was on time, she purposely elected not to wear the compulsory white gloves.

"Ethel would always see if she could get caught doing something wrong," Alice Meadows said. "It was like a game to her. When she did get caught and sent to the Dean of Discipline, she'd apologize profusely to Mother Bourke, crocodile tears and all. And then she'd brag to the girls how she again had duped Mother Bourke."

Because the girls were constantly watched by the nuns during the day, Ethel saved her best antics for after dinner, after the nuns had already retired to their rooms to pray.

"She was like a little kid," classmate Mary Bayo said. "She loved to short-sheet someone's bed, and she wasn't averse to using a pair of scissors to cut someone's bed sheets into shreds. Sometimes, she'd put gooey stuff in certain girl's beds, like toothpaste, or if she could steal it at dinner – pudding. Then she would steal people's stuff, hide it, and then lose it on purpose. To her all this didn't seem to mean much."

Even though she was thin, with toothpicks for legs and no visible muscle mass, Ethel was a terror playing field hockey.

"You'd have to brace yourself when she came running down the field because she'd run right through you," said fellow field hockey player Alice Meadows. "She was extremely tough, competitive, and enthusiastic."

An average student at best, Ethel never even considered a professional career.

"The church and the school were influencing girls like Ethel to get married and have babies. I remember her goal in life was to marry well and produce children. Any kind of career was out of the question."

Ethel received her high school diploma in June of 1945. None of the Skakel family were present at the ceremony, not even Big Ann.

It was a tradition that, after the graduating ceremony, the girls would have dinner and then spend the rest of the night telling their schoolmates what they intended to do with the rest of their lives. But not Ethel.

"That was our last night together," Alice Meadows said. "Right after we ate, Ethel left. Someone called from Greenwich and suddenly she was gone."

Chapter Fourteen

Ethel Skakel's College Years and the Kennedy Connection

After President Harry Truman twice ordered the atom bombing of Japan; first on August 6, 1945, of Hiroshima (which killed an estimated 90,000 to 140,000 people), and again on August 9, of Nagasaki (which killed an estimated 39,000 to 80,000 more), Japanese Emperor Hirohito got the message, and he waved the white flag of surrender.

On September 2, 1945, at approximately 9 am Tokyo time, the Potsdam Agreement, ending the war with Japan, was signed. Japanese Foreign Minister Mamoru Shigemitsu signed on behalf of the Japanese government, and General Yoshijiro Umezu signed for the Japanese armed forces.

Supreme Commander Douglas MacArthur next signed on behalf of the United Nations.

He said, "It is my earnest hope and indeed the hope of all mankind that from this solemn occasion a better world shall emerge out of the blood and carnage of the past."

Ten more signatures were made: by the United States, China, Britain, the USSR, Australia, Canada, France, the Netherlands, and New Zealand, respectively. Admiral Chester W. Nimitz signed for the United States.

The entire ceremony took a mere 20 minutes.

Back at the Skakel mansion in Greenwich, Connecticut, George and Big Ann Skakel celebrated the end of the war like they usually celebrated the end of the work week; by getting plastered. George Jr., Jim, and Rushton Skakel had not yet returned from overseas, but their Greenwich buddy, Sylvester Larkin, recently discharged from the Marines, was not aware of that fact. So, dressed in his military khaki dress uniform, Larkin marched up to the Skakel mansion and knocked on the front door.

The maid who greeted Larkin at the front door said none of the Skakels were home. But Larkin was not deaf, and he heard raucous familiar voices booming from the Skakel living room. Upon entering the living room, Larkin saw unbridled merriment he had never seen before and hoped he would never see again.

In the living room with George and Big Ann Skakel were three young Royal Canadian Air Force Pilots in full dress uniforms. A maid holding a large silver platter filled with water balloons stood off to the side, while George and Ethel, and the three pilots, all standing, took turns throwing and ducking water balloons, between bursts of laughter by the men and delightful squealing by Big Ann, whose blouse was drenched. The men, too, were soaked to the skin, and the walls, floors, and furniture were saturated.

Larkin just stood there dumbfounded and wholly embarrassed.

"They were so tanked-up and involved in what they were doing they didn't even know I had entered the room," Larkin said. "So, I made an about-face and left. I said to myself, 'Nothing's changed. The Skakels are still crazy!'"

Two weeks after the official Japanese surrender, Ethel Skakel was admitted to Manhattanville College of the Sacred Heart. Manhattanville College of the Sacred Heart was founded as the Academy of the Sacred Heart by Mother Aloysia Hardey in 1841, on Houston Street in downtown Manhattan. The institution quickly outgrew their small building, and they soon moved uptown to a new campus purchased from the estate of Jacob Lorillard. It was located between 125th to 135th Streets on St. Nicholas Terrace (to the East) and Convent Avenue (to the West); in the heart of New York City's predominantly black Harlem.

Mother Eleanor O'Byrne was the Manhattanville college president. In her recruitment speeches and fund-raising efforts, one of Mother O'Byrne's selling points was that "ninety percent of our girls are engaged before they graduate."

Mother O'Byrne emphasized in her speeches that "part of the Sacred Heart education was to train young women to be the partners of successful men, to act like ladies, and to be the mothers of tomorrow."

The Manhattanville girls often engaged in wishful-thinking while huddling around the campus statue of St. Joseph, who, as legend has it, would "help the girls find a good husband if they prayed hard enough."

In the 1930s - 1940s, the Manhattanville student body consisted of approximately 200 female students. Though small, the college made headlines across the country for taking a strong position promoting racial equality decades before the Civil Rights Movement. In May 1933, the students created the "Manhattanville Resolutions," a document that pledged an active student commitment to racial justice. This commitment was tested when the first African-American student was admitted to the college in 1938.

The alumni response to an integrated student body was mixed. While the vast majority of letters praised Manhattanville for its courageous action, President Grace Dammann, RSCJ, viewed the negative responses as an opportunity to open hearts and minds. At the annual Class Day Reunion, on May 31, 1938, she delivered a passionate speech entitled "Principles Versus Prejudices." In that speech she stated that education is the key to rising above bigotry.

"The more we know of man's doing and thinking throughout time and throughout the world's extent, the more we understand that beauty and goodness and truth are not the monopoly of any age nor of any group nor of any race."

Yet, when Ethel arrived at Manhattanville, to keep the neighborhood African-American residents at bay, the entire perimeter of the college campus was fortified by a ten-foot-high concrete wall, with steel spikes lining the top. The school gates were locked at night, and the girls were warned to "never leave the campus alone and to never stand at a local bus stop or use the local subway unless accompanied by a member of the staff."

Stories abounded, none of them proven to be true, that poor innocent white girls had been abducted in the area surrounding the school by black pimps. Then, the girls were allegedly drugged and forced into prostitution. Stories like this sent shudders down the spines of the white socialites entering Manhattanville, who had lived their entire lives in lily-white communities, and they only saw blacks when they worked as servants for their parents. When Ethel was admitted to Manhattanville, only three of the students were black, and there was not a single black nun in the entire Order of the Sacred Heart.

One of the female students later said, "We were all pretty much unaware of social and political issues. Our goals were to have fun, get out of college, and get married. We lived a terribly self-centered existence."

Sister Mary Byles was a campus liberal who preached integration to her students. She adopted a set of written rules, one of which said, "If I get on a Fifth Avenue bus and there's an empty space besides a Negro person, I will sit down beside that person."

As a result of the liberal principles taught at Manhattanville, parents, especially from the Deep South, yanked their daughters out of school, in some cases, even before they had finished their first semester.

"Sometimes the students that got along best with black people were the families who had black servants," Sister Byles said. "It was because they knew them. They understood and didn't look down on them. The black Mammies were very much loved by them."

However, these social issues meant little to Ethel and to her parents. Big Ann's only concern was that Ethel get a good Catholic education. Still, Ethel, ever the prankster, told her girlfriends at Manhattanville, that although her mother was a staunch Irish-Catholic, her father was a Jew.

One of Ethel's co-students, who actually believed this deception, later said, "She thought she'd shock us. You know – the thought of a Jewess at a rigid Catholic school like Manhattanville. But most of us were amused rather than shocked."

At first sight, Ethel Skakel and Jean Kennedy formed a bond that would persevere through many tragedies during the next two generations. Visually, they were exact opposites – Ethel was thin, high-spirited and kinetic – and Jean, fourteen months older than Ethel, was mousy, introverted, and slightly overweight. The bond became such that one would often finish off the other's sentences, and both would laugh at the hint the other was making a joke.

Except for the fact that the Kennedy clan portrayed themselves as staid and proper Irish- Catholics, their family backgrounds were not dissimilar. Both families were filthy rich, but as the Kennedys enjoyed their wealth under the quiet banner of pseudo-respectability, the wild and wooly Skakels flaunted theirs with defiance.

Ethel's and Jean's persona were as different as chalk from cheese, which may have been one of the reasons they got along so well.

"Ethel had a very magnetic personality," their classmate Kay Simonson said. "Ethel loved life and having fun. But Jean was, and still is, very much into herself. Jean is more private than Ethel and very shy. As a result she's misunderstood because most people think she's snobby."

"The two of them made an ideal combination," classmate Abbyann Day said. "One of them could do the outgoing stuff, and the other could be quiet and be a good friend and a good companion."

Another classmate, Anne Marie O'Hagan said, "Ethel was totally different from Jean. Ethel was not sophisticated when she came to college. She had not traveled a lot like Jean had. Her family wasn't important in political and social circles like the Kennedys."

By the shear strength of her personality, Ethel extracted Jean from her shell of reticence, and soon both were known on the Manhattanville campus as the purveyors of practical jokes.

One night, Ethel and Jean were debating what the good nuns wore to bed at night.

"Well, there's one way to find out!" Ethel said.

After the lights were out, Ethel activated the fire alarm, and in seconds, the inhabitants of the school were scurrying about searching for signs of fire and smoke; including the nuns who did so in their assorted types of nightwear.

One weekend, both Ethel and Jean had so many bad marks in their demerit books, they were not allowed to leave the campus on a weekday night to meet two paramours waiting outside the front gate in a new luxury car.

"This is ridiculous for us to be grounded at this age," Ethel said. "We're too damn old to be grounded."

Ethel's simple solution was to break into the nun's main office, extract the demerit book from a drawer, and dispose of it down the incinerator chute. This pleased about a dozen other girls, since they, too, had too many black marks in their demerit book to be allowed off campus during the week.

One of Ethel's biggest indiscretions at Manhattanville was when the 69-year-old Monsignor Hartigan from Australia arrived at the Manhattanville campus driving a brand new Cadillac. To Ethel, a priest, even a Monsignor, had no right to flaunt material wealth, while the Sacred Heart nuns lived humbly observing the vow of poverty.

"Can you imagine the gall of this man?" Ethel told Jean. "I'll fix his wagon."

On a large piece of white cardboard, Ethel printed in block letters, "Are the collections good, Father?

Then, she scotch-taped the cardboard message to the front windshield of Monsignor Hartigan's car.

What Ethel didn't know, or maybe she didn't care, was that Monsignor Hartigan was a world-renowned poet and author, whose works were published under the pseudonym "John O'Brien" as far back as 1906. His poetry was very popular in Australia, and was well received in Ireland and in the United States. And, because his Roman Catholic priestly vows did not include the vow of poverty, Father Hartigan had properly, and within the bounds of the Catholic Church's doctrines, earned the money to buy his new car (in 1911, the-then Father Hartigan was one of the first curates in Australia to own a motor car).

So Ethel, by leaving her inane note on the Monsignor's car, was falsely impugning the integrity of a respected author and poet, and more importantly – a man of God.

When the irate Monsignor spotted the note on his windshield, he decreed that no one could leave the Manhattanville campus until the perpetrator came forward and admitted her guilt.

To her classmates' dismay, it took Ethel five days to summon up the courage to fess up that she was the culprit.

One of her classmates told another, "I'd like to strangle that skinny bitch."

Another time, Ethel and one of her classmates visited the National Horse Show at Madison Square Garden in New York City. There, they met a member of the Irish riding team, and Ethel was so infatuated with the young man, she invited him for lunch. Not to give the appearance of impropriety, Ethel insisted her classmate join them.

The lunch date went just dandy, but the following day when Ethel and her friend again attended the horse show, the young Irish rider looked right through them like they were invisible.

Irate, Ethel snuck into the horse stable under the arena and painted the poor lad's horse kelly green.

In secular colleges, Ethel's actions would have most surely led to expulsion. But when the Sacred Heart nuns expressed their extreme displeasure with Ethel's outlandish actions, and this happened often, Big Ann Skakel, lugging George Skakel's dough, would ride to Ethel's rescue, delivering cash on the barrelhead to the good nuns of the Sacred Heart.

One of Ethel's classmates said, "The school always needed money for one project or another. It was like Ethel's parents owned a bank and were handing out interest-free loans."

Ethel's actions at school did not go unnoticed to the Kennedy clan's matriarch, Rose Kennedy, who was also a graduate of Manhattanville College.

"Mother thought we just weren't studying enough," Jean Kennedy said. "And mother also thought that Ethel was just a bad influence on me. I had graduated with honors from Norton High School, and at Manhattanville, my marks were steadily down. So, mother put a wall between us."

During the Christmas holidays of 1945-46, Jean Kennedy brought Ethel Skakel, then seventeen, with her on a skiing trip to Canada. There, Ethel first met Jean's 20-year-old brother, Robert "Bobby" Kennedy. As was Ethel, Bobby was built like a twig, and he stood maybe five feet and nine inches tall. Bobby had large ears which looked like radar antennas, and his hair looked like it had never been introduced to a comb. In addition to Bobby's unimpressive appearance, his high-pitched voice sounded like it belonged to a member of the female species.

For whatever reason, the thin and athletic Ethel became infatuated with Bobby, but, at first, the feeling was not mutual.

One weekend, Bobby invited Ethel to Harvard University where he was a student. Ethel took along her older sister, Pat, who was also attending college at Manhattanville, and in no time, Bobby was smitten with Pat Skakel; the sister who was more refined and didn't act like a tomboy.

According to The Kennedy Women by Laurence Leamer, "Ethel was totally taken by Bobby. It was endlessly humiliating, that of all the women in the world, Bobby should be dating Pat. But Ethel did not give up, and neither did her friend.

"Jean invited Ethel to come to Boston in the spring of 1946 to work on Jack's campaign (In 1947, John 'Jack' Fitzgerald Kennedy was elected U. S. Senator in the House of Representatives, representing the 11th Congressional district in Massachusetts). Ethel rang doorbells and passed out literature as fervently as anyone, spending as much time with Bobby as she could manage. Still, Bobby did not seem to think of Ethel as anything more than an amusing and sometimes annoying little girl.

"During Christmas, Bobby invited Pat to spend the holidays at the Kennedy mansion in Palm Beach. That was almost a declaration of intent, but Jean and Ethel plotted their own strategy. Jean invited Ethel to come as well, in yet another attempt to pry Bobby and Pat apart. In the end, Bobby and Pat split, not because of Ethel's overwhelming allure, but because Pat considered Bobby immature and too young. Ethel was there to catch him."

"Pat never really liked Bobby very much," said Pat's close friend Pat Norton. "I never felt, 'Whoops! Here's Bobby Kennedy, a big romance in Pat's life. It was more of a casual thing with Pat."

That differed with the assessments of other Manhattanville girls, including Mary O'Hagan, who said, "Pat was really crazy about Bobby. But in some way or another, Ethel stole Bobby away – stole his affections. Suddenly, Bobby's affections were turned towards Ethel. We felt it was awfully peculiar for the younger sister to steal the beau away from the older sister, if that's what happened. It was the big talk at Manhattanville, that Ethel was now dating Bobby instead of Pat. People were angry."

Nevertheless, by Ethel's junior year, she and Bobby were said to be "serious."

Ethel decided to return the favor to Jean, and she arranged a date with Jean and her brother, Rushton, who by now was known as the "quiet and sane" Skakel boy.

"Jean was a nice girl, but I just couldn't handle it," Rushton said. "The Kennedys were just not my cup of tea."

There was also another brief Skakel/Kennedy romance, and it involved Jim Skakel and Pat Kennedy, the sixth of nine Kennedy children.

"Jim was immensely attracted to Pat Kennedy, and they fell in love," said Pat Kennedy's friend Margaret Adams.

But after seriously dating for over a year, the relationship suddenly went kaput.

Some people said it was Jim Skakel's drinking that soured Pat on their romance. But Jim Skakel claimed it was he who ended the relationship.

"The Kennedys were just too clannish for me," he said. "If you went out with one Kennedy, you went out with all of them. So I said, 'The hell with it.' We were just not suited for each other."

By 1948, Ethel's junior year, Bobby Kennedy became a fixture at Manhattanville, picking up Ethel every weekend for dates in venues all over the northeast.

"Ethel was head-over-heels in love with Bobby," classmate Ann Marie O'Hagan said. "That's all she talked about and wanted. She couldn't wait for the weekends to see Bobby. All her conversations were about either Bobby, or the Kennedy family. It was Kennedy, Kennedy, Kennedy – and not much Skakel anymore."

"After every weekend date, we go scrambling up to Ethel's room at the college to get all the details about what had happened," said classmate Kay Simonson. "Sexual activity was unheard of. We'd talked about kissing and holding hands and stuff like that."

The truth was neither Bobby nor Ethel was outwardly demonstrative with their affection for one another. Both were prudish. Friends thought this was a nod to their rigid Catholic beliefs about no sexual activity before marriage. Holding hands in public was as hot as it got, and the casual observer might think they were a loving brother and sister, especially after noticing their almost identical facial characteristics.

As it was becoming more obvious to both the Kennedys and the Skakels that Bobby and Ethel would soon tie the knot, not everyone was happy about the situation.

George Skakel Jr. told his brothers, "I don't know what Ethel sees in that skinny prick, Bobby Kennedy. Every time I see him with Ethel, it pisses me off. And every time I hear his fucking squeaky voice, I want to strangle him."

To make matters worse for George Jr., Bobby was at the Skakel mansion virtually every weekend. He passed himself off as somewhat of a tutor on American history, when his grades at Harvard were barely average. In fact, considering his mediocre high school grades at Milton Academy in Milton, Massachusetts, it's doubtful he would have been admitted to a prestigious Ivy League school like Harvard if it weren't for his father's deep pockets; pockets Joe Kennedy emptied often to help any one of his sons, for a variety of reasons, academic, political, and otherwise.

"Bobby was very helpful when he came into the picture," Kay Simonson said. "We'd be up there in Greenwich and he'd sit on the couch, and we'd sit around him and cram for our tests and essays. It was something we looked forward to. He was a terrific help because he made the subjects so interesting and engaging."

On one Sunday afternoon at the Skakel mansion, while Big Ann held court with her gaggle of Catholic friends, intertwined with local Catholic priests mainly there for the free food and cocktails, brothers Jim and George Skakel Jr. watched as Bobby played teacher to a group of girls, including Ethel, in Big Ann's lavish Catholic library.

"Well, what do you make of this?" Jim asked his brother, George Jr. "Do you think Ethel is serious with the Kennedy boy?

"Well, there's no doubt that Ethel is smitten with little Bobby," the six-foot two-inch George Jr. said. "But there's something about him that just doesn't smell right."

"Yes, I know what you mean," Jim said. "But I just can't put my finger on it."

"Well, it's simple to me," George Jr. said. "It's common knowledge that his father cheated on his mother."

"Oh, you're talking about that little fling he had with actress Gloria Swanson in Hollywood?" Jim said.

"Little fling? They were walking around Hollywood like they were husband and wife, while Rose Kennedy stayed home and took care of his nine children," George Jr. said. "It's no fucking secret Joe Kennedy was banging Hollywood actresses two at a time. He owned a fucking Hollywood movie studio, for Christ's sake! And the way I heard it, an actress couldn't get a part in any of his films unless she spent quality time on her back."

"So you figure, like father, like son?" Jim said.

"Sure, why not?" George Jr. said. "Look at our father and his father before him. Both drunks. And look at us and Rushton, all drunks too, by any definition.

"I'm going to see how this plays out, but if I get wind of little Bobby cheating on our sister, I'll rip his head off and feed it to our dogs."

Chapter Fifteen

To Ethel's Dismay, Bobby Kennedy Falls for a British Actress in England

Bobby Kennedy graduated from Harvard in March of 1948 with a less than stellar record. In fact, Bobby's grades were so mediocre, not even his father's money could buy him into a big-time law school, like Harvard Law. So, Papa Joe Kennedy took his money, and he deposited it at the doorstep of Virginia Law School, hardly an elite venue at the time. Virginia Law School grudging accepted Bobby, but it noted in their consideration of him that he had "far from an outstanding record at Harvard."

Papa Joe decided that Bobby, who he called the "runt in the family," needed some worldly experience before he entered law school. So, he threw his checkbook at the Boston Post, and, with a written recommendation by Cardinal Spellman, he inveigled press credentials for Bobby as a "news correspondent." Bobby took his press credentials, and with the 6-foot 2-inch George Terrien as a paid companion, they set sail for Europe on the Queen Mary (Terrien later married Ethel Skakel's older sister, Georgeann).

"Old Joe wanted me to go along to take care of Bobby," Terrien said. "Joe wanted someone with a lot of seasoning to babysit for him."

So, while Ethel Skakel started her senior year at Manhattanville, Bobby was globetrotting all over Europe and the Middle East; writing featured articles for the Boston Post.

After traipsing around foreign ground for two months, Bobby returned to London. There, playwright, William Douglas Home, gave Bobby tickets for him and George Terrien to attend Home's new play, The Chiltern Hundreds, at London's Vaudeville Theater. The star of the play was the 21-year-old British actress, Joan Winmill, a blond and blue-eyed beauty, who took Bobby's heart for a glorious spin.

After the play, Bobby met Joan backstage, and in an instant, the last thing on his mind was Ethel Skakel.

"It was love at first sight," Joan said. "He looked so cute with his freckled face and white, toothy grin. His looks made me feel weak at the knees. When Bobby asked me out the following night, I accepted like a shot."

When Joan met Bobby, she was basically broke. She got paid very little for her acting, and her salary as a part-time cocktail waitress was a paltry $32 a week. She lived in a one-bedroom flat in a questionable neighborhood, with two other aspiring actresses.

Within a week, Bobby had gotten Joan, with his father's money of course, a lovely two-bedroom flat in a posh neighborhood.

"To Joan, it was like a fairy tale come true," said one of her actress roommates. "She was having a romance with the handsome son of a former British Ambassador. What could be wrong with that?"

George Terrien was in the middle of this intercontinental romance, and Bobby swore him to secrecy.

"Joan was a far different kind of girl than was Ethel," Terrien said. "She was sexy and sophisticated, and I never had a doubt that Bobby was in love with her. Shortly after Bobby met Joan, he told me, 'Ethel's fun but she's just a girl. Joan's a real woman.'"

Bobby spent hours bragging to Joan what a prestigious family the Kennedys were in America. And she lapped it up like a puppy dog licking ice cream.

"We had great times together," Joan said. "We went to the theater. We'd go to dinner. He'd bring me flowers. He was very romantic."

Incredibly, Joan claimed they never had sex. Bobby did a lot of begging and pawing, but it was all to no avail.

"I was able to reason with him," Joan said. "I told him if he didn't stop behaving like a dog, chasing me all over the flat, I'd throw a bucket of cold water on him."

It's not clear if George Terrien was playing the part of a double agent, but somehow Papa Joe Kennedy found out about his son's dalliances in England.

Joe Kennedy told a trusted political advisor, "Bobby is using his wrong head in England. If the United States press gets a hold of this story of Bobby dating a British actress it could develop into a scandal and embarrass the family. Bobby could seriously jeopardize Jack's chances at being voted in as a Senator in the Massachusetts House of Representatives."

When Bobby, who was deathly afraid of his father, found out that Papa Joe knew all about Joan, he tried to convince her that he was his own man and that his father could never tear them apart.

"Bobby treated his father's feelings more as a joke," Joan said. "He didn't feel there was anything for us to be worried about. He was like any son laughing at his father's foolishness. Bobby told me straight out that nobody was going to break us up.

"But as time went by, I realized he was so controlled by his father. He was clearly in the shadows of his brothers, and his father dominated much of his life."

At this point in time, Ethel didn't know about Joan, and Joan didn't know about Ethel.

Feeling the heat of his father's breath on his back, Bobby put an end to his and Joan's nightlife in London. Instead of going to opulent parties attended by the upper crust of London society, Bobby played it strictly low-key.

"If someone had seen us out in public together, something would have gotten written in the newspapers," Joan said.

His hat tipped down over his face and his overcoat collar snapped upward, Bobby would pick up Joan after her performance at the theater. With the hulking George Terrien running interference, they would trot to a little restaurant across the street, have a quick bite to eat, and then abscond to Joan's flat for the rest of the night, only to repeat the same routine the following day.

"For the most part, we kept our relationship very low-key," Joan said. "As a result, there was never any publicity."

Enter Murphy's Law, which states, "Anything that can go wrong, will go wrong, and at the worst possible time."

Ethel Skakel and Jean Kennedy decided it would be a wonderful idea if they jetted over to London to see the summer Olympic Games at the Empire Stadium, later known as the Wembley Stadium. But if the truth be known, if Joe Kennedy knew about Bobby's fling with Joan, so did his daughter, Jean, who was Ethel Skakel's best friend. Connect the dots, and it was clear Ethel and Jean had made the trip to Merry Old London to sabotage any chance that Bobby had of sowing his wild oats in someone other than Ethel Skakel.

Knowing the duo was on the way, Bobby met Ethel and Jean at the airport, and after settling them into a swank hotel, he took them to see Joan's performance at London's Vaudeville Theater.

Backstage after the show, Bobby made the faux pas of introducing Ethel as his sister Jean's friend and not his girlfriend.

"I vaguely was aware that Ethel was looking at Bobby and me almost as if she were jealous," Joan later said. "I didn't even know they were going together. He never told me he was dating Ethel. I just thought she was with his sister."

In August, Bobby and George Terrien headed back to the States, by luxury liner, both to attend Virginia Law School.

"I went to the ship with him, and before he boarded he put his arms around me tenderly," Joan said. "He told me, 'Don't cry, I'll be back next summer. I can't stay away from you.'

"I was really a struggling actress, and Bobby was a very caring person. He would sense what I needed, and he sent things to me without me ever asking. He sent me perfumes and soaps, chocolates, and elegant clothes, with famous labels like Sak's, Bergdorf's and Bonwit's. He told me he had swiped them from the closets of his sisters, Jean and Pat, who had so many glorious possessions, they would never miss them.

"We also exchanged piles of love letters. I considered myself to be in love. He epitomized everything I had ever dreamed of."

During school break in the summer of 1949, Bobby returned to London and resumed his clandestine relationship with Joan. When summer ended, he invited Joan on the ship with him to say goodbye.

"We talked about me coming to America to be with him," Joan said.

In May of 1950, Joan was waiting for word from Bobby about the details of her impending trip to America. Instead, she got a kick in the stomach.

He wrote her a letter, which simply said, "Dear Joan. I am getting married to Ethel Skakel."

"I was devastated," Joan said. "We were like boyfriend and girlfriend. It was like an old-fashioned romance. I was furious. But what could I do? So, I went into the drawer where I kept Bobby's love letters, lit a match and burned them."

Years later, Joan pondered her relationship with Bobby.

"Those times with Bobby were some of the happiest times I ever had then. But as time passed, I realized that Bobby and I were not suited at all.

"I am not a very athletic person as was Ethel. I had only two children. If I was to have eleven as Ethel did, I never would have made it. I also know I would never have fit in with the Kennedy family. Everybody in the family was very competitive, athletic, and had tremendous energy, especially Ethel. I'm not that way. As it turned out, Ethel was perfect for Bobby."

Chapter Sixteen

Ethel Skakel and Bobby Kennedy Tie the Knot

Back in the US of A, Big Ann Skakel was absolutely thrilled when she heard her daughter, Ethel, was going to marry Bobby Kennedy, whose family was at the zenith of American Catholic society. The Skakels were filthy rich alright. But the Kennedys, not quite as rich as the Skakels, were as good as it got when it came to respectability in Catholic circles, which was a characteristic the Skakels, to Big Ann's dismay, had never come close to achieving in the Catholic-controlled town of Greenwich. Big Ann felt that a Skakel-Kennedy liaison would put her at least on a par with her blue-blooded Catholic neighbors, maybe even a notch above.

George Skakel Sr. felt differently.

"Joseph Kennedy and his family are nothing more than vulgar Irish trash," George Sr. told his wife. "I made my money legitimately, through hard work and vision. Joe Kennedy made his dirty money by bootlegging during Prohibition and rubbing elbows with Italian hoodlums. Quite frankly, Joe Kennedy couldn't kiss my ass."

In May of 1950, Big Ann was in her glory when she planned and executed a luxurious wedding party that she felt would propel the Skakel/Kennedy union into the upper echelon of American society.

As usual, Big Ann was quite generous when spending her husband's money. She sent out twelve hundred invitations for the extravaganza, which was to take place at the Skakel mansion in Greenwich. For the ceremony itself, Ann had constructed a huge circus-like tent on her front lawn, with seating for as many as

1,500 people, just in case. Big Ann also hired more than 100 servants and a dozen bartenders to service the guests; some of whom were Greenwich police officers, making moonlighting money on the side, which was quite legal and a common occurrence in Greenwich. Famed Irish tenor, Morton Downey Sr., was brought in to headline the entertainment.

In the weeks leading up to the wedding, it was evident that Big Ann and Rose Kennedy, respective matriarchs of their families, did not see eye to eye; especially since Big Ann was over six feet tall and the diminutive Rose Kennedy barely reached five feet in her stocking feet.

"Ann Skakel had the habit of trying to intimidate people with her height and size," a Kennedy family friend said. "But Rose Kennedy was as tough as they came, and she would have none of that."

At her husband George's urging, Big Ann figuratively spit in Rose Kennedy's face, when, although she had invited dozens of her friends to stay at the Skakel mansion for the duration of the wedding party, there was no room for the Kennedys.

"They have plenty of cash, those Kennedys do," George Sr. told Big Ann. "Let them find and pay for their own place to stay."

Years later, Betty Skakel Medaille, Ethel's first cousin, said, "The Kennedy clan decided it would be convenient for them to stay at the Skakel house at Lake Avenue. But Uncle George and Aunt Ann decided it wasn't convenient; not for them, not for their family, and not for their friends. No one pushed Aunt Ann around, not even Rose Kennedy. Aunt Ann liked to have the privilege of inviting and not have it forced upon her. The Kennedys didn't like it at all."

An exception was made for Jean Kennedy and that was done by Ethel herself.

"She's my best friend, and she's staying at our house," Ethel told her parents.

The week before the wedding, the Kennedys stayed at their home in Hyannis Port, to avoid paying an even bigger check than the one they would have to swallow for staying a few days after the wedding at a Greenwich hotel.

George and Big Ann also decried the fact that when it came to picking up dinner checks at upscale restaurants, Joe Kennedy had short arms and deep pockets.

As was reported in The Kennedy Men: 1901-1963 written by Laurence Leamer, "Big Ann and George Sr. didn't begrudge spending a fortune on the wedding, but it irked Ethel's family that the Kennedys were so confoundedly cheap. When the two families went out together for dinner, the Kennedys were healthy enough when it was time to order the best food and the finest wines, but by the end of the evening their arms became so weak they were unable to reach out and pick up the check. This happened so many times and in so many ways that the Skakels concluded that they were not being appreciated for their largess, but were being played for chumps."

At the wedding, the Skakels got a measure of satisfaction, when, as the wedding party prepared to proceed down the aisle at nearby St. Mary's Church, Lem Billings, a Jack Kennedy crony from way back, arrived late for his seat up front as an usher. As Billings, an acknowledged homosexual, rushed down the aisle in front of the bride and her bridesmaids, he spotted some loose change on the floor. As he bent down to pick up his bounty, Ethel's brother, George Jr., who was trailing close behind, booted Billings hard in the butt, sending him sprawling face-first onto the floor.

George Jr. later told his brothers, "I guess I kick-started that wedding off with a bang."

The night before the wedding, John Kennedy held his brother Bobby's bachelor party at the Harvard Club. And the Skakel boys were born to party.

To counterbalance the bulk of the male Skakels, Bobby invited several members of his old Harvard college football team, of which Bobby, at 150 pounds, was a third-string tight end, who spend most of game time picking splinters out of his butt on the bench. All total there were thirty men at the party, and as the testosterone rocketed back and forth, it was a miracle no fights broke out between the opposing factions.

Leamer wrote in The Kennedy Men: 1901-1963, "The Skakel brothers and their friends arrived at his bachelor party like a wandering minstrel troupe of such spirited demeanor that they made everyone dance to their song. Bobby's old college football teammates were ready for the party too, and by the time the thirty or so guests left the Harvard Club they had consumed twelve and a half bottles of champagne, five bottles of Haig & Haig Pinch Scotch, half a bottle of rye, most of a bottle of gin, and a third of a bottle of bourbon.

"On their way out, one of Bobby's friends picked up a fire extinguisher and doused the room, causing over a thousand dollars' worth of damage, before staggering out into the New York night. The Skakels conceded nothing to the Kennedys, considering themselves their equal in wealth and position, vastly superior in their enjoyment of life and sense of humor, and lesser only in their lack of pretense. The Skakels did not have the Kennedys' public name, but they were an immensely powerful psychological force that changed the Kennedys far more than the Kennedys changed them."

While the boys were letting loose at the bachelor party, Rose Kennedy sat quietly alone in her home in Hyannis Port. The morning of the wedding, a limo took her to Greenwich.

As for Papa Joe, on the night before the wedding, he avoided his son's bachelor party and was busy in New York City, entertaining his latest paramour. On the morning of the wedding, he, too, was driven by limo to Greenwich.

Because Big Ann held numerous parties at her home, in the mid-1940s, she decided that maintaining a beauty salon on the premises, for her and her girlfriends' use, was the right thing to do. Still an old cheater at heart, Big Ann had bogus beauty salon business cards and letterheads produced, so that she could purchase supplies, including commercial hair dryers, wholesale from the major distributors.

On the morning of the wedding, the six bridesmaids had their hair done in Big Ann's Hair Salon. The labor was performed by a dozen beauticians that Big Ann had imported from the town of Greenwich.

After getting their hair and makeup done, the bridesmaids decided to head outside to the pool to enjoy some early morning cocktails. This got George Skakel Jr. to thinking.

He turned to his brothers, Jim and Rushton.

"Those girls must be looney," George Jr. said. "This is Skakel territory, and you know what that means!"

As if by instinct, the three Skakel brothers moseyed over to the gaggle of giggling girls, and one by one, they flung them into the pool.

"The bridesmaids got thrown into the pool," Big Ann later said. "Needless to say, their hair was ruined. But I know my boys, and I planned for the worst."

For the girls, it was back to Big Ann's Hair Salon for a re-hairdo, and their gowns were expertly dried and pressed in time for the wedding.

At the wedding ceremony, George Skakel Sr. escorted his daughter, Ethel, down the aisle. Ethel was dressed all in white, as were the six bridesmaids. The maid of honor was Ethel's older sister, Pat Skakel Cuffe, who had flown in from Ireland, where she now resided. Pat, who had a drinking problem since her teenage years, was noticeably tight, but far from wobbly drunk.

Congressman John F. Kennedy, dressed in a luxurious black tuxedo, was his brother's best man. Bobby's younger brother, Teddy, and George Terrien served as ushers, as did several of Bobby's football chums from Harvard.

As the wedding procession proceeded down the center isle of the church, Big Ann whispered out loud, "Where did Bobby get these characters?"

The ceremony was performed by the Reverend Terrance T. Connolly before more than 2,000 people who had crowded, like sardines, into the church.

The vows were exchanged, Bobby kissed the bride, and it was off to the wedding party extravaganza at the Skakel mansion.

During the festivities, Big Ann noticed Ethel was imbibing more than Big Ann thought appropriate.

She pulled her daughter to the side, and said, "You can't drink and take care of a husband, too."

Ethel did not have another drink at her wedding.

As for Joe Kennedy's spectacular tightness with the buck, one of Ethel's brother-in-law's, John Dowdle, had a solution that warmed George Skakel Sr.'s heart. Since George Skakel Sr. had footed the bill for the wedding, Joe Kennedy agreed to handle the expense of the honeymoon in Hawaii. Dowdle knew about Joe Kennedy's tightness with a buck, but Bobby Kennedy, himself, had stiffed Dowdle on several occasions when they were out on the town together.

Dowdle told Jim Skakel, "Whenever a check at a bar or restaurant came due, Bobby's standard M.O. was saying, 'Oh John, I left my wallet home. Could you handle this for me?'"

So, when Joe Kennedy sluffed off to Dowdle the assignment of making the arrangements for the Hawaii honeymoon, Dowdle gladly accepted the task.

First, he booked the newlyweds into the swank Royal Hawaiian Hotel on Waikiki Beach and then into the plush Hanamaui Resort Hotel on Maui. To add to Joe Kennedy's expenses, he told the management of the two hotels to add a 40 % tip to all expenses: drinks, food, gift shop, etc... Dowdle ordered fresh orchids to be delivered every morning to the Honeymoon Suite and a magnum of their best champagne every evening at 8 pm, sharp.

Bobby realized what was going on, but what could he do? Disappoint his new wife?

So, Bobby kept his mouth shut. And when the two breathtaking hotel bills for the honeymoon were presented to Papa Joe Kennedy, he almost burst a blood vessel in his brain.

After the newlyweds had jetted off to Hawaii, Dowdle told a friend, "We took great pleasure in arranging the most expensive honeymoon imaginable because we knew it would annoy the hell out of Bobby and his old man."

Chapter Seventeen

Kennedy Family Tragedies

After the union of the Kennedy and Skakel families had become a fait accompli, for the next generation, the Kennedy family experienced a roller coaster ride of monumental successes and unimaginable tragedies.

John F. Kennedy continued as the United States House of Representative for the 11th Congressional district in Massachusetts until 1953. In November 1952, with the backing of his father's money, added to a substantial amount of arm-twisting and deceit, JFK defeated incumbent Republican Henry Cabot Lodge II for the U.S. Senate seat. After losing to Estes Kefauver as the Democratic vice presidential candidate under the 1956 presidential candidacy of Adlai Stevenson, in 1960, again, with his father pulling the strings, and with more than a little help from the American Mafia, JFK became the thirty-fifth President of the United States.

At his father's urging, JFK named his brother Bobby as the Attorney General of the United States. In addition, Papa Joe, exhibiting monumental quantities of arrogance and stupidity, ordered Bobby to go after the same Mafia pals who had been so helpful to the Kennedys in the presidential election.

It was a blunder that would cost both John and Bobby Kennedy their lives.

The two Kennedy assassinations have been covered thousands of times in hundreds of different publications, so we will not go into them in great detail. The basic facts are these:

After Bobby Kennedy, as the new Attorney General, went after the same Mafia hoodlums who helped fix the presidential election in 1960 for his brother, it was only a matter of time before the inevitable occurred.

Rather than go after Bobby, the aggrieved Mafioso decided to kill the "head of the dog," (JFK) and the body (Bobby's tenure as Attorney General) would die. No matter how many times you hear that it was the "one bullet" nonsense, fired from the gun of the "lone gunman," Lee Harvey Oswald, that killed JFK, be assured that it was a complete fairy tale.

Also, be assured that everyone, from FBI Director J. Edgar Hoover to Bobby Kennedy, himself, knew it was a red herring to distract the American public from grasping the truth: The Mafia had been strong enough and wily enough to assassinate the President of the United States. J. Edgar Hoover either was powerless to stop it, or he knew about it in advance and had looked the other way.

As for Bobby Kennedy, he knew from day one that the Mafia had killed his brother. On the night of the assassination, Bobby told a friend, "I thought it would be me they killed, not Jack."

But Bobby Kennedy also knew, and Hoover frequently reminded him, that Hoover had a damning secret dossier on the Kennedy family that would blow the head off any illusions that the Kennedys were as righteous as they claimed to be.

Bobby was, as was his brother, and as was their father, a serial adulterer, who had bedded beauty after beauty, including the movie star, Marilyn Monroe, who, in 1963, had turned up tragically dead from an apparent suicide. One word from Bobby to anyone that differed from Hoover's version of the events of his brother's murder (and later the Warren Commission's version of the events), and Hoover was ready to release his Kennedy report for world-wide consumption.

Bobby Kennedy signed his own death warrant, when, after being elected Senator from New York in 1964, he foolishly decided to follow his brother's footsteps and run for President of the United States. Bobby had to know that the same people who had killed his brother would try to do the same to him if he ever tried such a bold move.

The same cast of Mafia characters, who killed his brother, were still alive and more powerful than before. And they used the same "pin it on the dope" formula as they did with Lee Harvey Oswald, using another dupe named Sirhan Sirhan.

On June 5, 1968, after celebrating a major win in the California Democratic Primary, Bobby, at the last moment, was misled by someone to exit through the kitchen because it was a "short cut to the press room." Waiting in the kitchen and working as a busboy was degenerate gambler, Sirhan Sirhan, who owed the Mafia more money for betting on three-legged horses than he could earn in a lifetime of bussing tables.

As Bobby passed through the kitchen, Sirhan jumped in front of him and fired three shots from a .22 caliber Iver-Johnson Cadet revolver. All three bullets hit Bobby in the front torso. But what was conveniently suppressed by Hoover from the public was that the two fatal shots were fired from a .38 caliber revolver into Bobby's head from behind.

After Hoover's death in 1972, and after still photos from the crime scene were examined, it was discovered that an phony "security guard," hired at the last minute, allegedly from a security firm which had no records of such a hiring, could not be located, nor was there any proof, except from the photos, that he ever existed.

As for the family patriarch, Joseph P. Kennedy, he suffered a stroke on December 19, 1961, which paralyzed his right side and limited his speech, for the rest of his life, to occasional murmurs, grunts, and groans.

Papa Joe lasted until November 18, 1969, when he expired at age 80. Whether he was cognizant of the fact, or not, Joe Kennedy Sr. outlived both his sons, John and Bobby, who died, respectively, at ages 47 and 42.

Chapter Eighteen

Skakel Family Tragedies

The Skakel family tragedies started on Tuesday, April 4, 1955.

The headline in *the New York Times* read:

> **Mr. and Mrs. George Skakel Die in Plane Crash**
> **Exploded in Mid-Air Over Oklahoma**
> **Were Flying to Coast on Business Trip**

The article said:

Union City, Oklahoma

George Skakel Sr. of Greenwich Conn., chairman of the Great Lakes Coal and Coke Corporation, was killed together with his wife in a plane crash last night.

Four bodies were recovered from the wreckage near this little farm community. The other victim was pilot, Joseph W. Whitney, of Stratford, Conn. The co-pilot of the two-engine company craft was John E. McBride, 31, also of Stratford.

Mr. Skakel, 63, and his wife, Ann, 63, had taken the plane in New York on a flight to Los Angeles. The crash occurred shortly after the plane refueled in Tulsa.

Before the crash, the pilot reported to the Oklahoma City airport tower that he was in trouble and would land in Oklahoma City. Nothing more was heard. Witnesses said they saw the craft at a low altitude, and then it exploded and burst into flames.

The news spread quickly throughout the Skakel family. Rushton and George Jr. flew in from the Great Lakes Coal and Coke Facility in St. Louis, where they worked for their father's company. Jim Skakel flew in from Los Angeles. Pat and her husband, Luan Cuffe, flew in from Dublin. Georgeann, the eldest Skakel family sibling, and Ann, the youngest, already lived in Greenwich. The six Skakel siblings congregated in Big Ann's library.

The only one missing was Ethel Skakel Kennedy.

George Jr. phoned Ethel in her apartment in Washington D.C., where Bobby was working for the Senate Permanent Subcommittee on Investigations.

Bobby picked up the phone, and even though he knew the senior Skakels had perished, he refused to let Ethel speak to her brother.

"Well, the six of us are in Greenwich, already," George Jr. said. "Have Ethel fly in, and I'll pick her up at the airport."

Bobby was irate.

"No! Ethel's not coming to Greenwich," Bobby said. "She will only come up after you make the funeral arrangements. And she will only come up for the funeral. But she's not coming up now!"

"You're a real tough guy on the phone," George Jr. told Bobby. "Let's see if you talk to me like that when you get to Greenwich; if you have the nerve to come."

When George Jr. got off the phone and told his siblings the bad news, the two other men cursed, but the three women burst into tears.

Finally, between sniffles, Georgeann said, "Ethel should be here with her family. Why does she put up with him? Why doesn't she come up here on her own? My God! Our mother and father are dead!"

"This is so typical of that vindictive little prick," George Jr. said. "He's a little Napoleon, and one of these days he's going to get his. I'll sort this out someday."

"You know Ethel always defers to her husband," Rushton said.

"It's the Kennedy bullshit, you know," said Jim. "Ethel's a Kennedy now, and fuck the Skakels."

Virginia Skakel, who was separated from Jim Skakel, also flew down to Greenwich to be with the family.

"A dynasty was gone," Virginia later said. "The mother and father ran everything. But I was surprised at the reactions when the two caskets were brought into the library. They were all basket cases inside, but outside they showed very little emotion."

On Friday, October 7, twenty-five priests said Mass at the solemn requiem High Mass (the Mass for the dead). As the priests intoned their prayers in Latin, the Manhattanville Choir sang Catholic funeral songs, including the "Song of Farewell" and "We Will Rise Again."

In the first row of the church, all seven Skakel siblings sat next to each other, but Bobby was warned to stay in the back of the church. Bobby and Ethel had arrived in Greenwich late the night before.

"I hugged her, but she didn't say a word," Virginia Skakel said. "There were no tears from her, or from any of them. Instead of crying, they laughed and drank. It was the only way they could cope."

Even though Big Ann Skakel was a Catholic and her husband was not, the Catholic Church allowed them to be buried side by side in the Catholic St. Mary's Cemetery, because of "Ann Skakel's longtime friendship, devotions, and sponsorship of the Catholic Church."

At the Skakel mansion after the funeral, instead of brooding, the Skakels were in full-party-mode.

"The house was crammed with so many people, it was like the black hole of Calcutta with a cocktail party atmosphere," cousin Berry Medaille said. "Ethel and Bobby didn't want to mingle with the herd. Ethel had the look of someone who wished she wasn't there."

Ethel told Bobby she wanted to stay with her family for a few days, but Bobby would have none of that. Instead of dining the evening of the funeral with the Skakels in Greenwich, Bobby took Ethel to a fancy New York City restaurant. No Skakels were invited.

After dinner, Bobby and Ethel boarded a plane back home to Washington D.C. Early the next morning, after Bobby had departed for work, Ethel headed to the Bethesda Country Club, where she played 18 rounds of golf with her friend Sarah Davis.

"Not once did Ethel discuss her parents, or what had happened to them," Davis said.

Georgeann Skakel Dowdle was put in charge of closing up her parents' mansion, selling off the furniture, and putting the house up for sale. She paid all the servants one months' salary in advance, and then she returned to her own home, not wanting to be in the way as the servants performed their final tasks.

A week after the house was supposed to be empty, Georgeann returned to the mansion and found several of the servants still working.

"What's going on here?" Georgeann said.

The servants told her that a man, who had come down for the funeral, had been living in the house for more than a month, and they just assumed this had been done with the approval of the Skakels.

Just then, the 23-year-old Teddy Kennedy came skipping down the steps from his bedroom upstairs, grinning like he hadn't a care in the world.

"What the hell are you doing here?" Georgeann said.

"I decided to stay in Greenwich after the funeral, and it was more convenient to stay here than staying in a hotel," Teddy said.

"You've got some nerve!" Georgeann said. "I'm going home to tell my husband, and you better be gone before he gets here!"

Georgeann rushed home and informed her husband, John Dowdle, the same man who had padded Ethel's and Bobby's honeymoon bill because the Kennedys were so stingy, what had just transpired.

"That cheap son of a bitch!" Dowdle said.

He rushed to the Skakel mansion, but when he got there, the servants told him that Teddy Kennedy had hastily vacated the premises just minutes before.

"He literally ran out the front door with three suitcases," one of the servants told Dowdle.

It took five years for the Skakels to sell the Skakel mansion, and when they did, it sold for a mere $350,000; less than half of what they were asking.

In order to pay the estate taxes, the Skakels needed to sell other properties, too. Bobby Kennedy had his eye on a specific property that the Skakels owned in Palos Verdes, California. Knowing from his wmife that the Skakels needed the cash and might entertain a lowball offer, Bobby, not willing to haggle with a male Skakel face-to-face, sent his brother-in-law, Steve Smith, the husband of his sister, Jean, to do the negotiating. Smith was known to be something of a tough guy himself, but George Skakel Jr. threw him out on his ear, without even hearing his offer.

George Jr. told his siblings, "If something's worth a dollar, the fucking Kennedys want to pay a dime."

Chapter Nineteen

Like His Parents,
George Skakel Jr. Dies in a Plane Crash

During the late-1950s to the mid-1960s, George Skakel Jr. ran Great Lakes Coal and Coke for the family. Although George Jr. wasn't a smart decision-maker like his father, and despite the fact that he was a functional alcoholic, the company still made good money on a regular basis. George Jr. was no doubt the spokesman for the family, and he was known to speak his mind to anyone; even a United States Senator and the future President of the United States.

One fine day in Martha's Vineyard Sound, in a Kennedy-owned sailboat, the duo of George Skakel Jr. and Jack Kennedy were racing another pair of boats. Kennedy assumed the role of captain, barking commands, while Skakel was thrust in the role of first (and only) mate. Skakel, following Jack's orders, was adjusting the sails in a way he knew would lessen the sailboat's speed rather than increase the speed, thereby causing them to lose the race.

Finally, tired of Kennedy's arrogant attitude, Skakel turned around, and said, "Look, Jack, are you going to keep screaming at me how to trim this sail, when I know damned well better than you how it ought to be trimmed?"

"Just shut up and do as you're told," Jack Kennedy said.

"Shut up and do as I'm told?" George Jr. said. "Just like you Kennedys, always giving orders when you should be listening."

"It's my boat, and I'm the captain," Jack said. "You're nothing but the first mate."

Skakel jumped out of the cockpit of the boat. He got into Jack Kennedy's face and gave him a snappy, naval salute.

Then he said, "Aye, Aye, Captain! I request permission to leave the ship, sir."

Before Jack Kennedy could open his mouth, George did an about-face and dived off the sailboat. He swam two miles to shore, leaving Captain Jack with a redder than normal face and no crew to finish the race with.

After the 1961 presidential inauguration ceremony, at the party in the Capitol Reception Room, George Jr. was taken aback at the pomposity of Jack and Bobby Kennedy, as well as their snooty staff. As Jack Kennedy strode to the reviewing stand, George Jr. noticed that the only non-Caucasian in the room was a black porter sweeping up in the back of the room.

George Jr. turned to his brother, Jim, and said, "The Kennedys claim to be liberals, and they didn't even invite one Negro to the reception room as a guest. I'll fix their wagons."

George hurried to where the black porter was sweeping, and he handed him his seating pass to the reception.

"Here you are, my good man," George said. "Enjoy the festivities!"

George Jr. and Jim Skakel stood in the back of the room and gleefully watched the shocked horror on Jack Kennedy's face when it was the black porter's turn to shake the new President's hand.

On September 25, 1966, George Jr., ever the adventurist, and twenty of his friends, headed on a ten-day elk hunting trip on a ranch in Idaho, where they planned to stay a week. The trip started in New York City where George Jr., along with several of the hunting crew, flew on a Great Lakes Coal and Coke-owned Convair 300 to St. Louis, where they picked up the rest of the hunters. The plane then continued to Boise, Idaho, where the hunters then boarded three separate small charter planes, which would take them directly to the ranch.

The plane George Jr. boarded along with three others, including Dean Markham, a close friend of Bobby Kennedy's, was piloted by Donald Adams, 38, an Air Force master sergeant in charge of radar traffic control at the Mountain Home Air Force Base. He had been a pilot for ten years.

As Adams was trying to land the plane, containing the four passengers and loaded with hunting gear, at the Crooked Creek Airstrip in a canyon in Riggins, Idaho, he overshot the runway. Adams touched the plane down, but then he flew back up and around trying to attempt a second landing.

As the plane was climbing out of the canyon, a wing clipped the side of a mountain. The plane spiraled downward, sheared several trees, and then crashed into a creek, killing all aboard, including George Skakel Jr. George Jr.'s 13-year old son, Mark, was on the ground at the Crooked Creek Airstrip, and he had watched in horror as the plane burst into flames.

Tom Wyman, a member of the hunting party, who later was a State Department official in the Kennedy administration, was also on the ground as the plane crashed.

"It did more than telescope," Wyman said. "The plane disintegrated."

In the following day's Idaho Statesman, the headline read:

Blame Pilot in Death of Five, One a Kennedy Kin

The article below the headline said:

Idaho Aeronautics Director, Chet Mouton, was quoted as saying, "It was a case of a man taking on more weight than he was equipped for. There was nothing wrong with that plane. Landing there is a calculated risk unless you are proficient. Adams was not a mountain pilot. Another problem was that this landing was attempted in the afternoon when the weather is hot."

The following day, the bodies were fished out of the creek by a helicopter. They were then transported to the Great Lakes Coal and Coke-owned Convair 300, which had taken them to Idaho, for their trip back to New York City.

When Ethel Kennedy heard of her brother's death, she was properly devastated; not so was her husband, Bobby, at least not for George Skakel Jr. His concern was for Dean Markham and his family.

After picking up Markham's children and bringing them to Washington D.C., Bobby told a friend, "My grief isn't for that lunatic brother-in-law of mine. He always had a death wish. But he took my best friend with him."

Suzie Markham, Dean's wife, was also bitter about George Skakel Jr.'s role in her husband's death.

A Markham friend said, "Down in the depths of her heart she was very, very upset that George had taken Dean with him. George was a wild man."

Not everyone blasted George Skakel Jr. for dying the way he had always lived his life.

Sportswriter Red Smith said in the New York Herald-Tribune, "Big George was all man, all sportsman, all battle, and we could not afford to lose him."

Conservative Columnist Willian F. Buckley considered himself a close friend of George Skakel Jr.

Buckley wrote in his syndicated newspaper column:

The death of George Skakel Jr. in Idaho was announced to the word via his prominent connection with Sen. Robert F. Kennedy; and indeed Mr. Skakel's sister is Mrs. Robert Kennedy. One wonders whether, absent that connection, his death would have been noticed on the front pages. No doubt the answer is no – his qualifications for public attention depending, by the rules of journalistic commerce, on his closeness by marriage to political glamour.

He otherwise emerged, in the obituary notices, as a young tycoon and sportsman, but he was, it is the purpose of this particular obituary to note, something rather special; someone whose death is worth mourning beyond his immediate circle of family and friends. Skakel was in the tradition of the total

American man, whose principal complaint against the cosmos is that we are destined someday to die.

George Skakel had an energy to his life, which, in this jaded age of general fatigue and instant ennui, of philosophical weltschmerz and forty-hour weeks and unconditional surrender to television sets and the passive life, made him seem almost eccentric, out of harmony with the rhythm of a senescent world, made him, too, impulsive, in mischievous and irresistible ways.

The range of his interests was phenomenal, his capacity to live and exploit the pleasure of earth – they call it a "lust for life," the kind of thing that great artists, writers, and statesman have had – Michelangelo and Victor Hugo, Thomas Jefferson and Winston Churchill. George Skakel had it.

On September 28, more than 200 mourners crowded into St. Mary's Roman Catholic Church in Greenwich for George Skakel Jr.'s funeral mass.

A Skakel family friend said, "It was quite a bizarre affair. Father Billy McCormack, who used to hang out at the Skakel house in the old days, led the Requiem Mass. But there in the church, the only thing on everyone's mind was that George Skakel was the world's biggest sinner and was probably burning in hell that very moment.

"The service was made even stranger by the bevy of George's blond, blue-eyed babes sitting in the pews crying their eyes out. 'The Swedish Mafia,' as we called them. After the service, I was standing with Ethel and even she was amused by the fact that there was a klatch of beautiful blonds who had been her brother's girlfriends.

"Despite what Bobby thought about George, Ethel adored her brother, and deep down she thought he could do no wrong."

George Skakel Jr. was buried next to his parents' graves in St. Mary's Cemetery in Greenwich.

Rushton Skakel was now in charge of Great Lakes Coal and Coke. However, Rushton, eternally affable and usually drunk, wanted no part of the gig. Without any input from his elder brother, Jim, Rushton designated his cousin, Joe Solari Jr., the son of Big Ann's sister, Ethel, to be president of a thriving enterprise headed by a Skakel since 1919.

Jim Skakel angrily said, "Rushton did this while the body of my brother George was still warm."

Solari, the son of an Italian immigrant, Joe Solari Sr., had a Northwestern bachelor and law degree, and he was a lieutenant commander in the U.S. Navy during World War II. After the war, Solari worked for Sterling Precision Corporation, the Federal Telephone and Radio Company, the Jefferson Electric Company, and the Peabody Coal Company. Just a month before his death, George Jr. had appointed Solari, 48, as group vice president. Before that, Solari had been the vice president and general manager of the company's Carbon Division.

Despite Solari's obvious capabilities, Rushton frequently referred to Solari as "my skinny Guinea flop wop cousin."

Before the year was over, another Skakel would be involved in a tragedy, and this one would involve an innocent 6-year-old girl. It would be the first indication of the Skakel's pull within Greenwich law enforcement.

Chapter Twenty

A Little Girl Dies in Greenwich

In November 1966, two months after her brother George Jr.'s death, Pat Skakel Cuffe, Ethel's elder sister, who had dated Bobby before Ethel, decided to give a grandiose Thanksgiving party for the Skakel family in her Greenwich home on Vineyard Lane. Pat's oldest daughter, Kick, on a four-day Thanksgiving leave from a Catholic boarding school, arrived at her parents' house in the late morning and immediately jumped into her shiny new 1966 Ford Mustang convertible that her father had given her as a "Sweet Sixteen" present. Her newly acquired Connecticut driver's license allowed Kick, still only 16, the freedom to drive her car without any restrictions.

Because it was an unusually warm day in Greenwich for late November, Kick wanted to cruise around Greenwich in her convertible with the top down. Kick invited her cousin, Little Georgeann, the daughter of Pat's older sister, Georgeann, to join her for a spin, but Little Georgeann declined the invitation.

"To be around Kick was like being around Uncle George," Little Georgeann later said. "She was always living dangerously. Mother made it clear that Kick was a bad influence."

At 1 pm, Kick and her mother decided to visit Royall and Sally O'Brien on Peckland Road. Royall had attended Georgetown University with Rushton Skakel, and over the years the families had remained close.

When Kick pulled the Mustang up to the O'Brien's driveway, the family was outside enjoying the warm weather. While Kick and Pat chatted with Royall and Sally, the three O'Brien daughters. Hope,

6, Sarah, 8, and Morgan, 9, romped around in the grass with their playmates, the two Martin sisters, who lived across the street.

Because of the beautiful weather, Pat and Sally decided to take a walk around the neighborhood.

Kick asked Sally, "Is it okay if I take the girls on a ride in my Mustang?"

"Sure dear," Sally said. "But be careful."

The two older woman started on their stroll, and as Royall O'Brien began tinkering in his garden, Kick took off in the Mustang convertible with the top down and the five little girls in tow. She stopped a few blocks away on Peckland Road and picked up her younger sister, Susan, 12. That made it seven people in a five-passenger car, a violation of the driving laws in any state.

There were several different versions of what happened next, but the fact is that about 90 minutes after Kick left the O'Brien residence, she returned in her Mustang. Royall O'Brien was still pottering around in his garden, and he watched as Kick jumped out of the car and headed to the front door of his house. He also noticed that his daughters and the two Martin girls didn't seem to be in the car.

Knowing that the two mothers were still on their walk and that no one would answer the door, Royall O'Brien yelled to Kick, who obviously didn't see him, "Hi, I'm over here. Where's everyone?"

Kick froze and seemed incapable of answering. Knowing something was wrong, O'Brien rushed over to the convertible. There, he spotted Susan Skakel sitting sunken in the front seat, with little Hopey unconscious in her lap.

As Kick approached her car, O'Brien screamed, "What happened to Hopey!"

With no emotion, Kick simply said, "She fell out of the car."

"Hopey was out, but she wasn't bleeding," O'Brien later said. "I didn't ask too many questions. I jumped right in the car and drove to Greenwich Hospital."

The doctors tried to revive her, but Hope O'Brien fell into a deep coma.

Royall O'Brien stood at his daughter's side for the entire ordeal. At night, as his wife, Sally, cared for her other two girls, O'Brien slept next to Hope, on a cot a nurse had brought into the room.

"Hopey's hand held my finger," O'Brien said. "She gripped me very tightly. But a few days later, her grip had loosened. She died on the seventh day."

On the day after the accident, the *Greenwich Times* reported: "Six-year-old Hope O'Brien was thrown out of a Mustang convertible driven by 16-year old Kick Skakel after hitting a man-made bump designed to slow down traffic. Miss Skakel told the police that she was driving between 15-and-20 miles an hour when it went over the bump."

The day after Hope O'Brien had passed away, Greenwich police chief, Steven Baran, blamed the "speed bumps" for her death. The Greenwich police also returned Kick Skakel's driver's license, which they had confiscated when she reported the accident.

When the *Greenwich Times* asked Baran whether charges would be brought against Kick Skakel, he replied, "I doubt negligence was involved in the accident. But there will be a coroner's inquest in a few days."

Neither the Greenwich police, nor the newspaper contacted the O'Briens. And no mention was made in the Greenwich Time of the fact that Kick Skakel was a member of the notorious Greenwich Skakel family, and was also the niece of Ethel Kennedy, the wife of Bobby Kennedy, the former United States Attorney General and presently a Senator from New York. Two months earlier, when George Skakel Jr. perished in the plane crash, his connection to the Kennedys was played up in every newspaper in the country.

Susan and Royall O'Brien, obviously grief-stricken, never questioned Kick about the accident, nor did they quiz their two little girls, who had been in the car at the time of the accident.

The real story began to break when an investigator from the Skakel's car insurance company phoned the O'Briens to get their version of the details of the accident, so that a financial settlement could be made. This was the first time Royall O'Brien had actually questioned his daughters about their version of the accident that killed Hope.

"It was just something that I had never thought about doing," O'Brien later said. "When Hopey was in the hospital, we were there most of the time, and in and out of the hospital a great deal. There wasn't a lot of discussion at that point concerning the actual accident and how it happened. I also felt it was a sensitive subject to bring up with the girls."

After the insurance investigator interviewed the O'Brien girls and the Martin sisters from across the street, an account of the events emerged that utterly opposed what the Greenwich Time reported that Kick Skakel had told the Greenwich police.

According to the four little girls' statements, Kick Skakel glided around Greenwich in her Mustang convertible with the top down. Her sister, Susan, sat next to her, and the other five little girls were packed into the back seat. After a period of time, two of the five girls in the back seat, including Hope, jumped back and sat on the trunk; their legs dangling onto the back seat.

Then Kick Skakel, for no apparent reason, began alternately stepping on the gas and hitting the breaks, causing the little girls to rock back and forth like they were in an amusement park ride.

Suddenly, Kick hit a speed bump, and Hope fell, not out of the car, but off the trunk of the car. Her head hit the pavement, and she never regained consciousness.

"That's the real way it happened," Royall O'Brien said. "I have never had occasion to question my daughters' account. They were eight and nine at the time. They gave me the innocent truth. They would have had no reason to lie. They couldn't have made up a story like the one they told me."

The coroner's inquest, held five days after the accident, cleared Kick Skakel of any wrongdoing in the death of Hope O'Brien.

"We were never invited to be present at the coroner's inquest," O'Brien said. "We were never in any kind of court over this case."

When the true events of the accident became known to all, the Skakel family, and Pat Skakel in particular, were understandably contrite. But the O'Briens gave them the brush off.

"Pat Skakel tried to be very solicitous," O'Brien said. "I only saw her once after the accident and that was when I went over to tell her not to call our house anymore. She was constantly calling, and it upset Sally.

"I was contacted by all of the Skakels, and they were solicitous, too. The only one who didn't call was Ethel. She's a very unemotional type; a frightening personality."

The O'Briens received a measly $25,000 insurance settlement for their little girl's negligent death from the Skakel's insurance company.

Nine years later, another young girl associated with the Skakels would meet her death in Greenwich. This time it was the result of a cold-blooded murder. The Greenwich police would then be accused of either being incompetent, or complicit in a cover-up.

In the following pages, the facts will show that one, or the other (and possibly both) was the grim truth.

Chapter Twenty-One

The Martha Moxley Murder Investigation Gets Off to a Rocky Start

On Halloween morning, Friday, October 31, 1975, Greenwich police officers Millard Jones and Daniel Hickman were chomping on sausage sandwiches in Car 22, parked on Old Post Road, when their police radio crackled to life. The voice on the other end told them to call the police precinct from a call box and not to use their police radio for any police communication until told otherwise.

Hickman directed their car to the corner of Post Road and Ferris Road, where the nearest red call box was located. He picked up the phone, and several seconds later he heard the voice of Detective Audrey Aidinis.

"Go to the Moxley residence as fast as you can," she told Hickman. "I don't know all the details, but we just got a call that someone may have been killed. Let us know what you've got when you get there."

With the police car's dome lights flashing and the siren blasting, Hickman arrived at the Moxley residence in less than ten minutes. When the two police officers jumped out of their car, they were confronted by panic and bedlam.

"Some folks were milling about the house, hysterically crying," Hickman said. "Mill Jones and I just looked at each other, wondering what we had. Then a girl said, 'She's down there! Down there!' Crying her eyes out. We went bolting down the slope and came to a big tree. We split up. Just on instinct. Jonesy went this way, and I went around that way. Then, I put on the breaks, and said, 'My God, Mill, over here!'"

Hickman bent over Martha Moxley's body, which was sprawled face down. He checked her pulse and found none.

Hickman glanced at his watch. It was exactly 12:30 pm.

"It was the first sign of foul play that I had ever run across," Hickman said. "I tell you, it sets your mind racing."

Jones ran to the Moxley house to use the phone. Soon, Walsh Lane and nearby Otter Rock Drive were teeming with uniformed police officers, detectives, emergency personnel, newspapermen, and curious neighbors who never thought this sort of thing could happen in their prestigious locale.

After Hickman alerted the precinct that they had a murder case, Captain Thomas Keegan rushed to the Moxley residence, and he took control of the crime scene. He was aided by Detectives Steven Carrol and Joe McGlynn.

Keegan marched up to Hickman.

"What have you done here so far?" Keegan said.

"Not a thing, Chief," Hickman said.

"Good. Now, you and Jonesy fan out over the area and see if you can find some evidence, blood or anything else that looks suspicious," Keegan said.

Several other cops did the same, and soon they discovered two large pools of blood 70 feet from the pine tree, where they assumed the killer had unmercifully beaten Martha. Then, they traced a path of blood from the two pools to exactly where Martha's body lay beneath the pine tree's leaves.

In the grass near the murder scene, the police also found three pieces of what they thought to be the murder weapon: the metal head and two pieces of the shaft of a Toney Penna 6-iron. The grip and approximately four inches of the shaft, were nowhere to be found.

At approximately 1 pm, Dr. Richard Danehower arrived at the Moxley residence. He had been summoned by Marilyn Pennington, a close neighborhood friend of the Moxleys, who was presently comforting Dorthy Moxley.

"I guess there was some question at the Moxley residence as to whether the girl was still alive," Danehower said. "Marilyn told me they needed someone from the medical profession to help make that decision and to present the facts to Dorthy Moxley."

After Dr. Danehower bent over Martha's body, he spotted a deep skull wound near the crown of her head; a wound that alone could snuff out a person's life.

"I could see that the wound had penetrated the skull," Dr. Danehower said. "I could also see the dura mater layer of the brain through the injury. There was no motion. No life."

Dr. Danehower went back to the Moxley residence. He spotted Dorthy sitting in her chair with her head down. He knelt before her and told her that her daughter was dead.

Almost simultaneously, the phone rang in the Moxley residence. Marilyn Pennington picked up the phone, and she heard the voice of David Moxley, Martha's father, who, although he was in charge of the New York office of the accounting firm Touche Ross, had been visiting a branch office in Atlanta. David was presently at the Atlanta airport ready to board a flight to take him to New York. He was oblivious to the horrific situation at home and was just calling to check in.

Marilyn scanned the room for help, and she spotted her husband, Lou, sitting on the couch next to Dorthy and holding her hand. Realizing help was not on the way, Marilyn bit the bullet and reluctantly spoke to David Moxley.

"I kept telling him to please come back to Connecticut," Marilyn said. "He persisted in asking me why, and I kept begging him just to come home because something serious had happened to Martha. Finally, he said to me, 'Is she dead?' I lost it and said, 'Yes, she's dead.' It was the most heartbreaking thing I had ever done."

Martha's older brother, John Moxley, was at an early Greenwich High School football practice when Coach Ornato approached him and put his hand on John's shoulder.

"Look, something's happened at home," Coach Ornato said. "Your family wants you home right away."

John jumped into his new Mustang and raced back to Belle Haven, minutes after Lou Pennington had left the Moxley residence to drive to the school to alert John as to the tragedy at home. Neither realized they had passed each other somewhere along the way.

When Pennington reached the football field and found out that John had already left, he jumped back into his car and raced back to the Moxley residence. He did not obey the speed limit, and he passed several red lights on the way. Lou figured that since Dorthy Moxley was in an almost catatonic state, and his wife, Marilyn, was not in much better shape, he wanted to be the one to break the news to John that his younger sister was dead.

As John Moxley made the turn onto Walsh Lane, he was greeted by a bevy of police cars. He spotted yellow tape draped across the front of his house with black lettering that screamed, "CRIME SCENE! DO NOT CROSS!"

"It could be something that you've never seen before in your life, but you walk into the picture and know exactly what is it," John later said. "There was no question in my mind that this was a major police event that involved us somehow."

John parked his car at the end of the driveway and hurried up to this house. But before he could get there, the beefy right hand of the rather-large Lou Pennington latched on to John's shoulder and stopped him in his tracks.

"I'm sorry, John, but your sister has been killed," Lou said.

"How was she killed? Was she shot or stabbed or something?"

"No, they think she may have been beaten to death with a golf club."

Instinctively, John launched an overhand right that could have felled an ox. Luckily for Lou, he was able to sidestep the blow.

John did a quick about-face, and he ran into the house yelling, "My sister! My sister!"

"I mean the light was on in my head, but nobody was home," John said. "Everything just shut down. I was in denial for years. Absolute denial. I just couldn't comprehend what had happened to my sister."

John ran into the house and into the arms of his mother, who was still sitting on the couch.

They hugged, and John said, "What happened?"

"I don't know," Dorthy said. "They found her by a tree."

Dorthy spent the rest of the day sitting on the couch trying not to break down. But every few minutes, she would cradle her head in her hands and weep uncontrollably.

"I said to myself I have to keep control," Dorthy said. "But Martha was my favorite person in the world, and I would never see her alive again."

Chapter Twenty-Two

The Greenwich Police Stumble Through the Investigation

Starting from the time that Martha Moxley's body was found, the Greenwich police's investigation resembled something from a Keystone Cop's movie. Whether it was inexperience or ineptness is up for conjecture, but the Greenwich police were anything but aggressive in their investigation immediately following the finding of the body.

According to Police Chief Magazine, "In murder investigations, many agencies follow the 72-hour rule, in which officers closely investigate the first 48 hours after the homicide occurred and the 24 hours prior to the homicide. Most homicides are precipitated by an event that occurred within the last 24 hours of the victim's life, so an effective investigative method is to dissect the last 24 hours of the victim's life and then aggressively investigate leads within the first 48 hours of the commission of the crime."

Greenwich Police Chief Stephen Baran, a 30-year veteran of the Greenwich Police Department, told the New York Times on the day of the murder, "We haven't had anything like this as far as I can remember."

This was the same Chief Baran who, nine years earlier, had said that Hope O'Brien's death was caused by "speed bumps" and that there was no negligence on the part of Kick Skakel.

Since this was the first Greenwich murder case in recent memory, it was no surprise that the detectives, who arrived at the scene of the crime, had no experience on how to conduct a murder investigation. Summoning their inner Inspector Clouseaus, the detectives indiscriminately fanned out and started knocking on front doors without examining the clues that were right in front of them.

"It was very disorganized at the beginning," retired detective Steve Carroll said years later. "Individual teams of detectives began canvassing the neighborhood. Everyone was out to make a collar."

One theory the police clung to for the first few hours was that the murder had been committed by an outsider, a vagrant, or a hitchhiker, who had somehow slipped through Belle Harbor security. But when they could uncover no hard evidence supporting that theory, the police finally concentrated on the murderer being a local.

Since Belle Haven, a community of 63,000 people, was considered such a crimeless district, with no murders having been committed in recent memory, newspaper people quickly arrived at the Moxley residence from as far away as New York City. By mid-afternoon on Halloween day, more than a dozen reporters had arrived, and they peppered the locals gawking at the murder scene with questions.

12-year-old Linda Skovron told the New York Times, "I've never been scared before. Things like this just don't happen in Belle Haven. Everybody is so rich."

One elegantly dressed woman, who refused to give her name, said, "I live practically next door. We used to walk a lot at night, and I think everybody felt quite secure. I guess I won't do that anymore."

Another woman, wearing an expensive tweed jacket, who would only give her name as "Mrs. Hill," said, "I've lived here three years. My girls go out jogging late at night, and we never gave it a thought. This will certainly make us stop and think."

A third woman sporting a full-length mink coat said, "What can you say about murder? Belle Haven is a fantastic place. I've lived here for 27 years and nothing like this has ever happened before."

Nick Bernard, a 16-year-old student at Greenwich High, told a reporter, "I don't see why anyone would want to kill her. It had to be some crazy person from somewhere else. I don't think anyone who knew her would hurt her."

One of the curious onlookers at the scene of the crime was the morose 15-year-old Michael Skakel, who was notorious in the neighborhood for viciously killing small animals, mostly chipmunks and squirrels, sometimes by cornering them and beating them to death with a golf club. At the time, Skakel was short and frail (he barely weighed 115 pounds), and he rarely smiled, like he had the weight of the world on his shoulders.

As Michael meandered around the edges of the crowd, a female newspaper reporter ran up to him, pen and notebook in her hand.

She asked Michael, "Is it true your mother was a steak-choke victim?"

The truth was that it was Michael's aunt (George Skakel Jr.'s wife), not Michael's mother, who had choked to death on kebob meat six months after her husband had perished in the plane crash in 1966.

Instead of answering, Michael began to sob uncontrollably. The newspaper woman did an about-face and looked for someone else in the crowd to interrogate.

A teenager who had witnessed the odd scene turned to another teenager, and said, "Michael Skakel likes to kill chipmunks and squirrels. How come he didn't kick that newspaper bitch in the ass?"

The other teenager replied, "Maybe it's because that newspaper bitch is big enough to fight back."

Chapter Twenty-Three

Police Try to Reconstruct the Night of the Murder

After the Greenwich detectives compared notes, they pieced together the last hours of Martha Moxley's life. They came up with the following scenario, which may or may not have been entirely accurate:

At around 8:30 pm on Mischief Night (also called Doorbell night), Martha Moxley, along with Helen Ix and Geoffrey Byrne, arrived at the Skakel residence. Michael Skakel was waiting outside. Minutes later, Michael and Martha were sitting in the front seat of his father's maroon Lincoln, which the Skakel boys refer to as the "Lustmobile," Helen and Geoffrey were sitting in the back seat. All four just sat there listening to music on the radio, and as of yet, neither boy had tried to put the moves on the girl sitting next to him.

This became a moot point when 17-year-old Tommy Skakel, his brother Michael's nemesis, bolted out of the house.

Tommy and his brothers, Rushton Jr., John, and Michael, and sister, Julie, along with their new tutor, the hulking Ken Littleton, had finished their dinner an hour earlier at the upscale Belle Haven Club. It was Littleton's first night on the job, and with Rushton Skakel Sr. away on a wild-game hunting trip, it was his job to keep the cantankerous Skakel male youths in line. Still, at dinner he said nothing while the underage Skakel brothers belted down several alcoholic beverages apiece.

As a result, when Tommy emerged from the house, he was not quite drunk, but he was more than a little high, a condition which applied to Michael, too.

Tommy pulled open the passenger door and said to Martha, "Move over."

She did as he requested, and soon, Tommy, as Michael seethed, was rubbing his hands on Martha's inner thigh.

Martha giggled and said, not too convincingly, "Tommy, get your hand off my thigh."

Tommy removed his wayward hand, but, to Michael's dismay, he continued to flirt with Martha.

At around 9:15 pm, Rushton Skakel Jr., John Skakel, and their cousin, Jimmy Terrien, emerged from the Skakel house.

"We're going over to Jimmy's house to watch the Monty Python movie," one of the older teenagers said. "Does anyone want to come with us?"

Tommy said no; he had some homework to finish was his later excuse. Michael said yes, and he asked Martha if she would like to accompany him. Martha, obviously smitten with the older Tommy, declined the invitation, as did Helen Ix and Geoffrey Byrne.

Rushton Jr., John, Michael, and Jimmy Terrien then drove off in the Lincoln.

After Helen Ix and Geoffrey Byrne strolled way from the Skakel residence, Tommy and Martha were left to their own devices.

This is where the sequence of events becomes confusing, and over the years the stories have changed as to who did what and went where, and at what time.

Helen Ix and Geoffrey Byrne, who were interviewed the day after Martha's body was found, said the last time they saw them Tommy and Martha were flirting on the side of the Skakel residence. Also, on the day after the body was found, Tommy told the Greenwich police that he went home at around 9:30 pm, and the last time he saw Martha, she was walking back to her house.

Martha's likely path (it was approximately 200 yards from the Skakel house to the Moxley property) was to cross the Skakel yard, cross Walsh Lane, and then head onto the Moxley property. On the grass of the Moxley property, the killer landed several blows on Martha's head with a golf club, and she fell unconscious onto the grass. The killer landed an additional 10-15 blows, which shattered the golf club into four pieces. Enraged, the killer grabbed one of the broken pieces of the club's shaft and plunged it into Martha's neck.

Because there was so much blood at the initial point of attack, the police concluded the killer had left, and then came back approximately 30 minutes later and dragged her under the pine tree, which was approximately 70 feet away. The killer then pulled down Martha's jeans and underwear, exposing her buttocks and down to her knees. An examination showed she was not sexually assaulted. The killer may have been interrupted, or maybe the sight of Martha's bloodied head had caused him to become impotent.

At around 9:30-9:45 pm, several neighborhood dogs began hysterically barking. It was Mischief Night, and most of the people who heard the barking thought it was just some unruly kids tearing up the town. Still, some of the neighbors went outside to see if they could determine the cause of the disturbance.

Nanny Sweeney was the Skakel's live-in house maid. She was so disturbed by the barking that she sent Ken Littleton outside to investigate. Littleton went outside and circled the Skakel house, but he could not find anyone or anything that might have caused the barking.

Strangely, the Skakel's dog, a hulking German Shepard named Max, did not bark.

Also at around 9:30-9:45 pm, Dorthy Moxley was painting the trimming around the windows of her second-floor bedroom. The night had turned chilly, and she had closed all the windows to prevent a draft from coming into the house. Still, she heard loud voices of at least one male teenager, and the bellowing sounded threatening rather than affable. The voices seemed to be coming from under the second-story bathroom window. Dorthy went into the bathroom and opened the window, but she saw nothing amiss. At around 11 pm, Dorthy went down to the first floor living room, turned on the television and began watching the 11 o'clock news.

At approximately 11:20-11:30 pm, John Moxley returned home after a night of tomfoolery with two pals. They started the night by buying eggs at a grocery store, and then, minutes later, they hurled them at a group of cheerleaders who were preparing for a football pep rally. Finished with their naughtiness for the night, the three teenagers attended a couple of parties, and then John returned home to get some sleep before an early morning football practice.

"Martha isn't home yet," Dorthy told her son. "I grounded her last week because she stayed out late. And before she went out tonight, I warned her about staying out late again. She said she'd be home early. This isn't like her. Making a promise and then breaking it."

"Okay ma," John said. "I'll get in my car and cruise around town. Maybe I can find her."

John traversed the Belle Haven neighborhood in his car for about thirty minutes, and then he returned home.

"No trace of Martha," he told his mother. "The town is almost deserted. I saw one person, and he was laying down drunk in front of the Ferguson house."

Dorthy tried to go to sleep, but it was of no use. Just after midnight, she decided to start dialing the phone numbers of Martha's friends. Dorthy hoped that maybe someone knew where Martha was, and if not, maybe they could point her in the right direction.

Dorthy's first call was to the Ix residence, which was almost directly across the street from the Moxley residence. Helen Ix told Dorthy that she had last seen Martha about 9:30 pm in the company of Thomas Skakel in front of the Skakel residence, and she gave Dorthy the Skakel's phone number.

Dorthy dialed the Skakel's number, and Julie Skakel answered the phone. Dorthy told her what Helen Ix had said about her last seeing Martha with Tommy.

"Tommy is sleeping right now," Julie said.

"Well, can you please wake him up?" Dorthy said. "This is so unlike Martha, and quite frankly I'm very concerned."

While Dorthy waited on the phone, Julie went upstairs to Tommy's bedroom. He was fast asleep, and when Julie shook him and asked him if he knew Martha's whereabouts, Tommy said, without getting out of bed or turning on the light, "I saw her (Martha) at our back door about 9:30 pm. I had to leave because I had to study for a test."

Julie relayed that information to Dorthy, but that only made Dorthy more concerned about the welfare of her daughter.

As the night progressed, Dorthy phoned the Skakels several more times. Julie answered each time, and when she went upstairs to question Tommy, she always got the same reply: "I don't know where Martha is."

Finally, Dorthy begged Julie to put Tommy on the phone.

After his sister shook him awake, Tommy reluctantly got out of bed and went downstairs to the phone.

Dorthy asked Tommy, "Do you have any idea where my daughter can be?"

"No, ma'am. I have no idea where she is," Tommy said.

Julie told Dorthy to call the Terrien's residence. Rushton Jr., John, and Michael Skakel had gone to the Terrien residence earlier, departing from the Skakel house around 9:30 pm, and Julie figured that maybe Martha had gone there with them.

Georgeann Terrien, George Terrien's wife and the eldest Skakel aunt, answered the phone. Georgeann told Dorthy her son wasn't home yet either, and she didn't know where he could be.

Dorthy then called the home of every teenager in Belle Haven who might know her daughter.

Not one person knew the whereabouts of 15-year-old Martha Moxley.

At 3:15 am, Dorthy woke her son, John.

"You have to go out and look for Martha," Dorthy said.

The first time John went looking for his sister, he was not overly concerned. He knew it was Mischief Night and that teenagers all over town were staying out late; raising havoc and plundering the small town. But John also knew, as Dorthy did, that Martha was not the type to stay out until the wee hours of the morning without calling home. Martha knew that her mother would be worried sick, and unless she had gotten drunk and passed out, she would have surely phoned home.

Gunning his car in all directions, John searched every nook and cranny of Belle Haven. He did not return home until dawn, when he told his mother there was still no sign of Martha.

At 3:38 am, Dorthy phoned the Greenwich Police Department to report that her daughter was missing. In big-city police departments, the police sometimes tell the person reporting a missing person that 24-hours must elapse before that person is believed to be missing. But that 24-hour period is waved if the missing person is a minor, or someone with reduced mental capacity. But in actual practice, most police departments, to cover their butts from a possible lawsuit, respond immediately to a report of a missing person.

As a result of her phone call, Patrolman Daniel Merchant hurried to the Moxley house, where Dorthy told him, "There is no reason to suspect that my daughter has runaway. And it's not like her to stay out so late."

"He (Merchant) gave me the feeling that he thought Martha was just at a friend's house," Dorthy said. "And that she had just not bothered to call home. Then, I started thinking that kids today are drinking beer. Kids are into drugs. Martha could have tried something."

Dorthy and Merchant made a thorough investigation of the house and the surrounding areas, but they came up empty.

Merchant then called headquarters, and two Greenwich police vehicles were dispatched into the area. For the next two hours, the two police cars fanned out all over Belle Haven, using flashlights from their side windows, as well as their headlights, to help them peer into the darkness.

Yet, they still could not stumble on the already-dead 15-year-old girl who was lying under a tree on her own property.

Around 7 am, Dorthy, now thoroughly exhausted, fell asleep on the window seat in her library. She awoke around 10 am, and she knew what she had to do.

Dorthy walked across Walsh Lane to the Skakel house, where she was greeted by the Skakel's German Shepard, Max, who did not take kindly to strangers traipsing into his territory (Yet, he did not make a peep the previous night when all the other neighborhood dogs were barking in unison). Max scared Dorthy half to death before Michael Skakel answered the door, looking rumpled, like he had slept in his clothes.

"When Michael answered the door he looked very disheveled," Dorthy said. "He looked a real mess, and he was barefoot. I noticed that very clearly."

After introducing herself, Dorthy said, "Martha didn't come home last night. Do you know where she might be?"

Michael barely belched out a "No."

Remembering that Martha was last seen in the company of Tommy Skakel, Dorthy said, "Are you sure she's not here?"

Without even checking any of the rooms, he again answered weakly, "No."

Dorthy went back home, and soon many of her friends arrived at her home to comfort her as the search for Martha continued.

When Georgeann Terrien discovered that Martha Moxley had been found murdered and that she was last seen in the company of Tommy Skakel, she immediately phoned Ethel Kennedy.

George Terrien later said, "When my wife called Ethel and told her the news, Ethel was a nervous wreck. Georgeann also told me that Ethel said she was going to call her brother-in-law, Ted Kennedy, right away. Ethel also called her other advisors. She said, 'We can't let this touch the Kennedys.'"

Joe Romanello was a teenager in 1975 and a close friend of Martha's.

Years later, Romanello said, "In 1975, we were a bunch of teenagers who didn't remember about Chappaquiddick."

Editor's note: In July of 1969, 28-year-old Mary Jo Kopechne was in the back seat of Senator Ted Kennedy's Oldsmobile, when, after a night of partying, he drove off a bridge on Chappaquiddick Island. Kopechne drowned, while Kennedy, married at the time, never tried to rescue her, and he swam safely to shore. He didn't report the fatal car accident for 10 hours.

"That stuff hadn't come out yet about Jack or Bobby, so we weren't biased at all," Romanello said. "But at the same time, we said, 'There's a lot of money here. This is Ethel Skakel Kennedy's family. This is the Kennedys.'"

Chapter Twenty-Four

Martha Moxley Calls Michael Skakel "An Ass" and "An Asshole" in Her Diary

The key clue to the murder of Martha Moxley was the fact that it was a rare golf club, a ladies' Toney Penna 6-iron, that was determined to be the murder weapon. Soon after the body was found detectives fanned out all over Belle Haven seeking to find anyone who owned a woman's set of Toney Penna irons.

After ascertaining that Tommy Skakel had reportedly been the last person to see Martha alive, Detectives Jim Lunney and Ted Brosko went to the Skakel residence to ask questions and to see if they could spot anything that might be a clue.

The two detectives did not have a search warrant.

Since Rushton Skakel was on vacation hunting wild game, it was Tommy Skakel who answered the door.

Tommy told the detectives he had last seen Martha at about 9:30 pm on the lawn of his house, but he had to leave her to write a report about Abraham Lincoln for school the following day. He gave the police the name of his schoolteacher, but when the detectives questioned the schoolteacher later that day, she looked puzzled.

"I'm an anthropology teacher," she said. "I doubt we discussed much about Abraham Lincoln."

Tommy Skakel also told the detectives that, after Martha had left the Skakel house, he had spent about twenty minutes watching *The French Connection* on television with Ken Littleton, a fact that Littleton verified.

As the detectives exited the house, they spotted a single golf club propped up against a storage bin. It was a Toney Penna 5-iron that had belonged to Rushton Skakel's late wife, Anne. The detectives noted that etched in the area below the grip was the name "Anne Skakel." That part of the matching 6-iron murder weapon was missing from the scene of the crime. Since the detectives had not obtained a search warrant, they had no choice but to leave the golf club at the Skakel residence.

A police report later said, "After an extensive survey, it has been determined that there were no other Toney Penna golf clubs in the entire Belle Haven area.

Donald Browne, the state's prosecutor said, "There was never any question that a Skakel club was the murder weapon."

On November 2, Chief of Police Baran told members of the press, "Golf clubs are not all that uncommon. There is nothing special in the fact that the murder weapon was a golf club."

For whatever reason, the general feeling around the Greenwich police department was that the wild and wooly Skakel kids were notorious for tossing golf clubs, amongst other things, around their properly. They could have easily left the 6-iron outside, where the real murderer picked it up and used it to bludgeon Martha Moxley to death.

Jerry Oppenheimer wrote in *The Other Mrs. Kennedy*, "The reason for the failure of the police department in the days after the murder was simple. Initially, the Greenwich police could not bring themselves to believe that the murder could have been committed by a local resident. Greenwich, and Belle Haven in particular, was populated by wealthy, powerful professionals, not the sort of people who commit violent crimes. And that naive assessment applied to the entire Skakel clan, despite that their long history of eccentric violent behavior was well known to the local police and longtime residents of the community."

After her daughter's death, Dorthy Moxley found Martha's diary. She felt a chill when she read her last entry.

Dorthy said, "Martha mentioned in the diary the Skakel boys. Up to that point, I didn't know she even knew the Skakels. She said she had to be careful because she didn't trust one of them. But she didn't mention which one."

Especially telling was Martha's entry on September 19, 1975, less than six weeks before she was murdered.

She wrote:

Dear Diary, Today was nothing extra special at school. Tonight it ended up w/me, my girlfriend Jackie, Michael, Tom, John, and David (four Skakel brothers) at the Skakel residence. Michael was so totally out of it that he was being a real asshole in his actions & words. He kept telling me that I was leading Tom on when I don't like him (except as a friend). Michael jumps to conclusions. I can't be friends w/Tom, just because I talk to him, it doesn't mean I like him. I really have to stop going over there. Then, Michael was being such an ass. They all started fighting because he was being such a big "he man." He kept calling Tom & John fags & they were ready to have a fist fight, so I said "Come on Jackie, let's go."

So, it was evident from her diary entry that Martha felt that Michael was the problem child in the Skakel family, not Tommy, or any of the other Skakel boys. It was also obvious from her September 19 post that Michael was jealous of his brother Tommy, and as a result of this jealousy, he was capable of resorting to violence when angered.

Yet strangely, it was Michael Skakel who was quoted in the newspapers the day after the murder saying that he had seen his brother, Tommy, talking to Martha on their lawn shortly *before* she left the Skakel residence.

Greenwich Deputy Police Chief David Grant, whose 147-member force seemed to be more concerned with protecting Greenwich residents from outsiders than from each other, had bridled at the conviction, widespread amongst the residents, that the killer had to have been a Belle Haven resident, in order to have found his way past the guard points, and in and out of the winding and dimly lit streets around the Moxley house.

"We have nothing to report," Deputy Chief Grant told the New York Times the day after the murder. "No leads. No motives and no suspects; from Belle Haven or anywhere else."

Despite Grant's personal comments, the *New York Times* wrote:

The seclusion of Belle Haven, which juts out into Long Island Sound, is reinforced by three private police guard posts on two main access roads and barricades that extend into the streets to impede unfamiliar traffic. It is possible for a resident to avoid the guard posts, but it would be highly improbable for a stranger to do it. Some streets, such as the one where Martha lived, have been chained off to become cul-de-sacs.

On November 2, the Greenwich police issued a nationwide search for the grip and part of the shaft of a stainless steel golf club used in the bludgeoning death of Martha Moxley.

According to the *New York Times*:

The usual 'all-points bulletin' went out over the national police teletype network after the police had already spent several days searching for the grip and shaft of the club in the woods surrounding the Moxley estate and in the shoreline weeds that surround the peninsula on which the estate stands.

In addition, the state's Chief Medical Examiner, Dr. Elliot Gross, announced after a six-hour investigation at Greenwich Hospital that the girl had been killed by repeated blows to the skull with a golf club.

Now, here is where members of the Greenwich Police Department, if they didn't outright lie, had a bad case of short-term memory loss.

As we have stated before, on the day Martha's body was found (October 31), police detectives Lunney and Brosko has spotted a Toney Penna 5-iron with a metal head in the Skakel house.

Yet on November 3, the *Times* wrote:

The police have already been looking for the complete set of golf clubs from which the murder weapon came. They would not say, tonight, however, whether a wooden-headed or metal-headed set had been used in the murder.

The search for the set of clubs was not confined to the privately patrolled Belle Haven estate area, where Miss Moxley and three teenaged friends had spent hours Thursday night about the dark streets and visiting friends.

Stephan Baran, the chief of police, suggested that the clubs might not prove a useful clue and finding the owner of the set might not necessarily lead to finding the killer.

And the fact that the murder weapon was a golf club does not, he added, strengthen the conviction among residents that the murderer must have either been a Belle Haven resident or at least someone familiar enough with the area to slip past two guard posts and through the maze of streets.

The Moxley neighbors felt differently than Chief Baran.

John Gentri was a radio personality who anchored a local radio show.

"I have six kids, and I lined them up for a family conference," John Gentri said. "I told them that no one goes out alone at night anymore, and no one goes anywhere without telling us. Not until that creep gets caught."

Gentri's son, Chris, who was friendly with Martha Moxley, and who had gone out on Mischief Night, said, "There was no weird man lurking in the woods. Whoever did it saw Martha that night and knew who she was. One of the people in the freakin' neighborhood did it. There was no guy who snuck off the Thruway behind Belle Haven. That's plain ridiculous!"

Again, on November 3, when quizzed by the press as to his reputation for protecting the rich in Belle Haven, Baran got downright testy.

"You can be certain that we would act if we had any evidence linking a person to the crime," he said. "We certainly do not have evidence at this time to substantiate any arrest."

Maybe not, but Chief Baran certainly had enough evidence concerning members of the Skakel family to make them his prime suspects, and it's curious that he did not think it necessary to do so.

The crucial 48 hours after the murder had passed quickly, and Greenwich police seemed in no hurry to ramp up their investigation.

On November 4, the Greenwich police, clearly over its head, called in the state police and asked them to send its mobile crime laboratory.

Police Chief Baran told the press, "This is the kind of equipment that the Greenwich police are not often called upon to utilize in this wealthy well-guarded community, which has always felt itself safe from the kind of violent attack that makes a murder investigation necessary. But I assure you that this is the only outside help the Greenwich police department will seek."

Chief Baran then uttered something he had been reluctant to say just one day before.

He told the press, "National statistics indicate that it's usually a member of the family, or a close friend who commits a murder. Not many murders are a mystery."

Chapter Twenty-Five

The Undisciplined Skakel Boys Had a History of Violence

The second generation of Skakel boys seemed to have parroted the recklessness of the past generation of Skakels; especially Tommy and Michael Skakel.

As his rowdy youngsters grew into teenagers, Rushton Sr. proved helpless to control them, especially since the death of his wife, Anne Reynolds Skakel, who died of cancer in 1972 at the age of 42. The boys took the death of their mother especially hard, and they repeatedly vented their rage in violent ways around the Skakel residence, sometimes beating up on each other, and sometimes taking out their rage on the family furniture. Rushton Sr. was a mental and physical wreck, and when the boys got completely out of control, he'd call his husky neighbor, Lou Pennington, to stop the boys from either destroying the house or sending a sibling to the hospital.

In 1963, Marie Kane was just 21 when she arrived in America from her home in Ireland's County Antrim. Her first job was in helping her family work as caretakers for Danish comedian Victor Borge, who owned a waterfront estate in Greenwich. In the summer of 1974, Kane took a job at the snack bar at the Belle Haven Beach Club, which is where she met Rushton and Anne Skakel.

"They offered me a job and I took it," Kane told the *Norwalk Patch* in 2013. "It was a full time, live-in nanny job, but they called me a governess."

Right off the bat, Kane realized the Skakel boys were an unruly bunch with a penchant for violence.

"The Skakels didn't like discipline," Kane said. "The kids or the parents. It's not like the parents were unkind to me, but their children were just out of control.

"I was raised with discipline and I thought it was very strange they didn't give me anything to discipline their children, especially if they (Rushton and Anne) weren't going to be their all the time. And those boys were never happy, always angry. Even when their parents were home."

Whenever Kane tried to regulate the boys on her own, they replied with vicious blows to various parts of her body.

"They used to kick me, too; Michael and Tommy," Kane said. "My legs were black and blue."

Kane showed the bruises to her Aunt Eileen.

"I said to my aunt, 'I don't have to take this in America, do I?'" Kane said. "And she said. 'No, you don't.' So, I told the Skakels, 'I'm leaving and I'm not coming back.' I lasted with them in Belle Haven for five or six months.

"Later I was shocked that Anne Skakel had gotten sick and had died of cancer. She was always the picture of health, and she loved to play tennis."

In 1974, George Boynton was a history teacher and soccer coach at Brunswick High. Although he was not a live-in tutor, as Ken Littleton would later be, Boynton did go over to the Skakels on weekday evenings to help Julie Skakel and the Skakel boys with their homework. Rushton Jr., John, and Julie were intent on learning and diligently did their work; not so Tommy and Michael.

"Tommy and Michael were bouncing off the walls," Boynton told Timothy Dumas in Dumas's 1998 book, *Greentown*. "They just could not concentrate. They had fallen behind badly in their schoolwork. To distract me, Tommy would often offer me food and alcohol. He had that game down nicely. Every two minutes he'd come over and talk to me."

When Boynton was tutoring the children, the cook, Ethel Jones, would serve him and the children in the dining room, while Rushton Sr. sat by himself in the living room watching television.

"When I came to say hello, he (Rushton Sr.) always had a glass of wine in his hand," Boynton said. "And when I went to say good night, he still had a glass of wine in his hand. He just had no fire in him. He was having a very rough time. I think he was blown away."

Boynton was also Tommy's and Michael's soccer coach.

"Michael had natural gifts, but no discipline," Boynton said. "He was easily distracted. He was bent on making trouble; tripping guys, hitting guys. I think Michael was the one most affected by his mother's death."

Yet, it was Tommy Skakel that Boynton had to dismiss from the team. Even though Boynton said that Tommy was by far the most talented soccer player of the Skakel boys, and playing soccer gave him confidence and an identity of his own, Tommy committed an unforgivable sin in a team sport – at game time, he abandoned his team.

"Tommy just decided, out of the blue, not to show up for a game," Boynton said. "So, I told him to leave the team. He didn't take it well. The next day he came to practice and begged me to take him back on the team. I told him, 'I'll tell you what. If the kids on the team say you're back on the team, you're back on the team. Come see me after practice.'"

While Tommy watched from the sidelines, Boynton assembled his team on the field.

"I asked the team what we should do about Tommy Skakel, and it was unanimous," Boynton said. "The boys said, 'No way! We don't want him back.'

"I told Tommy what the team had decided, and he was very, very upset. He walked away in tears. He obviously didn't take rejection too well."

Boynton also felt the key incident that was responsible for transforming Tommy and Michael Skakel from difficult to incontrollable was the death of their mother.

"Without a doubt, that's what did it," Boynton said. "Anne Skakel was easily the most impressive woman I've ever met. Call it what you will. A commanding presence. Charisma. When she walked into a room, you just kept your mouth shut and paid attention. When she died, the family just unraveled."

A family friend said after Rushton Sr.'s death in 1999 from "brain illness" that "Anne Skakel seemingly was Rushton Skakel's emotional compass. Her death left Rushton Skakel with a deep sense of loss and emptiness in his life. He numbed the pain with alcohol and prescription drugs, and he was hospitalized on several occasions for alcohol abuse."

The family friend also said, "Discipline was lax in the household before Anne Skakel's death. And after her death, it veered towards non-existent as Rushton relied on tutors and caretakers to look after his children during his frequent travels."

Chapter Twenty-Six

Without Any Evidence or Motives, the Greenwich Police Make Neighbor, Edward Hammond, Their Chief Suspect

On November 1, 1975, even though two Skakel family boys appeared to be the likely suspects, the first person the Greenwich police put the screws to was the 26-year-old Edward Hammond, a queer-duck-of-a-man, who lived next door to the Moxleys. It was an elderly neighbor, Jeanne Wold, who pointed the police in Hammond's direction.

A few hours after Martha Moxley's body was found, Wold, who was not physically well and slowly going blind, went to the Greenwich Police Station and spoke to Captain Thomas Keegan.

She told him, "This may be nothing, but Edward Hammond is a strange one, alright. Back in April, I was sitting in a chair on my porch when I heard strange noises around the corner of my house. I got up and walked to the side entrance.

"One set of doors had been opened. A dark haired, sturdily built man was rattling the French doors to the living room, trying to open them. That man was Edward Hammond of 48 Walsh Lane.

"I said to him, 'Edward, what on earth are you doing?'

"He just turned around and walked away as if nothing happened. Then, the next day he came to my front door with this peculiar excuse that, the night before, he had wanted to see my new dog. Of course, I didn't believe him. That man is a strange one, alright. He's a loner and a bad drinker. And he seems awkward when talking to women.

"I'm not saying Edward killed Martha, but I think he should be investigated."

The truth about Hammond was that he was melancholy from the recent death of his father, and as a result, had become more than a social drinker. Hammond was a Yale graduate and a veteran of the United States Army. He was presently attending Columbia Business School and living with his mother at 48 Walsh Lane.

Based on the rantings of an old, sick, and nearly blind woman, on Halloween night, just hours after Martha Moxley's body had been found, police arrived at Hammond's home.

"Where were you last night at around 9:30-10 pm?" the detectives asked.

"I was sitting home watching *The French Connection* on television," Hammond said.

Not convinced about the validity of Hammond's explanation, the detectives read Hammond his rights and took him handcuffed in an unmarked car to the Greenwich Police Station.

Two other detectives, after allegedly getting permission from Hammond's mother via a signed "consent to search" form, searched the Hammond residence, but they found nothing incriminating.

When Mrs. Hammond arrived at the Greenwich Police Station, she was dismayed to discover that her son's clothes had been confiscated, and he was now wearing prison-issue scrubs.

The police noted in their report that Hammond's beige-colored pants had "blood stains on the upper left leg." Hammond's blue men's shirt, sized 17-34, had "unknown stains," and his red knitted sweater, color red, had an "unknown type of stain in the chest area."

After giving a signed statement, Hammond was released into this mother's custody.

"But don't be taking any trips," a detective told Hammond. "We might have to talk to you again."

The tests on Hammond's clothes determined that the stains on Hammond's pants were his own blood, and the stains on his blue shirt and red sweater turned out to be nothing but food stains.

On November 13, Captain Keegan and Detective Joe McGlynn interviewed Hammond at the Greenwich Police Station. This time, Hammond was represented by an attorney, and, after conferring with his attorney, Hammond agreed to take a polygraph test. The test was deemed "inconclusive," because Hammond, an alcoholic, was taking the drug Antabuse, which, combined with alcohol, makes the person taking it violently ill.

A week later, Hammond took the polygraph again, and this time he passed with flying colors.

After he passed the polygraph, two Greenwich detectives drove Hammond home. Hammond was sitting alone in the back seat, when suddenly, the detective in the front passenger seat spun around holding golf club head in his right hand.

He barked at Hammond, "Do you know what this is?"

"No sir, I don't," Hammond said.

"This is the golf club head that was used to kill Martha Moxley!"

"Why are you torturing me like this?" Hammond said. "I passed your polygraph, and I told you I don't know anything about the murder."

Investigative reporter and author, Leonard Levitt, said in his 2004 book *Conviction: Solving the Moxley Murder*, that in 1983, while he was working for *New York Newsday*, he was able to contact Hammond by phone. Hammond was now living in Venezuela and working for Lloyds of London. His mother had passed away a year earlier, and Hammond had not been back to Greenwich since her funeral.

"It used to be so enjoyable in Belle Haven," Hammond told Levitt. "But the way the police treated me changed one's view and coloring."

"I have one question," Levitt said. "Why did your clothes have your blood stains that night?"

"I cut myself shaving," Hammond said.

Chapter Twenty-Seven

Tommy Skakel and Ken Littleton Give Each Other Alibis For the Time of Martha's Murder

Having put Edward Hammond on the back burner as a murder suspect, the Greenwich police focused on Tommy Skakel, who was allegedly the last person to see Martha Moxley alive, and Ken Littleton the live-in tutor, who was on his first day of work at the Skakel's house on the night Martha was murdered.

Littleton, 23, a recent graduate of Williams College, was 6 foot 3 inches with shoulders like a linebacker. Starting in the fall of 1975, Littleton taught science and physical education at the exclusive Brunswick School, where three of the Skakel boys, Rushton Jr., Tommy, and Michael, went through the motions of attaining some form of education. Their father, Rushton Skakel Sr., thought that Littleton's bulk combined with his mental acuity would make him the perfect person to discipline his sons, while teaching them the basics of a high school education.

On the night of the Moxley murder, Rushton Sr. was on a hunting trip in the Vermont woods, and Littleton had moved into the Skakel master bedroom on the second floor in the rear of the house. What especially got the Greenwich police's attention was the fact that the master bedroom had a terrace that faced Walsh Lane and had a clear view of the Moxley house.

As we stated earlier, on the night of the Moxley murder, at around 7 pm, Littleton had taken the Skakel boys to the Belle Haven Club for dinner. Despite the fact that all three Skakel boys were underage, all imbibed either beer, wine, or alcohol for the duration of their stay, which ended about 8:30 pm.

Littleton was surprised that no one at the club said anything about the under-aged boys drinking, and he didn't want to make waves on his first night on the job.

When the Skakel boys got home from the club, they were greeted by several friends - male and female - including their cousin, Jimmy Terrien. Littleton went upstairs to finish unpacking, and at 9:30 pm, the Skakel's live-in housekeeper, Nanny Sweeney, came upstairs and asked Littleton to investigate outside as to why the neighborhood dogs were barking so aggressively. Littleton did as Nanny Sweeney requested, searching the area on both sides and in front and back of the house, but he could find nothing that would cause the dogs to be so belligerent.

"It must be the neighborhood boys stirring up trouble on Mischief Night," he told Nanny Sweeney.

At around 10 pm, Littleton said he was joined in the master bedroom by Tommy Skakel, and they spent about 20 minutes watching *The French Connection* on television.

"Tommy came up about twenty minutes before the chase scene," Littleton told the Greenwich police.

The Greenwich police checked with the local television station, and they determined that *The French Connection* chase scene started at 10:03 pm and ended at 10:30 pm.

As soon as the chase scene ended, Tommy Skakel left the master bedroom, and Littleton claimed he stayed in the master bedroom for the rest of the night.

The next day, Littleton was raking the leaves and doing yard work when all the commotion started. He could not believe that on his first day on the job, a horrible murder had been committed right across the road from where he was employed.

"I said to myself, 'How the hell did I get myself involved with this family (the Skakels),'" Littleton said.

When informally interviewed by the Greenwich police at the Skakel residence soon after the body was discovered, both Littleton and Tommy Skakel basically told the same story concerning the night before.

Later that evening, Tommy and Littleton were interviewed separately by the police; this time at the Greenwich police station. Both repeated the stories they had given earlier that day at the Skakel residence, which gave them both alibis for the estimated time of the murder, which the police report said was approximately 10 pm. The police administered Tommy Skakel a polygraph test, which he reportedly passed, but Ken Littleton was not given a polygraph.

On Sunday, November 2, Rushton Skakel Sr. returned from his hunting trip. He was greeted by Detectives Jim Lunney and Ted Brosko, the two men who had spotted the Toney Penna 5-iron at the Skakel residence on the day Martha Moxley's body was discovered.

The two detectives wrote in their report, "Since the golf club, which was still at the Skakel home, was similar to the one that caused the death of Martha Moxley, investigators proceeded to the Skakel home in an attempt to obtain the golf club."

The two detectives still did not have a search warrant, but they convinced Rushton Sr. to sign a "consent form," which gave them permission to make an informal search of the house. There were conflicting reports on why a legitimate search warrant had not been obtained.

Chief of Detectives, Tom Keegan, who had replaced Baran as Chief of Detectives said years later, "We figured we didn't need a search warrant because Rushton Skakel was totally cooperative at the beginning, and he gave us carte blanche inside the house."

Detective Lunney had a different take.

"We were afraid if we asked him he might have said, 'Get out!'" Lunney said. "We were afraid we'd lose what access we had."

Detective Steve Carroll was even more blunt than Lunney.

"When it came to the Skakel's, the Greenwich police treaded very lightly," Carroll said. "Maybe it was the Skakel money. Maybe it was their position. But I believe I was subconsciously intimidated by them."

Because Rushton Skakel had not yet realized the severity of the situation, Detectives Lunney and Brosko exited the Skakel residence in possession of the Toney Penna 5-iron, with Anne Skakel's name etched in just under the grip. Still, despite the missing Toney Penna 6-iron from the Skakel residence, they felt they still had no concrete evidence to indict anyone in the Skakel family.

"Everyone knew the Skakel kids left things all over their property," a Greenwich police officer said. "They could have left the 6-iron outside, and anyone could have picked it up and committed the murder with it."

On November 3, Rushton Sr. took his son Tommy down to the Greenwich police station to take another lie detector test. The test was inconclusive. The reason given by Greenwich police was that, due to the Moxley murder and investigation, Tommy had not gotten much sleep. On November 9, Tommy took another polygraph, and this time he passed.

As for Littleton, he was informally interviewed by the Greenwich police at the Skakel residence on November 5. A pair of Wrangler 36-30 jeans with possible blood stains on it, along with a pair of blue pair of Tretorn sneakers, also with possible blood stains on it, had been found in a black plastic garbage bag outside the Skakel garage during the "informal search" three days earlier. The jeans had a laundry stamp on the inside right pocket that said, "Matthai – B."

The detectives asked Littleton how he and the Skakel boys were dressed on the night of the murder.

"We dined at the Belle Haven Club," Littleton said. "And they have a strict dress code. We all had to wear ties, a jacket, and trousers. No one wore jeans."

On November 9, the detectives questioned Rushton Sr. about the jeans. Rushton said he thought the jeans belonged to Michael.

"While he was in summer camp in New Hampshire, Michael swapped jeans with another boy," Rushton said. "I believe the Matthai – B is the name of the other boy."

When the sneakers and the jeans were examined at the lab, the stains turned out to be boat paint. However, a long blond hair, similar to Martha Moxley's was found on the jeans.

A few days after Martha was murdered, the Greenwich police decided to administer a polygraph to Dorthy Moxley and her son, John.

"It was a tough thing for us to do," Detective Steve Carroll said. "But we didn't want to rule anybody out. What if the mother and daughter had an argument or something? Or maybe she had a fight with her brother, John. We had to consider everyone."

The Moxleys readily agreed to the polygraphs.

"Nothing was happening in the case, and I wanted to do everything possible to move things along," Dorthy Moxley said.

Both Moxleys passed the polygraph.

Since Ken Littleton's November 5, interview had been "informal," the Greenwich police interviewed Littleton again on November 14 at the Greenwich police station. This time the interview was taped, and Littleton was released after signing a written statement as to his version of the events on the night of the murder.

On November 20, Greenwich detectives contacted the authorities in Massachusetts in order to do a background check on Littleton. The report came back saying that Littleton had "no criminal record and came from a quiet family."

On December 11, the Greenwich police, having gotten nowhere in six weeks of investigations, interviewed Helen Ix and Geoffrey Byrne, the two teenagers who had been in the back seat of the Skakel's "Lustmobile" on the night of the murder. The teenagers said at about 9:30 pm they both had witnessed Tommy Skakel and Martha Moxley engaged in "sexual horseplay" near the back of the Skakel residence.

Based on this new evidence, the Greenwich police developed a theory concerning the sexual shenanigans perpetrated by the two teenagers and witnessed by at least two other teenagers.

One Greenwich detective said, "What if Martha and Tommy had engaged in light sexual foreplay, but Tommy wanted to go further and Martha didn't. That could have set Tommy off."

On December 13, Detectives Carroll and Lunney asked Tommy Skakel to appear before them at the Greenwich police station. Tommy came alone, without any legal representation, and without his father, who, at this juncture, was again deep into the bottle. The two detectives talked Tommy into allowing them to take samples of his hair. Tommy agreed, and Lunney took several samples of Tommy's hair from his head.

In the weeks following the murder, before Tommy Skakel had been identified as a possible suspect, most of the Skakels fell all over themselves trying to comfort and placate the Moxleys.

"We received sympathetic visits and phone calls from virtually all of the Skakels," Dorothy Moxley said. "The only one we never heard from was Ethel. She never called us, never wrote us, never left a message. I don't know. Maybe she felt the further she distanced herself from the Skakels, the less damage it could do to the Kennedys.

"But Rush and the others were wonderful from the beginning. I remember seeing Tommy at Martha's funeral, and I went over to him and gave him a big hug. I didn't know Tommy, but I felt since he was the last one to see her it must have been hard on him to know that she'd been killed. I don't remember thinking that he was the one who, maybe, killed her.

"I remember Rush used to come over and visit and tell us how sorry he was. He came over one night and said he had just been to an A.A. meeting. He came in drinking a big glass of bourbon. He said, 'This is really terrible what happened to Martha. I wish it could be solved. I hope you don't think it was Tommy.'"

Rushton Skakel Sr., and his brother Jim had not been particularly close in years; especially since the death of George Jr. when Rushton put Joe Solari, against Jim's wishes, in charge of Great Lakes Coal and Coke.

A few weeks after the Moxley murder, Jim Skakel decided to find out how deep the Skakel family was involved in the murder. Without telling his brother Rushton, or anyone else in the Skakel family, Jim contacted a friend who was an operative for the Pinkerton Detective Agency.

"Just find out how involved my nephews are in the Moxley murder and then get back to me," he told the Pinkerton. "But please don't get my name tangled up in all this."

The Pinkerton did his due diligence for a few weeks, and then he told Jim Skakel, "This is a complete mess. There are all sorts of theories floating around, and from what I could squeeze out of them, your nephew Tommy Skakel is emerging as a prime suspect. But the Greenwich police is screwed up and in over their head. They have no evidence at all; only theories with no meat. But this could get really messy, and my advice for you is to stay out of it and see how things shake out."

Jim Skakel did exactly what the Pinkerton advised; blood only ran so deep with the Skakels. It was different with the Kennedy family, where blood was paramount and everyone not a Kennedy was a rank outsider.

Christmas was approaching, and the residents of Greenwich quietly grumbled that the Greenwich police seemed to be dragging their feet on this case. On December 21, 1975, the discontent of the locals prompted Police Chief Baran to release a report to the press that said, "We are doing all we can in investigating the Moxley murder. We have interviewed more than 200 people, some of them two and three times."

Rumors began circulating throughout Belle Haven that the Greenwich police, and in particularly Chief Baran, were too busy protecting the rich and influential rather than digging deeply into the case.

When Chief Baran heard these rumors, on December 23, he hastily called a press conference.

Baran told the press, "You can be certain that we would act if we had any evidence linking a person to the crime. We certainly do not have evidence at this time to substantiate any arrests. We are still searching for the missing shaft and grip of the golf club that was the murder weapon. We have used metal detectors over a wide area, trees have been examined, lakes and ponds have been drained and the shorefront has been searched, all to no avail.

"We do not intend to utter the name of anyone until we have someone we are confident is the right person. I think there is some irresponsible journalism going on at the present time. Kids would mention a name and unfortunately it gets into the press. It's almost character assassination."

Chief Baran then dropped a bombshell when he admitted that, after an autopsy by the coroner, the previously stated time of death for Martha Moxley had been changed from 10 pm on the night of October 30 (remember the barking dogs) to anywhere from 9:30 pm October 30, to 5 am on the morning of October 31, which opened up the possibility of numerous other people being murder suspects.

"We have pursued that," Chief Baran said. "But there is no way of tightening it up."

Since the time of the murder was expanded five hours into the next morning, the residents of Belle Haven were more than a little apprehensive. They now wondered if their pristine community had been invaded by outsiders. Could it have been a transient, perhaps bent on burglary; someone who came on foot? However, there were no reports of strange noises that night, either from the New England Thruway or the Penn Central Railroad station less than a mile away from the Moxley residence.

On the eve of the first Christmas without her daughter, Dorthy Moxley seemed more confused than irritated with the police investigation.

On December 24, she told the press, "We don't know anything about the ongoing investigation. The Greenwich police have been good to us. We know they are doing their best. We feel strongly that this will be solved, but we don't know anything because the police don't tell us anything."

Chapter Twenty-Eight

Rushton Skakel Hires an Attorney and the Stonewalling Begins

In mid-January the Greenwich police finally came to the realization that Tommy Skakel was their best bet as a murder suspect, but they didn't have enough evidence to indict him. So, they decided to contact Rushton Skakel Sr. and request Tommy's school records from the Whitby School, where Tommy had spent most of his school years before attending Brunswick High. At first, Rushton Sr. seemed amendable to the Greenwich police's wishes.

"Do whatever you want," Rushton told the detectives. "Be my guest. I want this matter cleared up as soon as possible."

On January 16, Rushton Sr., on his personal stationery, gave the Greenwich police written permission for the release of all his son's records, medical and psychological, from the Whitby school.

But then saner minds prevailed.

Enter Christopher Roosevelt, a former United States Justice Department attorney, who was on the school board at Whitby. Roosevelt was also quite friendly with the Kennedy family.

After receiving the written request from the Greenwich police for Tommy's school records, Roosevelt phoned the Greenwich detectives in charge of the case: Detectives Carroll and Lunney.

He told them, "If you arrest Tommy Skakel, I guarantee you he will be represented by the finest lawyers in the state of Connecticut."

The detectives assured Roosevelt that no arrests were imminent and that they were just on a "fact-finding mission to shed some light on Martha Moxley's murder."

"Then shed your light someplace else," Roosevelt said.

And then he banged down the phone.

Roosevelt immediately phoned Rushton Sr. and convinced him that releasing Tommy's school records was not in Tommy's best interests. Rushton Sr. finally saw the light, and he immediately hired Emanuel Margolis, considered one of the top criminal attorneys in the state of Connecticut. Margolis agreed with Roosevelt's assessment of the situation, and he drafted a letter and told Rushton Sr. that he should personally hand-deliver the letter to Greenwich Police Chief Baran. Rushton did so on January 22.

The letter said:

Dear Sir:

This is to inform you that I, Rushton Skakel, hereby withdraw the 'Authorization to Release Medical and School Records' concerning my son, Thomas Skakel, executed January 16, 1976. This withdrawal shall take immediate effect.

After delivering the letter to Chief Baran, Rushton Sr. went home and had a cocktail or two. Then, he strolled down the street to visit his close friends, Cissy and Robert Ix. Less than a half hour after arriving at the Ix residence, Rushton Sr. was rushed by ambulance to Greenwich Hospital.

Detectives Lunney and Carroll, not yet privy to the fact that the letter had been delivered to their boss, were alerted that Rushton had suffered some sort of physical malady at the Ix residence.

They rushed over to the Ix house, where Cissy Ix told them, "Myself and Rushton were sitting in the study, and I left for a moment to get some more refreshments. When I returned Rushton's face was pale, and he was holding his chest."

Detectives Lunney and Carroll then raced to Greenwich Hospital. In Rushton's room they were greeted by Father Mark Connelly, a celebrity priest who frequently said Mass on television. He also considered himself a Skakel family advisor. After Father Connelly told the detectives that the doctors did not think Rushton Skakel had suffered a heart attack, but rather had "stress related" chest pains, they requested a few moments to talk to Rushton Sr.

"Yes, but make it quick," Father Connelly said.

Rushton Sr. then informed the detectives about the letter he had just hand-delivered to Chief Baran, and then he added, "My attorney, Emanuel Margolis, is handling things from now on. There will be no more private conversations between the Greenwich police and members of my family."

Editor's note: In 1981, the controversial Margolis, a Jew born and raised in Brooklyn New York, defended the first Amendment rights of the Ku Klux Klan, winning a case that allowed the Klan to stage a rally in Meriden, Connecticut.

Margolis knew that the Skakel family had endlessly deep pockets. So, he insisted that he represent, not only Tommy Skakel, but also the entire Skakel family, Ken Littleton, Nanny Sweeney, the maid - Amelia Rodriguez, the cook - Ethel Jones, and the gardener - Franz Wittene.

On January 31, the Greenwich police made a request, in writing, to Margolis, to administer Sodium Pentothal, the generally accepted truth serum, to Tommy Skakel.

Margolis replied, in writing, "Not only will I not let you administer truth serum to Thomas Skakel, but I will refuse any request for you to interview him again."

Chief Keegan then sent Detectives Lunney and Carroll to Margolis's office in Stamford, Connecticut.

There, they told the attorney, "We have enough evidence right now to indict your client. So, if Thomas Skakel is innocent of this crime, it would be in your client's best interest to cooperate with this investigation."

"And what might that evidence be?" Margolis said.

"We have witnesses that saw your client speaking to Martha Moxley right before she was killed – about 9:30 pm," the detectives said. "And we have the murder weapon: the head of a Toney Penna model 6-iron – the only iron missing from a set found at the Skakel residence."

Margolis smiled. He figured they had nothing on Tommy Skakel, and now the Greenwich police had confirmed his suspicions.

"As for the girl's time of death, I'm sure you know that the coroner's office has rejected Greenwich police's initial contention that the time of death was 10 pm," Margolis said. "All that nonsense about barking dogs was just that - nonsense. It was Mischief Night. Teenagers were out terrorizing the town. That's why the dogs were barking.

"Now as for the golf club, what you have proves absolutely nothing. The Skakel family leaves golf clubs all over their property all the time. Anyone could have picked up the club and committed the murder."

Margolis stood from his chair behind the desk. He paced to his office door and held it open.

Then, he smiled and said, "Now if you please, gentlemen. I have a client I am meeting with in a few moments."

Without saying goodbye, the two detectives exited the office.

In April of 1976, six months after the Moxley murder, with no arrests, and Rushton Skakel no longer cooperating with the investigation, the Greenwich police finally applied for a formal search warrant of the Skakel residence. However, their request was turned down by the state's attorney, Donald Browne, because "too much time had elapsed."

Detective Steve Carroll was exasperated that the Moxley murder investigation had apparently hit a dead end.

Detective Carroll said, "There was a point in time, months after Rushton Skakel withdrew his cooperation, that we all met up at Prosecutor Don Browne's office; me, Jim Lunney, Chief Tommy Keegan, and Jack Solomon, a State cop. We were discussing the case. What we had, and what we didn't have.

"Finally, I said to Don Browne, 'Why can't you convene a grand jury; have them bring in a true bill, or not a true bill?' A 'true bill' is the grand jury's finding of grounds for arrest. I was talking about Tommy Skakel.

"Browne said to me, 'Don't tell me how to run my business. And then he turns to Chief Keegan and says, pointing to me, 'I don't want him up here anymore.'

"In 1991, fifteen years later, I'm reading the newspaper and I see Don Browne saying it's too late to convene a grand jury. I said to myself, 'Yeah, sure it is now, but it wasn't in 1976.'"

Chapter Twenty-Nine

David Moxley Seeks Help in Finding His Daughter's Murderer

By February 1, 1976, the entire town of Greenwich was buzzing with the rumor that Tommy Skakel had killed Martha Moxley. Rushton Skakel, convinced of his son's innocence, heard these rumors. So did the Moxleys.

Ever since Martha's murder, the Skakels and the Moxleys had maintained a seemingly cordial relationship, but as it became clearer that the Greenwich police was either incapable or reluctant to act on the possibility of a Skakel connection to the murder, their relationship became edgy.

Rushton Sr. decided to take the bull by the horns and pay the Moxleys a visit.

After gruff greetings by the Moxleys, Rushton asked if he could speak to them for a moment.

"We're listening," David Moxley said.

Still feet from the front door, and not being invited by the Moxleys to have a seat either in the kitchen or in the living room, Rushton Sr. told David and Dorthy Moxley, "I've heard the same rumors that you have, and I have taken steps to put your mind at ease. I've had my son, Thomas, examined by several doctors, medical and psychiatric, and all the results have come up negative. Thomas did not, and, in fact, was not and is not capable of such violent acts."

"So, why don't you turn those results over to the police?" David Moxley said.

"I wish I could, but I can't," Rushton Sr. said. "My attorney has advised me against doing so."

"In that case we have nothing further to discuss," David Moxley said.

David Moxley then led Rushton Skakel to and then out the front door.

"It got so I couldn't even talk to the man," Dorthy Moxley said years later. "I couldn't be in the same room with him. How could I be in the same room with someone who I thought was covering up for someone in his house who murdered my daughter?

"I remember one time me and my husband were playing tennis, and Rushton was playing in the next court, and I thought, 'I just can't play. I cannot be around this man.'"

John McCreight was an associate of David Moxley at Touche Ross. He had served as a police consultant in Detroit, revamping their entire police system, before entering the Apollo Space Program. In 1968, he moved to Touche Ross, and in four years he was a partner in the firm.

On the night after Martha's body had been discovered, McCreight, who called himself "Columbo in a slightly better raincoat," phoned the Moxley residence and spoke with David Moxley.

"David, the Greenwich police is out of their league on this one," McCreight said. "They haven't had a homicide there in three decades. They will never be able to solve this. Let me get you some help with friends I have in the Detroit police department."

David Moxley appreciated the overture, but his head still was spinning from the day's horrifying turn of events, and he had not yet considered that the Greenwich police might not be up to the job of finding his daughter's murderer.

"Outside my house it's crawling with law enforcement people," Moxley said. "The local police has even called in the state police. I think I'm okay here."

"David, I've been all through this many times before," McCreight said. "After a couple of days, it gets much harder to solve a homicide. It's like a half gallon of ice cream you bring home from the supermarket. You put it on the counter and it's as hard as a rock. But it doesn't take long for it to turn to nothing but slop."

David Moxley promised John McCreight he'd contact him if, after a reasonable amount of time, the Greenwich police was unable to come up with the killer.

By the beginning of February, the Greenwich police were still floundering in the dark, and no arrests seemed imminent. Newspapers in Greenwich and in nearby New York City, ran editorials suggesting that the Greenwich police should call in outside help from a police department that was proficient in homicide investigations.

"We don't rely on anyone!" Chief Baran told the *New York Post*. "Just recently, valuable paintings were stolen from the home of famous art collector Joseph Hirshhorn. We not only apprehended the perpetrator, but we recovered the paintings, which are now hanging in the Smithsonian in Washington."

After reading Chief Baran's remarks in the newspaper, David Moxley picked up the phone and called John McCreight.

"Did you read what Chief Baran said in today's *New York Post*," Moxley said.

"Yes, and his baloney about comparing an art thief to a murderer is simply astounding," McCreight said. "What are the chances of anyone solving a homicide if they've never solved one before? Almost zero."

The next day, McCreight planted himself in Chief Baran's office. He told the chief if the Greenwich police did not seek help from a police force more proficient in homicide investigations, the Moxleys would hire private detectives to do the job of the Greenwich police.

"And furthermore," McCreight told Baran, "I will contact all the local newspapers, including those in New York City, to inform them of what you are forcing the Moxleys to do."

Chief Baran, fearing the negative publicity, sent Detectives Lunney and Carroll to Detroit accompanied by McCreight.

McCreight said in Timothy Dumas's *Greentown: Murder and Mystery in Greenwich, America's Wealthiest Community*, "Early on, the police had confirmed my fears of that first night: that they were completely out of their depth. And their challenge was exacerbated by the sophistication of the people they were dealing with. A lot of sophisticated people live in Belle Haven – smart, well-informed, and the police were outgunned. Way, way outgunned."

When Detectives Lunney and Carrol, and McCreight arrived in Detroit, they made a beeline to the offices of the Detroit Homicide Squad, who investigate close to a thousand homicides a year. Detectives Lunney and Carrol came prepared, bringing with them all pertinent notes, plus slides and photographs that showed not only the topography of the area near the murder scene, but also identified who lived in which house in the neighborhood.

Lunney and Carroll huddled for 10 hours with the best homicide detectives in Detroit, and what the Motor City Homicide Squad told the Greenwich detectives confirmed what Lunney and Carroll had already suspected.

The Detroit Homicide Squad concluded that the murderer "lives in the neighborhood and was acquainted with the victim." And that "he's a troubled young man with an explosive temper."

The description of the murderer screamed Tommy Skakel, but it also identified with his younger brother, Michael, who Martha Moxley wrote unfavorably about in her diary just six weeks before she was murdered.

But they still had no concrete evidence to seek an indictment; at least according to the state's attorney, Donald Browne.

Detroit Detective Gerard Hale accompanied Detectives Lunney and Carroll back to Greenwich to take a closer look at the evidence. He also re-interviewed Helen Ix and Geoffrey Byrne, who had been with Tommy and Michael Skakel and Martha Moxley on the night of the murder. It took some prodding, but Hale induced the two teenagers to give a slightly different version of the events than they had given on their first interview with the Greenwich police.

Hale wrote in his report, "The two teenagers told me that they had witnessed a shoving match between Thomas Skakel and Martha Moxley outside the Skakel residence on the night of the murder. It consisted of Thomas pushing Martha and Martha pushing Thomas. At one point, Thomas pushed Martha down and either fell on her or got down on top of her. This point is not clear because it happened partially out of the view of Helen and Geoffrey behind a brick wall."

The day after Hale's report, reporters from the *Greenwich Time* confronted Tommy Skakel outside the Brunswick School. When they told him about Helen's and Geoffrey's statements, he said, "I don't remember anything like that."

He ended the interview by storming away.

Hale was also critical of how the Greenwich police handled the case from the day of the murder. He told reporter, Len Levitt, who, in 2004, wrote the book *Conviction: Solving the Moxley Murder* about the Moxley-Skakel murder case, but was then working for the *Greenwich Time*, "There should have been a thorough, formal search of the Skakel residence as soon as possible after the murder. If Rushton Skakel was as cooperative as the Greenwich police say, why not go and do it immediately? Then, if he refused, they could have asked for a search warrant."

Hale then told Levitt what Greenwich town folk were thinking since Martha Moxley's body was found.

"When it came to the Skakel's, the Greenwich police were treading very lightly," Hale said.

Chapter Thirty

Rushton Skakel Fires Ken Littleton

In late March of 1976, with the Skakels still not cooperating with the investigation, Detectives Lunney and Carroll visited the Brunswick School. Their mission was to speak to the close friends of Tommy Skakel to see if they could pry loose some incriminating evidence against him.

The problem they faced was that Tommy Skakel had no close friends at the Brunswick School.

Detective Lunney wrote in his report, "It appeared that all of his friends are relatives. The consensus of opinion is that Thomas Skakel is a strange kid and that he is obviously aware of his family's wealth."

A few days after Lunney wrote his report, Fred Wittine, the Skakel's former gardener and occasional chauffeur, who had just retired and moved to upstate New York, showed up at the Greenwich Police Station and asked to speak with the detectives handling the Moxley murder case. Formerly, Wittine had been represented by Emanuel Margolis, but now that he was no longer employed by the Skakels, he decided to tell all he knew about the Moxley murder from the perspective of someone who was inside the Skakel household and was privy to information the Skakels did not want public.

According to Wittine, the person the Skakels were seeking to protect was not Tommy Skakel, but instead his brother, Michael.

"For some reason, the Skakel family was treating Michael extremely nice since Martha Moxley was murdered," Wittine told the detectives. "Before October 30, he was treated just like the rest of the family; no better, no worse."

The problem for the Greenwich Police Department was that they not only didn't have enough incriminating evidence to indict Tommy Skakel, they had even less evidence implicating his younger brother, Michael.

In May of 1976, Tommy Skakel decided he was tired of being harassed by the Greenwich press and the Greenwich police. Rushton Skakel attempted to enroll Tommy in a private school in New York City, but several parents of students, presently attending that school, knew about the Moxley-Skakel murder connection. These parents banded together and threatened to remove their children from that school if Tommy Skakel was admitted as a student.

Knowing that he would have this same problem in a school anywhere near Greenwich, Connecticut, Rushton enrolled Tommy at the Mountain School of Milton Academy in Vershire, Vermont, 260 miles north of Greenwich, Connecticut.

In mid-April of 1976, Rushton Skakel fired Ken Littleton, for reasons that are not clear.

According to an article written by Skakel cousin, Robert Kennedy Jr., in the January/February 2003 issue of *The Atlantic*, Littleton was fired by Rushton Sr. because "Police visited the Skakel home and reported that Littleton had wrapped his car around a tree in a drunken accident and then abandoned it."

There is no record of a police report substantiating Kennedy's claims.

However, there was an April 2 police report, written by Detectives Lunney and Carroll after they had interviewed Cissy Ix. Detroit homicide detective Gerald Hale had also participated in the Cissy Ix interview.

The report said, "Cissy Ix felt strongly that Thomas Skakel was not involved in the fatal assault of Martha Moxley. She also felt strongly that Ken Littleton should be checked out as a suspect. She could not understand why Mr. Skakel kept Littleton in his employ because he didn't contribute anything to the household. Mrs. Ix also stated that 'girlie' magazines were found in Littleton's room and that he was in the habit of visiting the Skakel's gazebo in the nude."

In late 1977, the Moxleys, sick of seeing the Skakels, moved out of Greenwich and settled in New York City. Months later, they relocated again to Annapolis where David Moxley piloted his 42-foot cruiser on Chesapeake Bay. In 1988, David Moxley died of a sudden heart attack, and Dorthy then moved to New Jersey.

In 2001, Cissy Ix visited Dorthy Moxley in New Jersey. With Cissy was her daughter, Helen, who had been with Tommy and Michael Skakel, and Martha Moxley on the night Martha was murdered.

The two elder women had never been especially close friends and they hadn't seen each other in years. Yet, Cissy Ix had the audacity to say to Dorthy Moxley in Dorthy's own home, "So much time has passed by. What's the use of pursuing something that happened more than a quarter century ago? Haven't the Skakels suffered enough?"

Resisting the urge to slap Cissy Ix's face, Dorthy Moxley simply said, "Would you feel the same if it had been your daughter, Helen, who was murdered? Helen is here today with you. Martha is not here with me."

Dorthy then politely escorted Cissy and Helen Ix to and out of the front door.

On April 3, 1976, the day after they interviewed Cissy Ix, Detectives Lunney and Carroll visited Ken Littleton at the Brunswick school. At the time, Littleton was still employed by the Skakels. Littleton refused to speak to the detectives without his attorney, Emanuel Margolis, being present. He also refused to sign a police-written statement that he felt the police had slanted to incriminate Tommy Skakel.

In 2003, after the Robert Kennedy Jr. article in *The Atlantic* hit the streets, Littleton insisted there had been no car accident, and he could only speculate on the cause of his dismissal.

"I never understood why he (Rushton Sr.) had turned against me," Littleton said. "I just think he wanted to separate himself and his family from me when the police began to pressure me."

Littleton never considered the obvious reason for his dismissal: to point the finger of guilt away from the Skakel boys, Littleton was being set up as a patsy.

When he fired Littleton, Rushton Sr. refused to pay Littleton's last month's salary. This was certainly a curious action on Rushton Sr.'s part. The Skakel family had money coming out of their ears, and Littleton's monthly salary was surely less than what Rushton Sr. spent in a monthly period on alcoholic beverages, just for himself. It was only after the headmaster at Brunswick School contacted Rushton Sr. and demanded that Littleton be paid that Rushton reluctantly agreed to do so. Still, refusing to pay Littleton's last month's salary may have been a subtle way for the Skakels to further tarnish Littleton's reputation.

Using his last month's salary as seed money, Littleton hired his own attorney, John Meerbergen. Meerbergen immediately notified the Greenwich police that he, and not Margolis, was representing Littleton and that his client would agree to be interviewed by the Greenwich police, with Meerbergen present. The interview took place on April 22, and again Littleton refused to sign a written statement implicating Tommy Skakel in the murder of Martha Moxley.

Littleton told Detectives Lunney and Carroll, "What you're asking me to sign is a statement supplying circumstantial evidence against Tommy. I will not do that because I don't think Tommy did anything wrong."

In July of 1976, while school was in summer recess, Ken Littleton was arrested for grand larceny on Nantucket Island, where he had been working as a bar bouncer. He was accused of stealing, on four separate occasions, $4,000 worth of items from three stores and a boat. After pleading guilty, Littleton said that he was drunk all four times that he had resorted to thievery. He was so drunk, he maintained, that, for reasons he could not explain, he had buried one of the items and could not remember where he had buried it.

As a result of his guilty plea to the grand larceny charges, Littleton received a suspended sentence of seven-to-ten years in prison and five years of probation.

However, Littleton's arrest and guilty plea in Nantucket put him in the crosshairs of the Greenwich police department.

"Those incidents in Nantucket cried out for our attention," Greenwich Chief of Detectives Keegan said.

On October 19, Littleton, still employed at the Brunswick School, agreed to take a polygraph test administered by the Greenwich police. According to the Greenwich police report, "Kenneth Littleton was given the test three times, and it was the opinion of the examiners that Kenneth Littleton was not truthful in answering the key questions."

During his polygraph, Littleton continued to deny "any involvement or knowledge regarding the (Moxley) murder."

According to the Greenwich police, the polygraph indicated that Littleton had lied when he said he "did not kill Martha Moxley," lied when he said he "did not hit her with a golf club," and lied when he said he "didn't know who did kill Martha Moxley."

Littleton later said he didn't believe his polygraph was accurate because he had been upset and ashamed because of his arrests in Nantucket, and this nervousness had negatively influenced his performance during the polygraph.

After Littleton's supposedly failed polygraph, the Greenwich police informed the Brunswick School about Littleton's summer arrests and guilty pleas in Nantucket, and as a result, Littleton was fired.

Still thinking that Littleton was their man, the Greenwich police asked Littleton, in the presence of his attorney, John Meerbergen, to take a sodium pentothal test. The Greenwich police felt that under the influence of the so-called "truth serum," Littleton might say something that would implicate himself in the Moxley murder.

Even though Littleton verbally agreed to come back to the police station for the truth serum test, his attorney John Meerbergen put the kibosh on that.

"This case is too hot and heavy," Meerbergen told Littleton. "There is absolutely no way I would advise you to take the sodium pentothal test. In your mental state, you might say anything while you're unconscious. Besides, there is no need for you to prove your innocence. It's their job to convince a grand jury that there is probable cause to try you on a murder charge. Why help them try to prove their case?"

Littleton then told the Greenwich police he was advised by his attorney not to take the truth serum test.

Because he was now out of a job and was feeling the heat in Greenwich, Littleton took a job as a teacher at the private St. Luke's School in New Canaan, Connecticut, fifteen miles northeast of Greenwich. But the Greenwich police had a hardon for Littleton that would not go away. They paid a visit to St Luke's and informed the hierarchy about Littleton's arrest and guilty pleas in Nantucket.

Littleton was fired again.

"It just didn't seem like a good situation for us," said a St. Luke's school official. "Kenny is an extremely talented science teacher and had a great relationship with the students. And he was well thought of by other teachers. I told Kenny that once he cleaned up this Nantucket business, he could reapply for his job here."

In 2002, Chief Keegan, who had, just months after the Moxley murder, considered Ken Littleton his leading suspect, told Lindsay Faber of the *Greenwich Time*, "When one considers that it was his first night in the house, and that the handle of the golf club, the murder weapon, was removed from the scene, in my view he was not a real logical suspect. If he were responsible, it is very unlikely that he would know that Mrs. Skakel's name tag was present and took the handle from the scene."

Why did Chief Keegan, over the years, have this monumental change of heart concerning Ken Littleton's guilt? Or did he, from the beginning, despite his posturing, know that Littleton was the unlikeliest of suspects and that someone in the Skakel household had killed Martha Moxley?

Chapter Thirty-One

Seventeen Months After Martha's Murder and Still No Arrests

On June 24, 1977, the *New York Times* did a follow-up article on the Moxley murder. The title read:

WHO KILLED MARTHA MOXLEY?

A TOWN WONDERS

The article said, in part:

In large measure and particularly because the police now believe they have traced the golf club used in the murder to a collection of clubs belonging to the Skakels, the investigation has become the story of police efforts to establish the guilt or innocence of two young men. One is Thomas Skakel, a nephew of Ethel Skakel Kennedy, widow of the later Robert F. Kennedy. The other man is Kenneth Littleton, a 24-year-old former Greenwich private school teacher, who, on the night of the murder had moved into the Skakel home.

Emanuel Margolis, a Stamford lawyer who represents young Skakel, said that nothing was proved by the police belief that the golf club came from a collection usually kept in the hallway of the Skakel home.

"Clubs were left all over the property all the time," Margolis said in an interview. "Anyone could have picked one up from the grounds."

Mr. Margolis also said that neither Thomas, nor his father, Rushton, chairman of the board of Great Lakes Coal and Coke Corporation, was available for interviews by the press on the Moxley case.

This was the first time it had been reported in the press, not to mention the prestigious *New York Times*, that "Thomas Skakel, a nephew of Ethel Skakel Kennedy," was, in fact, a suspect in the brutal murder of a lovely 15-year-old girl.

This did not go over well in the Kennedy camp in Hyannis Port.

Senator Ted Kennedy, who, in 1969, most likely avoided a manslaughter charge in the drowning death of Mary Jo Kopechne on the island of Chappaquiddick, was quick to turn up his nose at the Skakels, whose mansion in Greenwich, as was reported earlier, he once surreptitiously lived in rent-free for a month because it was convenient for him to do so.

Having read the article in the *New York Times*, Ted was apoplectic when he discovered that his sister, Ethel Skakel Kennedy, had invited Rushton Skakel Sr. to an affair where Ted was also expected to attend.

Ted Kennedy's aide, Richard Burke, remembered the incident well.

Burke said, "Ted knew about her brother Rushton's trouble. He said to me, 'Just make sure that guy (Rushton) doesn't get near me.' Ted didn't want Rushton Sr. near him because he didn't want to wind up in a photograph with the father of a suspected murderer."

As for Ken Littleton, after he was fired from his job at the St. Lakes School in New Canaan, his life nosedived into a drug-induced spiral from which he never fully recovered.

Running from his demons, as well as from the Greenwich police, Littleton moved to Florida where he was arrested three times for drunken driving, trespassing, shoplifting and disorderly conduct. He got married and divorced. Then, he moved to Canada where he worked on a loading dock. He drank incessantly and did drugs, and he became increasingly unstable. In Canada, Littleton underwent psychiatric treatment when it was discovered that he was both bi-polar and manic depressive.

Ken Littleton, after leaving Canada in 1982, bounced from town to town and from country to country. He even spent two years down under in Australia. By 2002, Littleton, now 50 years old, had settled into a tiny apartment in Boston's Beacon Hill District. He could only find part-time work and was basically supported by his girlfriend, Anne Drake, with whom he had lived for the past five years. Neighbors described the once-hulking Littleton as a "quiet, unassuming man who keeps to himself."

In 2002, his mother, Maria Littleton, told the *Greenwich Time*, "He was such a nice, beautiful boy. I don't know how he got involved in this (the Moxley murder). I don't know why they kept pointing the finger at him."

Maria Littleton also told the *Greenwich Time* that her son, who she raised as a good Christian boy, had become a brooding shell-of-a-man who was "unable to hold jobs, tried to commit suicide and abused alcohol and drugs." She said that her son had become paranoid to the point where he thinks that the Kennedy family and the Skakel family have collaborated together, and are "out to get him."

"This has ruined my family," Maria Littleton said.

Chapter Thirty-Two

***After Michael Skakel Was Arrested
for Speeding in Upstate New York,
His Father Dumps him at the Elan School
– a Detention Camp for Incorrigible Youths.***

It went unnoticed at the time – it didn't even make the Greenwich newspapers – but in March of 1978, at 4 am, Michael Skakel, now 17 years old, was driving near the Windham Ski Resort, in upstate New York. Rushton Skakel had recently purchased the resort as a winter getaway for his family. In the car with Michael was twenty-one-year-old Debby Diehl, a family friend.

"Controversy always surrounded them (the Skakels)," said Jimmy O'Connor, the previous owner of the Windham Ski Resort. "Something would always happen. Invariably something would happen."

A car had been disabled on the side of the road, and two state police officers were tending to the people involved. One of the police officers stepped onto the road and signaled for Michael to stop. But Michael, knowing his blood alcohol content was well above the percentage used to determine that a driver is legally drunk, not only didn't stop, but he tried to run down the police officer.

"Apparently the Skakel vehicle disregarded the signal and continued on, almost hitting the police officer standing in the middle of the road," said Windham Police Chief George Tortorelis. "The other officer who was in the car gave chase to the Skakel vehicle. It turned into a high-speed chase."

The chase ended when Michael smashed his car sideways into a telephone pole. Debbie suffered a broken leg, but Michael was unhurt.

The officers arrested Michael Skakel and charged him with speeding, unlicensed driving, failure to comply with an officer's order, and drunken driving. He spent a few hours in the police cooler, and at 9 am he appeared before a local judge. Fortunately, his father, Rushton, was notified, and he arrived in court with his bankbook.

As to the charges of speeding, unlicensed driving, and failure to comply with an officer's order, Michael pled guilty. But Michael had refused a blood alcohol test both at the site of the accident and in the local jail, and he insisted that when he was arrested he was as sober as the judge now presiding over his case.

After Rushton Skakel posted bail, Michael, still in cuffs, was driven to a local airport. There, two men in white coats dragged Michael, kicking and screaming, into a waiting plane, which deposited him in Poland Springs, Maine, where the Elan School is located. Elan is a rehabilitation facility that calls itself a "last resort for trouble youths."

When Greenwich Detective Jim Lunney heard about the incident, he phoned the Windham police station. Chief Tortorelis told Lunney, "Michael Skakel has been causing numerous problems for his family. With his father's permission, we sent him to the Elan School for rehabilitation."

When Detective Lunney contacted the Skakel family to find out what the deal was, he was instead put in touch with family lawyer, Tom Sheridan.

"This is private family business," Sheridan told Lunney. "Leave Michael alone. He's making progress, and we don't need outside influences which might cause him to relapse."

It cost Rushton Skakel $44,000 a year to take his troubled son off his hands and out of the newspapers.

The Elan School practiced a controversial behavior modification program that relied on "shouting sessions, long hours of sitting face-first in a corner, and boxing matches to rid unruly students of their anti-social mindset." At Elan School, if a student even smiled without permission, they could spend as much as 12 hours cleaning urinals with a toothbrush.

In 1997, Sandra Scarry, a New Jersey professor, sent her daughter to the Elan School. She told the *New York Times,* "It's no place any loving parent wants to have to send their child. You have a sense that you've just handed over your child to strangers, and you hope they know what they are doing."

When Sarah Levesque was only 14 years old, her parents sent her to Elan for two years. Four years after her release, she said, "I don't think I'd be alive today if I hadn't been sent there. But I have nightmares to this day about it. I wake up crying at least once a week. Elan saved my life, but I feel haunted by it."

After escaping several times, and being returned by his father to the Elan School each time, Michael settled into the daily routine, which included group therapy sessions.

However, during his two years at the Elan School, Michael would say things at these group therapy sessions that would come back to haunt him a quarter century later.

Chapter Thirty-Three

Tommy Skakel Starts a New Life

For the next several years the Moxley murder case lay dormant. Greenwich Police Chief Thomas Keegan, who was instrumental in treating the Skakel family during the Moxley murder investigation with kid gloves, retired from the Greenwich Police Force and moved to Surfside Beach, South Carolina. In 1989, Keegan was elected to the House of Representatives, representing District 106 (Horry County). He would serve eight two-year terms.

As for Tommy Skakel, with many of the Greenwich populace thinking he got away with murder, Tommy took it on the lam, traveling extensively throughout North America, Europe, and Africa.

Years later, concerning his wandering ways, Tommy said, "I got tired of walking around Greenwich and hearing people say, 'He did it.' I just wanted to get away from Greenwich."

In Africa, Tommy was bitten by an insect, called the Anopheles mosquito, and the result was a bad case of malaria; the symptoms of which would haunt Tommy for several years.

In 1987, Tommy married Anne Gilman from Boxford, Massachusetts. The newlyweds migrated to the tiny town of Stockbridge, Massachusetts, in Berkshire County, population 1,800 and 130 miles north of Greenwich. Although Tommy was never charged with the murder of Martha Moxley, his wife, Anne, said the murder case hung over his head like a guillotine (In 1998, former Greenwich Police Chief Keegan testified before a grand jury that Tommy was charged with the murder of Martha Moxley in 1976, but he could not produce the paperwork to back up his statement).

"My husband went through a lot of pain," Anne Skakel said. "Being wrongly accused, no one ever comes back and says they're sorry."

"I've lived with this most of my life," Tommy told the *Associated Press* in 1998. "It's been devastating over the years."

Chapter Thirty-Four

The Stamford Advocate *and* Greenwich Time *Ask Journalist, Len Levitt, to Investigate the Moxley Murder Case*

In 1982, investigative journalist Len Levitt received a phone call from an old friend. His name was Ken Brief, the editor of two small Connecticut newspapers, The *Stamford Advocate and Greenwich Time.* Levitt, a graduate of the Columbia School of Journalism, had previously worked for the *Detroit Press* and had been a correspondent for *Time Magazine*. But it was at *Newsday*, a Long Island daily newspaper, that Levitt and Brief had met, and they maintained a friendly relationship over the years. In fact, it was Levitt who had suggested to Brief that he leave *Newsday* and apply for the editor's job at the two small Connecticut newspapers.

As Levitt reported in his book *Conviction: Solving the Moxley Murder*, Brief said, "Look Len, there's something bothering me here in Greenwich. Wherever I go around town people are still talking about the unsolved Moxley murder and the Skakels. Why don't you spend a few months up here and look into this for me?"

Brief sent Levitt several clips from the Moxley murder case that dated back to the night of the murder. Levitt read about the murder weapon being a 6-iron taken from a complete set of golf clubs found at the Skakel residence. Levitt also read about the Greenwich police's obsession with Ken Littleton as the murder suspect. Most telling, he read a quote in a March 1976 *Associated Press* article attributed to Fairfield County State's Attorney Donald Browne, who said that, "A particular family has clearly impeded the police investigation."

Browne also said that, "short of a confession, a solution to the case seemed unlikely."

It was obvious to Levitt that the family Browne was referring to was the Skakels.

When Levitt arrived at Brief's office to start working on the case, Brief said, "Well what do you think?"

Levitt replied "It looks like someone has gotten away with murder."

The first two people Levitt sought to interview was David Moxley, Martha's father, and Bob Ix, the husband of Cissy Ix and the father of Helen Ix, who was with Martha on the night of her murder.

Both men treated Levitt like he had leprosy and refused to see him. From years working on the newspaper beat, Levitt knew the Greenwich police might get surly if they were approached by an outsider who questioned them as to why no arrests had been made in such a high-profile murder case. So, he bit the bullet and called Dorthy Moxley. She agreed to meet with Levitt, but she still wanted to know, "Why, seven years later, is a newspaper still interested in Martha?"

Levitt said, "The *Stamford Advance and the Greenwich Time* have asked me to take a fresh look into the case."

Levitt interviewed Dorthy Moxley in her apartment on the Upper East Side of New York City. He learned that the Moxleys had moved to Greenwich in 1974 from Piedmont, California. He also learned that Rushton Skakel, even though he hardly knew the Moxleys, sponsored them for membership at the Belle Haven Country Club in Greenwich, and also, that he sponsored David Moxley at the University Club in Manhattan. But unfortunately, Dorthy Moxley could provide very little information about her daughter's death that wasn't already public knowledge.

Dorthy told Levitt, "The Greenwich police have been very good to us. They have been compassionate and kind. I feel they have been loyal to us."

Dorthy then referred Levitt to John McCreight, the associate of her husband's at Touch Ross, who had, when it was obvious the Greenwich police were in over their heads and deferential to the Skakels, brought the Detroit police's homicide chief, Gerald Hale, into the Moxley murder investigation.

At first, McCreight was cautious about talking about the case. But when Levitt asked him, "Did Hale write a report?" McCreight put the conversation on hold while he tossed that question around in his mind.

Finally, McCreight answered, "Yes."

It took two more meetings with McCreight until he finally agreed to show Levitt Hale's report.

"He said he would show the report to me, but only with stipulations," Levitt said. "The first was that I could not quote it in my story. The second was that I could reveal the content only to my editor. And third, that the newspapers' lawyers draft a letter confirming our agreement."

Years later, when Levitt asked McCreight why he had agreed to release Hale's report to him, McCreight said, "You were the only engine for the next leg of the trip. Your newspaper was the only open road. And there was something else. I felt I could trust you."

Levitt read the report and it contained mostly everything he had already known about the night of the incident.

Then, like a pearl in a sandy oyster, a new clue materialized.

As Levitt already knew, Geoffrey Byrne and Helen Ix had been sitting in the back of the Skakel "Lustmobile" at approximately 9:30 pm on the night of the Moxley murder. Martha Moxley and Tommy Skakel had just exited from the front seat of the car.

Hale wrote in his report, "Jeff and Helen stated that it appeared as if Martha and Thomas were 'making out.' This, after careful questioning, consisted of Martha pushing Thomas and Thomas pushing Martha. At one point, Thomas pushed Martha down and either fell or got on top of her."

Levitt knew that the statement by itself meant very little. Even if Martha had engaged in playful petting and kissing with Tommy, there was absolutely no proof that he had brutally murdered her.

Later in the report, Hale stated that Tommy had received a severe head injury at the age of four (he accidentally fell out of the back seat of the family car). As a result, "He would become violent frequently and quite suddenly. He would jump up from the table, begin to throw things about, turn over beds, pull phones from the wall or threaten siblings.

"He would lose consciousness, and the episodes varied from 15-20 minutes to as long as 2-3 hours. His father was able to control him, but only physically. There is evidence that these rage reactions continue to this day."

Considering Tommy Skakel's past history of violence, considering that he was reportedly the last person seen with Martha Moxley before she was murdered, and considering the day Martha Moxley's body was found two Greenwich detectives had spotted a set of Toney Penna golf clubs in the Skakel house missing the six-iron murder weapon, it was inconceivable that Tommy Skakel was not immediately considered the top suspect by the Greenwich police.

If Tommy had been the chief suspect, the Greenwich police no doubt would have asked for a search warrant for the Skakel residence. They would have confiscated all clothing and shoes in the house belonging to Tommy Skakel. Then, they would have tested them for blood stains and hair fibers that could have connected the clothing to the death of Martha Moxley.

The Greenwich police did ask for a search warrant for the Skakel residence, but, inexplicably, the request was rejected by the state attorney.

The Hale report said, "Search warrants for clothing, shoes and other golf clubs have been denied by the State's Attorney, Mr. Donald Browne."

The Hale report did not speculate as to the reasons for Browne's actions, and with the rumors circulating in Greenwich the past few years about a police cover-up, it got Levitt to thinking.

"I wondered why," Levitt said. "Had there been a dispute between the Greenwich police, who had sought the warrant, and the state's attorney Browne, who had refused it. If so, did the rumors of a cover-up refer to him?"

Levitt knew he had to speak to Hale personally, and to do that he would have to make a trip to the Motor City.

After John McCreight acted as a go-between, Levitt saw Hale in his office on Beaubien Street, two floors above the press room where Levitt had worked as a young crime reporter.

Both men agreed that the Greenwich police, based on the circumstances on the night of the Moxley murder, should have immediately focused their case on Tommy Skakel.

"But why didn't they?" Levitt asked, half expecting Hale's reply to indicate a cover-up.

Instead, Hale said, "It was because, when it came to the Skakels, the Greenwich police treaded very lightly."

It was common knowledge around Greenwich that the police officers, who were not exactly pocketing bloated yearly salaries, depended on the locals for extra moonlighting work, which was perfectly legal in Greenwich. Some acted as bouncers at local bars, or as security at private parties. Others worked as private security guards at local jewelers and banks. It was not uncommon for a uniformed Greenwich police officer, while supposedly "on duty," to be spotted eating lunch or dinner in the kitchens of one of the numerous Greenwich mansions.

As their meeting was winding down, Hale told Levitt that the Greenwich Police Department had unrealistic expectations when it came to the reliability of polygraph tests. The Greenwich police had initially hung their hat on Ken Littleton being the murderer because he had performed so abysmally taking such tests.

"I tried to tell the Greenwich police many times that a polygraph is not an investigative tool," Hale told Levitt. "For it to be effective, investigators must know the subject and his reactions. A polygraph is just short of voodoo. I've seen them cause a lot of harm in homicide investigations if they are not properly given."

"What do you mean by 'not properly given?'" Levitt said.

"If, say, they gave the polygraph too soon, too early in the case, before the police knew the details, before they knew the proper questions to ask," Hale said. "I heard tapes of Tommy's test. Professionally, it did not clear anyone."

As for the sad-sack, Ken Littleton, who was psychologically beaten like a piñata by the Greenwich police, Hale told Levitt, "There could be many reasons for his failing the polygraph, including fear, nervousness, and improper questioning by the person giving the test. There's a difference between asking, 'Do you know something about the case?' and 'Did you kill Martha Moxley?'

"I've investigated over 1,000 homicides. I believe the Moxley case is solvable, even at this late date. What the Greenwich police must do is question each suspect's friends - the wives, ex-wives and girlfriends – to determine if such behavior – not necessarily killings, but violent behavior – is repeated. It will not be easy. It will take time, money, and manpower, but it can be done.

"Keep up your investigation. It might prod the Connecticut authorities into restarting theirs. I feel strongly about the Moxley case. Years later it still haunts me. Whoever killed Martha Moxley should have never gotten away with it. That's why I'm saying these things to a newspaper reporter."

Levitt's next move was to interview Chief Thomas Keegan and Detective Jim Lunney; both of whom had been involved in the Moxley murder investigation from the beginning. He did so at the Greenwich police station,

Before the interview even began, Keegan told Levitt, "I'm not closing the book on this. I have every intention of bringing this case to trial. I believe I know who killed Martha Moxley, but I cannot prove it."

"I assume you mean Tommy Skakel?" Levitt said.

Keegan didn't say anything; he simply nodded.

"I told this to the Moxleys," Keegan said. "As a mother, she has a right to know what people close to the investigation feel. I waited a long time to tell them. They are haunted by this."

Levitt later checked this out with Dorthy Moxley, and she confirmed what Chief Keegan said he had told her.

"I was shocked when he told me," Dorthy said. "Not by whom he identified, but that he actually said it."

Levitt then asked Keegan about Michael Skakel, and Keegan said he was never a suspect.

Keegan was still buying the erroneous time of death as being 10 pm (the dogs barking), when the coroner's report had widened the time frame from 9:30 pm to possibly as late as 5:30 am.

Keegan told Levitt, "Michael had driven with his brothers at 9:15 pm to their cousin Jimmy Terrien's home, which is about a 15-20 minute ride from the Skakels. Martha had been murdered around 10 pm. Michael could not have returned in time to kill her."

It was astonishing that the Greenwich Chief of Police would rule out Michael Skakel as a suspect on the basis of "barking dogs" and unilaterally disregard the coroner's ruling on the possible time of death.

Is this the cover-up the people of Greenwich have been whispering about for the past seven years?

When Levitt asked about Ken Littleton, it was Lunney who opened his yap.

"Lunney began to say he believed Littleton may have participated with Tommy," Levitt said."

As Lunney spoke, Keegan began pumping his arm up and down in an obscene motion, indicating Lunney didn't know what he was talking about.

That ended the interview.

A few days later, Levitt interviewed Keegan and Lunney again.

"I asked Keegan after finding the matching golf clubs, why hadn't he obtained a warrant to search the Skakel house for the clothing and shoes Tommy wore the night of the murder to test for traces of Martha's blood or clothing fiber," Levitt said.

Keegan spit out the same nonsensical excuse the Greenwich police had been jerking the public around with for the past seven years.

"They gave us carte blanche," Keegan said. "We were afraid if we asked Rushton to conduct a formal search he might have said, 'Get out!' and we would lose any access we had."

Levitt next approached retired Greenwich police officer, Steve Carroll, who had been Lunney's partner during the initial murder investigation.

Carroll said that, from the first day, the Greenwich police pursued the theory that some Greenwich outsider had killed Martha Moxley.

"We looked at people with drinking problems and violent tempers, oddballs or loners, a lesbian couple, a retarded girl," he told Levitt. "We had no shortage of suspects."

Carroll tried to explain to Levitt the inexplicable: Despite all the early evidence just screaming Tommy Skakel was the most likely suspect, why wasn't Tommy more actively investigated right out of the gate.

"We were too willing to believe Tommy," Carroll said. "The questions the first night were too casual, too informal and not thorough enough. One of the detectives, who questioned him, liked kids and was overly friendly. He did not press Tommy on details. For example, we never satisfactorily determined what clothing he wore that night, so we could test it for blood stains.

"Maybe it was the Skakel money. Maybe it was their position. Maybe I was subconsciously intimidated. But we eliminated rather than zeroing in."

Levitt then interviewed Fairfield County State Attorney Donald Browne. When Levitt asked him why he didn't obtain a search warrant of the Skakel residence, he hunched his shoulders and claimed he couldn't remember. Then he blurted out, "Probably too much time had elapsed."

After doing his due diligence and interviewing everyone he could, connected to the Moxley murder investigation, Levitt came to the conclusion, that rather than a police cover-up, "It seemed like in the beginning of the investigation, the police had instinctively shied away from the Skakels."

Yes, but why had the Greenwich police "instinctively" shied away from the Skakels? Where they afraid they would lose their moonlighting jobs catering to the Belle Haven blue-bloods? Or, were they afraid because of the Skakels' connection to the powerful Kennedy family?

As we reported previously in this book, the day after Martha's body was found, Ethel Skakel Kennedy told her older sister, Georgeann Terrien, that she was going to call her brother-in-law, Ted Kennedy, right away.

Georgeann's husband, George Terrien, later said, "Ethel also called her other advisors. She said, 'We can't let this touch the Kennedys.'"

Forty-one years after the murder of Martha Moxley, the above questions still haven't been suitably answered. And in all likelihood, they never will.

However, a clue to what possibly transpired was provided by John F. Kennedy Jr.

As was reported in *RFK Jr.* by Jerry Oppenheimer, "John Kennedy Jr. had his own private theory. He was convinced that Michael's older brother, Tommy, was somehow involved in the murder.

"Moreover, he claimed to a friend that his Uncle Ted, along with a prominent Kennedy brother-in-law and a close family friend, were allegedly involved in paying 'hush money' to certain officials to protect Tommy. 'John,' the friend stated years later, 'told me that Tommy Skakel was involved in the Moxley murder, and the family had been paying off people for years to cover up the whole thing. When John said that Tommy was involved, I took it to mean that Tommy did it. But being involved in a murder doesn't mean that Tommy was the one who actually murdered her. It could have been one of Tommy's brothers and that Tommy was involved in it somehow.'

"According to what JFK Jr. had told his friend, 'Teddy had been running the cover-up for years, seeing to it that certain people were paid off.'

"The alleged conspiracy, according to JFK Jr., had also involved Jean Kennedy Smith's husband, Steve Smith, who oversaw the Kennedy family finances and managed campaigns for JFK, RFK, and Ted Kennedy. When Smith died in 1990 at the age of sixty-two, Ted described him as, 'The wisest advisor. There wouldn't be a Camelot without Steve Smith.'

"Regarding the alleged plan to protect Tommy Skakel, JFK Jr. told his friend, 'Money went into Kennedy accounts via contributions to certain people. But he didn't go into detail. We had this big fight, and I was yelling at him (JFK Jr.). I suggested to John that he come forward and help the parents of the girl who had been murdered, and he gave me a lot of bullshit that there was nothing he could do.'"

Unfortunately, John Kennedy Jr. is not alive to verify those quotes.

On July 16, 1999, Kennedy Jr. departed from Fairfield, New Jersey, at the controls of his Piper Saratoga light aircraft. With him was his wife, Carolyn, and his sister-in-law Lauren Bessette. The plane was scheduled to arrive at Martha's Vineyard Airport. It did not.

Three days later, Coast Guard divers found the three bodies at the ocean floor, 120 feet below the surface.

John F. Kennedy Jr. was 38 years old.

Chapter Thirty-Five

Len Levitt Continues His Investigation

After interviewing Fairfield County State attorney Donald Browne, journalist Len Levitt knew he needed to get his hands on the Greenwich department case file on the Moxley murder. He asked Captain Keegan for the file, and Keegan refused.

A lawyer for the *Stamford Advocate and Greenwich Time* filed a formal complaint with the state's Freedom of Information Commission. The Greenwich police department fought this request tooth and nail. But after six months of going back and forth, on December 9, 1982, a lone commissioner heard the complaint. Levitt argued the newspaper's side, and Keegan, decked out in his neatly-pressed dress police uniform, medals dangling, preached the side of the Greenwich police.

In July of 1983, the commissioner said that since the police investigation has been dormant for seven years, with no one actively investigating it, there was no reason not to release the documents. The commissioner decreed that "Keegan was to release over 400 pages of documents and to provide an inventory for those he maintained were confidential."

"We had won," Levitt said. "The file detailed a pattern of missteps worse than I had imagined."

From the report, Levitt learned that the police had wasted time looking for a nonexistent hitchhiker. He also discovered that the police had badgered Edward Hammond, the next door neighbor, for forty-eight hours, with no explanation in the report as to why he had suddenly become the chief suspect.

Levitt also discovered that the police had misled the public as to when exactly they found the complete set of Toney Penna irons in the Skakel house. And they couldn't even get the date right.

On the report, dated October 30, 1975, one day before Martha Moxley's body was found (the writer obviously meant October 31), it stated, "At 5:45 pm, the investigators had an occasion to be in Rushton Skakel's home. They observed the following described golf clubs located in a storage bin in a room located on the north side of the house, first floor."

Yet, as was reported earlier in this book, in a *New York Times* article dated November 3,

Greenwich Police Chief Baran said the set of Toney Penna golf clubs had not, as yet, been found. The *Times* also reported:

The police have already been looking for the complete set of golf clubs from which the murder weapon came. They would not say, tonight, however, whether a wooden-headed or metal-headed set had been used in the murder.

The search for the set of clubs was not confined to the privately patrolled Belle Haven estate area, where Miss Moxley and three teenaged friends had spent hours Thursday night about the dark streets and visiting friends.

Stephan Baran, the chief of police, suggested that the clubs might not prove a useful clue and finding the owner of the set might not necessarily lead to finding the killer.

Why did Chief Baran, three days after the set of Toney Penna irons were located at the Skakel residence, tell the *New York Times* that they were still looking for them? And why did Baran say that even if the clubs were located, "they might not necessarily lead to the killer."

"So, there it was," Levitt said. "They (the Greenwich police) had wasted two days – the crucial forty-eight hours – searching for a transient and browbeating Hammond while the killer was someone under their own noses at the Skakels. Not only had they failed to confiscate the clubs immediately, they hadn't sought a warrant to immediately search the house for the missing shaft/handle, or for the bloody clothes and shoes the killer had worn."

Levitt next interviewed the elder Moxleys, Dorthy and David. First, Levitt interviewed Dorthy at her luxury apartment at the

River House, overlooking the East River in Manhattan. The first thing Dorthy told Levitt was that no one, not her husband, nor her son, John, was willing to discuss the death of Martha any longer. They wanted to move on, and they had decided the best way for them to do that was to completely eliminate Martha from any part of their conversations.

"More than I ever realized, Dorthy was alone," Levitt said.

Dorthy told Levitt years later as to why she agreed to this interview eight years after her daughter's death.

"It was that someone cared," she said. "I was just glad that someone was interested. It was so important to me because my family wouldn't talk about it. When no one cares, you feel despair.

"Until you came, no one encouraged me. Not the police. Not a soul. It wasn't that you were going to solve Martha's murder. I didn't want to hurt myself by thinking that. But it was that you wanted to talk about Martha, and I needed that."

David Moxley was a tougher nut to crack. They met at David's office at Toche Ross in Manhattan and before Levitt asked his first question, David told him, "Please make it clear when you write your story that the initiative for this meeting did not come from us."

As we have stated before in this book, a few months after the murder, Rushton Skakel had medical experts examine his son, Tommy, and when he told Dorthy Moxley that the test proved Tommy was innocent, Dorthy begged him to share his findings with the police. Rushton refused, saying he was doing so at the advice of his attorney.

When the Greenwich police realized that they were at a dead end in the investigation without those tests, they turned to David Moxley.

"I, in effect, brokered an agreement between Rush Skakel and the Greenwich police," David Moxley told Levitt. "The Greenwich police initiated the idea. They felt I could do more with the Skakels than them."

David came to an agreement with Rushton that was utterly worthless. Both would hire doctors to examine Tommy Skakel, and the two doctors would share the results with each other. But under the agreement, neither the police, David, nor David's lawyer would see the results.

That, in effect, ended the Greenwich police's investigation of the Moxley murder.

Just before Levitt left his meeting with David Moxley, David finally opened up a bit.

"In hindsight, I should have pushed back," David said. "I should have gotten aggressive as hell. Within twenty-four hours, I should have brought in outside detectives and outside lawyers. I should have offered a reward. There would have been an uproar, I tell you that."

Chapter Thirty-Six

The Stamford Advocate *and* Greenwich Times *Refuses to Run Levitt's article on the Moxley Murder Case*

In February 1983, Len Levitt started a full-time job covering the New York City Police Department for *Newsday*. But as far as he was concerned, the Moxley murder article was just about ready to be published. He just needed to speak to a few other people to tie up loose ends. One of the last people he interviewed was Tommy Skakel, who was then living at a horse farm near Bedford, Connecticut.

By this time, Ken Brief, the editor at the *Stamford Advocate and Greenwich Times* had assigned Kevin Donovan, a reporter for the *Advocate* to assist Levitt with his final interviews. Since he was now working full-time with *Newsday*, Levitt had to take a day off work and ride with Kevin to see Tommy at the horse farm.

When Tommy opened the front door, Levitt saw a balding twenty-five year-old man with stooped shoulders. He was wearing glasses.

When Kevin asked him what he had been doing the past few years, Tommy said, "I haven't spent too much time in Greenwich. I wanted to live my life and get out of the way and be myself. I would go to a restaurant and go shopping in Greenwich, and people would talk about it. Like who the hell are these people to judge me? What gives them the right?"

Kevin then asked Tommy about the night of Martha's murder; about him and Martha making out and then him falling down on top of her.

"I don't remember anything like that," Tommy said. "The last thing I remember is saying goodbye to Martha and going back into my house. I didn't know her. Michael liked her. I didn't."

Both Levitt and Donovan were shocked at Tommy's answer. How could he not remember, as several witnesses had said, making out with Martha and then sliding down on top of her on the grass?

Levitt made a mental note about the most telling thing Tommy had said: *"Michael like her. I didn't."*

This was the first time anyone had brought Michael Skakel into the conversation concerning Martha's murder. And it was his own brother, Tommy, who did it.

Levitt then traveled to Ottawa, Canada to speak to Ken Littleton. Littleton was now living with Mary Baker, who he would soon marry. He didn't have a job.

Littleton told Levitt, "I fully cooperated with the Greenwich police through the end of school at Brunswick. Even after I got in trouble I was cooperative."

In 1977, when the Greenwich police asked him to take a polygraph, Littleton complied with their request.

"I was naïve. I didn't see any harm," Littleton said.

The first trick the Greenwich police used was that after they strapped Littleton into the polygraph, they said, "Okay, we'll be back in a few minutes to take the test."

Then, they disappeared for a full twenty-five minutes, causing Littleton to stew in his own juices. When they did come back and started the polygraph, the first thing they said was not a question. Instead, they yelled at Littleton, "You killed Martha Moxley!"

Littleton vehemently denied that he had.

So, they brought him into a different room, where Chief Keegan was sitting. They again strapped him to the polygraph, and this time it was Keegan who yelled, "You murdered Martha

Moxley!"

Again Littleton denied the accusation.

And this was the polygraph, for years, the Greenwich police said Littleton had failed.

"I never knew Martha Moxley," Littleton told Levitt. "I never saw Martha, and I had nothing to do with her murder. And I didn't think Tommy did either.

"But when the police questioned me in 1976, I did give the police circumstantial evidence about someone else."

"Who was that?" Levitt asked.

"Michael," Littleton said. "I would have termed him an alcoholic. I thought Tommy was a good kid, but I was scared of Michael."

Littleton told Levitt that when he was golfing with Jimmy Terrien at the Greenwich Country Club, Michael was in a threesome just in front of them.

"When we caught up to him, I saw that Michael had crushed the head of a chipmunk and put a tee through it like a crucifix," Littleton said. "At the next hole, there was a squirrel with his head crushed in. When we finished the hole, Michael came up to us with a crazed expression on his face, and he told us how he had run down the animals.

"Up in Windham, Michael used to flush out pheasants from the bushes and shoot them. I saw him run one down before it could get in the air. Another time he shot a hawk in a creek.

"But when I told the police about this they told me Michael couldn't have killed Martha. They said if the murder occurred at 10 pm, he was at the Terrien home and couldn't have returned in time."

Len Levitt was now ready to submit his story to Ken Bright. He had put the finishing touches on the article, concentrating on the bungling of the Moxley murder investigation, from day one, by the Greenwich police.

"The story was to run on the day before Halloween, the eighth anniversary of Martha's death," Levitt said. "I had worked on it for nearly two years.

"But as the publication day approached, Ken told me it was not quite ready. He said loose ends remained – trivial things such as dates, quotes, and transitions. I thought nothing of it then. How was I to know what lay ahead?"

Bright told Levitt that he would wait, for maximum impact, an entire year to publish the Moxley murder report. That meant it would run on the day before Halloween, 1984, nine years after the murder.

But the following year, again, the story did not run. This time Bright said there were unspecified "legal concerns."

The same thing happened again on the day before Halloween 1985 – there was no Moxley murder article in the *Stamford Advance*, or in the *Greenwich Time*. The reason Bright gave Levitt was that the new publisher, Steve Isenberg, had objections to running the story.

"As I remember, Ken seemed afraid of it," Levitt said. "It was a very tough story. And as an editor you had to have a lot of self-confidence to go with a story like that. I think someone was putting pressure on him."

A few days later, Bright told Levitt that Steve Isenberg, the man who had objections to publishing the Moxley article in the Connecticut newspapers, was now moving to a new job. He would be the new associate publisher of *Newsday*.

In other words, he was going to be Len Levitt's new boss.

It took a full two years before Levitt ran into Isenberg at the offices of *Newsday* in Long Island.

When they did meet, Isenberg just smiled and said, "You know Len, your Moxley story will never appear, not just in Connecticut, but in any *Times-Mirror* publication. I poisoned the well."

Levitt was too stunned to reply.

"I had become a journalist because I dreamed of righting wrongs," Levitt said. "Here the Moxley family had been lost with nowhere to run. The local papers, the *Stamford Advance* and the *Greenwich Time*, had been their last resort.

"I had begun this case believing the police had engaged in a cover-up," Levitt said "I had been wrong. The cover-up was by the newspapers that had hired me in refusing to tell me why they had killed the story."

Len Levitt's ace-in-the-hole was that, although the newspapers wouldn't touch the Moxley story, he felt he had enough information to write a book about the incident. This did not sit well in with Isenberg.

The two men had lunch, and when Levitt brought up the fact that Isenberg had said he "poisoned the well" in the Moxley matter, Isenberg denied he ever said such a thing. He said that either Levitt had imagined it, or was mistakenly attributing it to him.

"I would never say such a thing," Isenberg said. "And if you write it in your book that I did say it, you will be doing me a great disservice."

The hidden implication was that if Levitt, with no proof (recordings) or corroboration, wrote Isenberg's quote, it would be a black day in Dodge City for Levitt. He could be sued, or worse, blackballed in the newspaper industry.

An honest reporter was being buffaloed by dishonest publishers.

Was there a quid-quo-pro between the Northeastern newspapers and the Kennedy/Skakel cabal?

Or were the newspapers just afraid to take on a political powerhouse like the Kennedys? Or was it both?

Or, was it nothing more than editors and publishers deciding that the Moxley murder was no big deal more than ten years after the fact.

Chapter Thirty-Seven

The New York Post Runs Len Levitt's Story on the Moxley Murder

For the next several years, there was no movement in the Moxley murder case.

Then, on March 29, 1991, William Kennedy Smith, the son of Steven Smith and Jean Kennedy Smith, decided to do a little bar hopping in Palm Beach, Florida, with his notorious uncle Ted Kennedy and his cousin Patrick Kennedy. After several stops at assorted bistros, they wound up in the glitzy night spot, Au Bar, which one local journalist said "trust-fund idlers, obscure blue bloods, dolled-up society matrons and erstwhile celebrities like Roxanne Pulitzer hung out."

At Au Bar, Patrick hooked up with 27-year-old waitress Michelle Cassone, and Kennedy-Smith, now 30, cuddled with Patricia Bowman, a 29-year-old single mother. Ted Kennedy sat quietly at the bar by himself and made love to his Chivas on the rocks, with just a splash of club soda.

Closing time came, and the two Kennedy boys invited their newfound female friends to a nearby family holiday waterfront estate called La Guerida (Bounty of War) for a few more drinks. While Kennedy-Smith strolled the private beach with Bowman, Cassone and Patrick snuggled in the living room, drinking wine.

At one point, Uncle Teddy staggered into the living room. He wore no trousers and his baggy undershorts were decorated with red interlocking hearts. Showing unusually good grace, the portly Teddy did wear a "long-tailed shirt," which gave him a tiny semblance of respectability.

Patrick, noticing that Cassone was uncomfortable with Uncle Teddy's mode of attire, suggested they go for a breath of fresh air. Teddy assumed he was invited, and soon all three sat on the sea wall outside the house and spoke of the "importance of family."

Meanwhile on the beach, Kennedy-Smith decided to completely disrobe, and he jumped into the cold surf. Then, according to Bowman, he galloped back onto the beach, and when she refused to get naked and jump into the water with him, he pushed her down onto the sand and roughly raped her.

Bowman then ran back to the house and called her friend, Anne Weatherly Mercer, who drove to the Kennedy mansion, picked up Bowman, and drove her to the Palm Beach Police Station, where Bowman filed a rape report against Kennedy-Smith.

The alleged rape of Bowman by a member of the Kennedy family was big-time news, and the sordid story was splashed across the newspapers and television stations in America, as well as across the Western world. Then out of the blue, a rumor surfaced that Kennedy-Smith had been at the Skakel residence in 1975 on the night of the Moxley murder.

A few articles popped up here and there speculating on the rumor, and one caught the attention of John Cotter, the city editor of the *New York Post*. Cotter had worked with Len Levitt at *New York Newsday* (a New York City offshoot of *Newsday*), and he knew about Levitt's problems about getting the Moxley story published in the *Stamford Advocate and Greenwich Times*. He sent a reporter to interview Levitt, giving Levitt the opportunity to extract a little revenge and maybe force the Connecticut newspapers to finally publish his Moxley murder story.

When the *Post* reporter asked Levitt if the newspaper's failure to publish his story was part of the cover up, Levitt let loose.

"I saw this as an opportunity to shame Isenberg and pressure Ken (Bright) into publishing the story," Levitt said. "I described how he (Bright) had hired me years before to investigate

Martha's murder and how we had obtained the police report, showing that the Greenwich police had discovered the missing golf club inside the Skakel house the day after the murder, yet failed to obtain a warrant to search the house. I described how the newspaper had refused to publish my story.

"My interview ran in the *Post* on May 1, 1991."

The *New York Post* headline read:

Fla Case Revives Probe of Kennedy Kin in '75 Sex Slaying

As if by miracle, on June 2, 1991, without contacting Levitt for any further addendums to the story, Ken Bright relented and published Levitt's article on the Moxley murder in the *Stamford Advocate and Greenwich Time*.

"It appeared on page one, and it filled four pages," Levitt said. "It ran virtually as I had written it years before."

Dominick Dunne was an investigative journalist, novelist, and movie producer, and he frequently appeared on television discussing how members of the American rich interacted in a favorable way with the American judicial system.

Dunne said in his book, *Justice: Crimes, Trials, Punishments*, "While I was covering the William Kennedy Smith rape trial for *Vanity Fair*, a rumor circulated that Willie Smith had been an overnight guest at the Rushton Skakel house in Greenwich the night Martha Moxley was killed."

On October 31, 1991, 16 years-to-the-day after Martha Moxley's body was found under a sad tree on the outskirts of the Moxley property in Greenwich, Connecticut, William Kennedy Smith's rape trial started in a courthouse in West Palm Beach, Florida.

"In the end the rumor turned out to be bogus," Dunne said. "Willie Smith had not been in the Skakel house that night. But my curiosity had been aroused. 'What happened to that case?' I asked someone I knew in Greenwich. 'Nothing,' I was told. At that point sixteen years had gone by since the murder. 'Remind me exactly what happened,' I said."

Author's note:

In a ten-day trial, even though three separate woman testified that Kennedy-Smith had sexually assaulted them, the Palm Beach jury found him not guilty of the rape of Patricia Bowman. The jury deliberated just 77 minutes.

After the verdict in the Kennedy-Smith rape trial, Dunne started asking more questions about the Moxley murder. When he discovered that Martha had been killed on October 30, a chill crept down his spine.

Dominique Ellen Dunn was a young American actress and was also the daughter of Dominick Dunne. At the tender age of 18, her first acting appearance was in the television film *Diary of a Teenaged Hitchhiker*. Her most famous role was that of Dana Feeling, the teenage daughter of a family who were terrorized by ghosts in the 1982 film *Poltergeist*.

On October 30, 1982, seven-years-to-the-day after the Moxley murder, Dominique was in her West Hollywood home on Rangely Avenue, rehearsing for the miniseries *V* with actor David Packer, when the phone rang. It was her ex-boyfriend, John Thomas Sweeney, a sous-chef at the L.A. hot spot Ma Maison, who, when they were together, had made a habit of using Dominique's head for a punching bag. Just a few weeks before, after he had tried to choke her, Dominique gave Sweeney the gate, ejecting him from her Rangely Avenue home. She then changed the locks on the front and back doors of her home.

When she realized who was on the phone, she screamed to Packer, "Oh God, it's Sweeney! Let me get him off the phone!"

Ten minutes later, Sweeney showed up at the Rangely home, and for some reason, Dominique agree to speak to him on the porch, while Packer remained inside. Packer later said he heard smacking sounds, two screams, and a thud. Packer ran out the back door of the house, and he spotted Sweeney in the bushes by the driveway kneeling over Dominique.

"Quick, call the police," Sweeney screamed.

When the police arrived minutes later, Sweeney met them out front with his hands held high in the air.

"I just killed my girlfriend, and I tried to kill myself," Sweeney told the police. "Man, I blew it. I killed her. I didn't think I choked her that hard, but I don't know, I just kept on choking her. I just lost my temper and blew it again."

Dominique, not quite dead, was taken to Cedars-Sinai Medical Center in Los Angeles, where she was placed on life support. For the next four days, doctors performed brain scans that ultimately showed she had no brain activity due to oxygen deprivation. Finally, on November 4, 1982, her parents (Dunne was divorced from Ellen Beatrice Griffin) allowed the doctors to remove her from life support. Dominique Dunne was just 19 days from her twenty-third birthday.

Just before Dominique's life-support equipment was removed, her father leaned down to say good-bye.

"I kissed her on her head," Dunne said, "and said to her, 'Give me your talent.'"

After Dunne rejected a plea bargain that would have given Sweeney seven-and-a-half years in prison, Sweeney went on trial in November 1983. At Sweeny's trial, the jury decided the strangulation death of Dominique Dunne was voluntary manslaughter, and the choking a few weeks before was a misdemeanor assault. The maximum sentence for the two charges was six-and-a-half-years, and with good time and work time deducted from his sentence, Sweeney spent just two-and-a-half-years in prison.

After the trial and subsequent funeral of his daughter, the senior Dunne spoke for his family, including his two sons, Alexander Dunne and the actor Griffin Dunne, "Not one of us regrets having gone through the trial, or wishes that we had accepted a plea bargain, even though Sweeney would then have had to serve seven-and-a-half years rather than two-and-a half. We chose to go to trial, and we did, and we saw into one another's souls in the process.

"We loved her, and we knew that she loved us back. Knowing that we did everything we could has done, for us, was the beginning of the release from pain. We thought of revenge, the boys and I, but it was just a thought, no more than that, momentarily comforting. We believe in God and in ultimate justice, and the time came to let go of our obsession with the murder and proceed with life.

"Dominique is buried near two of her mother's close friends, the actresses Norma Crane and Natalie Wood. On her marker, under her name and dates, it says 'Loved by All.' I knelt down and put the yellow rose on her grave, and said, 'Good-bye, my darling daughter.'"

Chapter Thirty-Eight

Dominick Dunne Writes the Novel Season in Purgatory, *Based on the Moxley Murder Case*

After gathering all the facts he could on the Moxley murder, Dominick Dunne decided he needed to speak to Dorthy Moxley.

"Somehow I felt drawn to her," Dunne said. "I wrote her and asked if I could come see her. I said I wanted to talk about her daughter's murder. In those days she was media shy. She did not ask me to her house. Instead, we met at a coffee shop in the Baltimore/Washington Airport.

"I asked her why she had moved away from Greenwich, since that meant there was no one there to keep the case alive. She said she could not bear to look out her windows at the Skakel house. She said she didn't know who killed her daughter, but she was sure someone in that house either had done it or knew who had. She told me that the day after the murder there were limousines with out-of-state license plates parked in the Skakel driveway."

Dunne, who had written three best-selling novels that had all been made into a television mini-series, thought he could do the same with the Moxley murder.

"I told Mrs. Moxley that I thought I could write another novel based loosely on her daughter's murder," Dunne said. "Since no facts were known publicly at the time, I said it might turn the spotlight on a long dormant case. She said she wasn't sure."

"Then I told her that I was, too, the parent of a murdered daughter. Our daughters had been born a year apart, and each was viciously attacked by a man she knew on October 30, although in different years. That marked the beginning of our friendship. She said okay, I could write the book."

"I was eager to have anybody help me who would, and he was eager for some information for his book," Dorthy Moxley said.

Not to open himself up to a lawsuit by the Skakels, Dunne wrote *A Season in Purgatory*, changing names (the Skakels were called the "Bradleys"), and changing the instrument of murder from a golf club to a baseball bat.

A Season in Purgatory, which, in 1993 became an instant best seller, was described on Amazon.com thusly:

They were the family with everything. Money. Influence. Glamour. Power. The power to halt a police investigation in its tracks. The power to spin a story, concoct a lie, and believe it was the truth. The power to murder without guilt, without shame, and without ever paying the price. They were the Bradleys, America's royalty. But an outsider refuses to play his part. And now, the day of reckoning has arrived.

In the introduction to his October 2000 *Vanity Fair* article called "Trail of Guilt," on how he came to write a *Season in Purgatory*, Dunne quoted from the *Great Gatsby* by F. Scott Fitzgerald to describe both the Skakels and the Kennedys:

THEY WERE CARELESS PEOPLE . . . THEY SMASHED UP THINGS AND CREATURES AND THEN RETREATED BACK INTO THEIR MONEY OR THEIR VAST CARELESSNESS, OR WHATEVER IT WAS THAT KEPT THEM TOGETHER, AND LET OTHER PEOPLE CLEAN UP THE MESS THEY HAD MADE.

In late-1993, Dan Rather of the *CBS Evening News*, picked up on the story and did a seven-minute segment on how a best-selling novel had reopened the 18-year-old Moxley murder case.

"Martha Moxley was back in the news, and I was on television quite often talking about her murder," Dunne said. "I learned that in certain houses in Greenwich the subject was being discussed again for the first time in years. But no one came forward."

Not everyone was impressed with Dunne and the quality of his work, but it was hard to question its effectiveness.

Robert F. Kennedy Jr., a first cousin to Michael and Tommy Skakel, said on *Larry King Live*: "I think you know Dominick Dunne is what Dominick Dunne is. He's not a journalist. He's a gossip columnist. And he entertains people. That's how he makes his money, and he has this formula where he finds notorious crimes, and he connects them to wealthy people. And it's a formula that's worked very well for him. It's produced a whole bunch of mini-series and best sellers, and it's a formula that has appealed to the public. The problem is he doesn't really even pretend to be accurate."

Dunne responded to RFK Jr.'s comments a few weeks later, also on *Larry King Live*, which was guest-hosted by Bob Costas.

After watching a clip of RFK Jr. ripping his integrity, Dunne told Costas, "I've seen this clip so many times, and I mean it's just ludicrous. I wrote a novel, for Pete's sake. A work of fiction based on a true story. Robert Kennedy is someone I have absolutely no respect for whatsoever.

"My only motivation in this has been Mrs. Moxley. No one understands the pain she's experienced like I do."

It's not as if Dunne had this uncontrollable urge to hurt the Kennedy, or the Skakel family. If anything, at first, he was a Kennedy groupie.

"When I first met him," said Dunne's friend Fred Eberstadt, "he admired the Kennedys very much, and wanted to like them and be liked by them."

Through a friend, in 1950 Dunne attended Robert F. Kennedy's wedding to Ethel Skakel. And he later befriended Peter and Pat Kennedy Lawford, who were neighbors in Santa Monica.

Even though Dunne had attended the wedding of his parents, RFK Jr. became the attack dog against Dunne for the Skakel family.

In 1993, he told *New York Magazine*, "In 1991, Dunne publicly declared the guilt of the Skakel family when he first heard about the crime, without having looked at a single police report.

"The formula that Dominick Dunne has employed to fulfill his dreams has done damage to a lot of people he's left in his wake. Dunne wants to write about two things, both of which are easy to sell: high-profile crimes and famous people. So, he's forced to try to make connections between his high-profile protagonists and the crimes. He's very clever about the way he does it. If you look at how he couches his accusations, it's always 'Somebody told me this.' 'An anonymous source said this.' So, he's not saying it's true, but the average reader misses that nuance.

"For some reason, the voice of this *pathetic creature* has been amplified by the willingness of talk-show hosts to allow him on to spout this stuff, and by his publishers, who publish stuff without fact-checking."

Jeffry Tobin, a former prosecutor turned journalist, was a friend of Dunne's. He defended Dunne to *New York Magazine*, saying, "I think Robert Kennedy Jr. is full of shit. Period. What he said (about Dunne) is a joke."

Replying to RFK Jr. calling him a "pathetic creature," Dunne told Mark Stein in *Macleans*, "I don't give a fuck about what that little shit has to say. That little fucking asshole!"

While Dunne was signing autographs in the Tattered Cover Book Store in Denver on his book tour for *A Season in Purgatory*, a tall, attractive, and well-dressed African-American woman approached him.

"I have some information on the Moxley murder," she told him.

They agreed to meet later at the Brown Place Hotel.

"She said she was a forensic psychologist, and early on she had been hired by the Greenwich police to do work on the case," Dunne said. "For some reason, which she did not explain, she either left or was let go. She had with her the autopsy pictures of Martha Moxley's body, which no one but the police had ever seen."

The woman handed Dunne several 11-by-14 inch photos that absolutely horrified Dunne.

"They were simply awful to behold," Dunne said. "It's one thing to discuss being bludgeoned by a club. It's quite another to see the effects of such an attack. One of the blows had taken off a portion of the right side of Martha's scalp, which was hanging by a piece of skin down over her face. You could see the wound where a short, pointed piece of shaft had been stabbed into the side of her neck. In one full shot, you could see that her jeans had been pulled down. I felt faint. I said to myself, 'He had to have been drunk, or stoned to have done this to her.' I said that I did not want to see anymore."

At her request, Dunne did not write down the woman's name in his notebook. He later claimed that he had completely forgotten her name.

As she was leaving, she told Dunne, "It wasn't Tommy."

And then she repeated herself.

"Up until then, Tommy Skakel had been the major suspect in the case," Dunne said. "I was convinced that he had done it and had said so on television. Her words haunted me."

After his book tour was finished, several members of the Greenwich Police Department visited Dunne at his Connecticut home. Trying to make nice, they presented him with a Connecticut Division of Criminal Justice coffee mug, a Connecticut State Police plaque for the wall in his den, and a Connecticut State Police shirt.

Then, they politely told him, "Please stop criticizing our police work on the case. It's impeding our ongoing investigation."

Dunne agreed to take it easy on the Connecticut State Police.

"In the pleasant conversation that ensued, I told them that I had seen photos of the autopsy," Dunne said. "They looked stunned. I said someone had shown them to me in Denver. I saw them look at each other, very upset."

"She stole those pictures," one detective said.

"I do not know the mystery behind the story, but their certainly is one," Dunne said. "All my attempts to track down my informant have come to naught."

Did Dominick Dunne really try to locate the well-dressed African-American woman who had shown him the Martha Moxley autopsy photos? And even if he did not write down her name at her request, is it possible that he had completely forgotten it?

Or did Dunne make a promise not to reveal the woman's identity; a promise that he kept?

Journalists have gone to jail rather than reveal the sources for their stories.

Dominick Dunne was a top-rate journalist.

Chapter Thirty-Nine

The Greenwich Police Finally Re-Open the Moxley Murder case

On August 8, 1991, Greenwich Police Chief Ken Moughty, who had replaced Chief Keegan, held a news conference at the Greenwich Police Headquarters, announcing the reopening of the Moxley murder case. State Attorney Donald Browne, who had been reluctant to reopen the case in the past, stood at Chief Moughty's side, next to his chief investigator, Jack Solomon, a gumshoe who was steadfast in his beliefs and not one to easily change his mind.

Next to Solomon was the man who Chief Moughty had selected to represent the Greenwich Police Department in the reopening of the case.

His name was Frank Garr.

Frank Garr (his father had changed the family name from Carino) was a medium-tall and stockily-built handsome man, who had moonlighted in the past as a film and television actor. Of course, he mostly played cops. In 1967, at the age of 22, he had been sworn in at the Greenwich Police Department, making him one of the few Italians on a mostly-Irish police force.

When he had had the audacity to grow a moustache, one of his bosses was heard saying, "That's all we need. Another guinea with a moustache."

As a member of the Greenwich police force, Garr moonlighted as a driver for the Greenwich elite. He also provided security at parties and even spent time behind the stick serving as a bartender.

Author's note:

Garr also provided security for football great Frank Gifford, whose daughter, Vicki, had the misfortune of marrying serial philanderer Michael Kennedy, the son of Ethel Skakel Kennedy and Robert Kennedy, and the brother of RFK Jr. Their sixteen-year marriage ended in disgrace after Vicki caught Michael Kennedy in bed with their babysitter, Marissa Verrochi, the daughter of Boston businessman, Paul Verrochi, a major fundraiser for the Democratic Party.

Marissa was 15 years old when the trysts with Michael Kennedy started, and sex with someone under the age of sixteen constitutes statutory rape in the state of Massachusetts. A conviction could have resulted in as much as a life sentence.

However, Marissa, through her attorney, told the state's attorney that she would not participate further in the investigation and would plead the Fifth Amendment if called to testify.

As a result, the charges were dropped.

Frank Garr had the disadvantage of entering a 16-year-old murder case where all of the detectives, who had previously worked on the case, Keegan, Looney, and Carroll, had all retired and could offer him little help, even if they were predisposed to do so. Besides, none of them had put a dent in the case in the past, and a new fresh set of eyes, without any preconceived notions, was exactly what this case needed.

"The only thing I had was the case file, the thousands of pages of Greenwich police reports," Garr told Len Levitt.

"I must have read the complete files twelve times," Garr said. "I became an encyclopedia."

As a result of the announcement of a $50,000 reward for information that led to the arrest and conviction of the killer, from his first day officially on the job, Garr's phone rang off the hook. The strange thing was that although it was generally accepted in Greenwich that either Tommy Skakel or Ken Littleton had been the murderer, the only phone tips Garr received were about Michael Skakel, 15 years old at the time of the crime.

"Not that anyone said Michael did it," Garr said. "The callers said things like, 'I just want you to know that Michael was out of control.'"

One of the tips phoned in concerned Michael Skakel, while he was attending the Elan School after his 1977 car accident in Windham, New York. It came from a man named David Bowlin of Santa Monica, California.

Since he had been convicted of several crimes, including burglary and drug possession, Bowlin was not exactly a model citizen. And one of his illegal escapades had landed him in the Elan School at the same time as Michael Skakel.

Len Levitt stated in his book *Conviction: Solving the Moxley Murder*, "The report from Bowlin, which was taken over the phone by Lieutenant Thomas Perry of the Palm Beach Police Department, said, 'Bowlin told Lieutenant Perry that he had just seen the television program *Hard Copy*, which speculated, falsely, that William Kennedy Smith had been at the Skakel house the night of the Moxley murder.' The program had also mentioned earlier news accounts that Thomas Skakel, a member of the Kennedy family, was a suspect.

"According to Lieutenant Perry, Bowlin related that the mention of this murder made him think that an acquaintance, Michael Skakel, might be involved. As a teenager in 1977, Bowlin had been sent to Elan when Michael was there.

"Bowlin knew Michael was related to the Kennedy family and stated that Michael had told him he had been taken from the ski slopes and delivered to the facility. The relationship to Thomas Skakel, and the proximity in time to the murder, made Bowlin think Michael Skakel may have been involved and that he was sent to the facility to hide him from investigators."

While perusing the file on the Moxley murder, Garr found a torn napkin that said that Michael Skakel's polygraph test had been cancelled. Garr knew that Tommy Skakel had taken such a test, but this was the first indication that Michael had been scheduled to take one, too.

Garr phoned retired Detective Lunney, who had no remembrance of any scheduled Michael Skakel polygraph.

"Maybe it was cancelled because Michael was only fifteen at the time and was too young unless his father gave consent," Lunney speculated.

"I'm thinking to myself maybe it was scheduled, but the old man put the kibosh on it," Garr said. "I'm asking myself why would he do that if he hadn't objected to Tommy."

In late 1991, Garr drove over to Belle Haven to interview Cissy Ix, who, from the night of the murder, seemed to be protecting the Skakel family, or at least pooh-poohing any possibility that someone in the Skakel family had been involved in the Moxley murder.

Garr was pleasantly surprised when Cissy, 16 years after the fact, opened up a bit about the night of the murder.

"While still protective of Tommy, as she had been with Dorthy (Moxley) years before, Cissy had no qualms saying she always felt that Michael and Jimmy Terrien should be looked at," Garr said. "With all his problems, Michael had always been a suspect in her mind, and she even told this to Chief Keegan. Keegan, however, had been dismissive. He had never questioned Michael's story of having gone to the Terrien's home. And if the murder had occurred at 10 pm, Michael couldn't have returned in time.

"Cissy added that two or three weeks after the murder she had gone to Tommy's room and asked him what had happened that night. 'Why don't you go and ask Jimmy Terrien?' Tommy had told her."

Garr also interviewed Greenwich resident Andy Pugh, who was a close friend of Michael's at the Brunswick School.

Pugh, who also had alcohol problems, had attended several AA meetings in Greenwich in the mid-1980s, when Michael was in attendance.

According to Len Levitt, Pugh told Garr, "When Michael had gone to Elan, the speculation was that the murderer was either

Tommy or Littleton. But the more I thought about it over the years, the more it pointed to Michael. The killer was not a stranger. It was someone within the household. I found myself thinking, 'Is it possible it was him?'

"Pound for pound, Michael was the strongest kid I ever met. And he liked her. She liked him, but he liked her more."

Pugh also told Garr he had seen Martha and Michael play-wrestling, and that Michael could be "very aggressive and violent when drinking."

Yet, it was Skakel family friend, Andrea Shakespeare, who threw Frank Garr for the biggest loop and got him to change his way of thinking.

When Garr interviewed Andrea, she was living in Massachusetts, married and the mother of three children. Garr brought Connecticut state investigator, Jack Solomon, along for the ride. Solomon had insisted for years, that because of Littleton's perceived failed polygraph, he was Martha's killer, and so far, nothing could change Solomon's mind.

Andrea told the two detectives that on the night of the murder she had been inside the Skakel residence drinking tea with Julie Skakel. At around 9:30 pm, she heard two female voices outside that she recognized as those of Martha's and Helen Ix's. But she never actually saw either girl.

Andrea then dropped a bombshell when she told Garr that, to the best of her recollection, when the Skakel car pulled away from the house with Tommy Skakel driving and Jimmy Terrien riding shotgun, Michael was not in the back seat of the car.

She told Garr, "I was always under the impression Michael was in the house when the car left. I don't know why that is my recollection. All I can say is that he didn't go."

"That was the first time anyone connected to the investigation had said that Michael didn't go to the Terrien's home," Garr said.

If Michael Skakel was still at the Skakel residence, then he, not Tommy Skakel, and not Ken Littleton could have murdered

Martha Moxley. There was no definitive proof, but for the first time, an investigator in the Moxley murder case considered the possibility that Michael Skakel could have killed Martha Moxley.

Still shoveling through the old files of the case, Garr came up with a memo from Detective Rich Haug, dated September 10, 1980. It seemed that Dorothy Rogers, an incorrigible teenager, who had been at Elan from June 1978 to June 1979, had been brought in for questioning about a fire that had been set in her parent's house. When repeated offenders are being questioned in a police station with the possibility of being arrested, it's common for them to try to give up information on other persons in order to cut a sweet deal for themselves. So, what Dorothy Rogers, then 19, had told Haug had to be taken with a grain of salt.

Still, she claimed when she and Michael were at Elan, they had become pals and had spoken often. One night, he confessed to her that he was drunk and might have killed Martha Moxley.

Still, this was an old memo from a girl whose credibility was doubtful at best. But Frank Garr was a bulldog, and he had a bone in his mouth he didn't want to let go.

Using standard police procedure, Garr dug up Dorothy's date of birth. He searched for her driver's license, social security number, and any possible work history, but he came up empty. He then got a tip that she might be in Anaheim, California, but according to the Anaheim Police Department's vice squad, she was little more than a derelict and an alcoholic. Garr contacted her parole officer and found out she was presently living in Graham, North Carolina, population about 15,000, 25 miles east of Greensboro and 550 miles southeast of Greenwich.

Garr jumped on a plane, and using the information provided by Dorothy Rogers's parole officer, he was able to locate her.

"She looked like a drunk," Garr said. "She had a lot of hard miles on her. Her teeth were bad. She looked drawn. Here she was just a back-country Greenwich girl who anyone could see had once been attractive, and now she looked like trailer trash."

Dorothy explained to Garr how she had nosedived from the tony town of Greenwich to the boot camp called the Elan

School. She said that she had stolen her parent's car and had gotten off with a warning. When she did it a second time, her parents shipped her off to Elan.

"Michael, she remembered was already there when she arrived," Garr said. "At a dance, she asked him about the Moxley murder. He told her the police believed either he or his brother Tommy was responsible.

"So, she's telling me this, and I'm thinking there is no way Michael was a suspect then. For Michael to claim the police thought he might be responsible for this murder, or that the police might arrest him and charge him with the murder was, in my eyes, an example of what we call 'consciousness of guilt.'"

Dorothy also told Garr that Michael told her that on the night of the murder he had gotten zonked. He said that he had blacked out, and although things were fuzzy in his head, he might have killed Martha Moxley. He said that his attorney had recommended that he take refuge in Elan so that he could avoid being charged with murder.

Garr knew that even though Dorothy wasn't in the best of shape physically, her testimony could be useful in the future if he was able to build a case against Michael Skakel. He told her to stay available, just in case he needed her.

For the next few years, Dorothy was in and out of prison, mostly for violations related to her alcoholism. Still, she kept her word and stood in touch.

"Sometimes she would call me from various prisons," Garr said. "She'd say, 'Frank, I just want you to know where I am.'"

In Garr's mind, what finally crystalized the murder case against Michael Skakel, was a meeting with Larry Zicarelli, who, six months after the Moxley murder had replaced Fred Wittine as the Skakel's chauffeur and all around handyman.

According to Len Levitt, a friend of Zicarelli's had phoned the Greenwich police station, and set up a meeting between Garr and Zicarelli to discuss the strange happenings in the Skakel household after the Moxley murder. At this meeting, Zicarelli told Garr that every Friday he drove Michael to New York City for a 4 pm psychiatrist appointment.

"One Friday morning Michael came downstairs shouting at his father," Zicarelli told Garr. "He raced outside screaming, 'You're not my father!' Then he jumped into a car in the driveway and tried to drive it through a fence. I ran outside to the car, and Michael pulled out a switchblade and pointed it at me. 'Start driving the car or I'll stab you the death!' he screamed. I turned to Rushton, who nodded his approval, thinking it might calm Michael down.

"I talked Michael into putting away the knife, then I drove him to the city. But on Park Avenue, he jumped out, and without a word, ran off. I didn't know what to do, so I drove to Rushton's office at Great Lakes Coal and Coke nearby. There, they told me that Michael's appointment had been changed from 4 pm to 2 pm. And that's where Michael had probably gone.

"I drove over to the psychiatrist's office and waited for Michael to appear. Sure enough, an hour before his appointment, he showed up, and I asked him why he had run off. He told me, 'You're the only one I can trust.' I bought him lunch and then waited for him to finish his appointment. When he came out, he was in tears.

"He got into the car, and we headed back to Greenwich. But while I was driving over the Triborough Bridge, Michael jumped from the car. 'I've done something very bad. I'm in a lot of trouble. I've either got to kill myself or leave the country,' he shouted as he crossed traffic lanes and began climbing up one of the bridge's spans.

"I stopped the car, chased him, and pulled him down. Then, I drove back to Greenwich."

Zicarelli handed in his resignation the following day.

Zicarelli also told Garr that Detectives Lunney and Carroll had pulled him aside one day, while he was still working for the Skakels, and asked him to "keep an eye out and call them about anything suspicious."

But even though he had secretly met with the two detectives over the years, he never mentioned the bridge incident.

Zicarelli told Garr that in early 1992, he had related the incident on the bridge to his friend, Edward Jones. Jones, who had seen newspaper articles in the Greenwich newspapers about the Moxley murder investigation being reopened, called the Greenwich police.

Garr asked Zicarelli why it took 16 years for him to tell his story about the bridge incident.

"I was afraid," Zicarelli said. "I was so afraid of those people. My wife told me, 'Don't ever say anything to anyone. Don't cause any trouble. Besides, there was nothing going on in the investigation all those years."

"There is now," Garr said.

Still, with all the evidence accumulated by Frank Garr against Michael Skakel, by mid-1992, Donald Browne, the state's district attorney, still refused to file charges against him. The reason was that Jack Solomon, who had been a detective under Browne for 25 years, despite all the evidence to the contrary, still insisted Ken Littleton was their man. And Browne believed him. The reason Solomon gave Browne why he was certain Littleton was Martha Moxley's killer was because he had failed two polygraphs 16 years earlier.

What both lawmen should have known was that polygraphs are inadmissible in court because they are not infallible.

Remarkably not infallible.

Finally, on December 14, 1992, after weeks of trickery and deception, Solomon finally conned Littleton, who was living in Ottawa, Canada, and weak of mind, to come to Greenwich to take a third polygraph. Of course, with his brain total mush, Littleton failed again. But, because of Littleton's mental condition, Solomon could wipe his butt with the polygraph, but he could not use it alone as a cause for an indictment.

So, Solomon decided to take another shot at Littleton, this time with more force and much more bravado.

Just before Littleton was to leave the Greenwich police station and head for the airport to take a flight back to Ottawa, Canada, Solomon invited Littleton into the police library for a little chat. Frank Garr was the third party in the room.

The average person walking the streets is unaware of this, but when interrogating suspects, law enforcement agents are allowed to lie or tell half-truths. It happens every day in police stations all throughout America. A frequent ploy is to separate two suspects to a crime, and then tell one, or the other, or both, that their pal in the next room is spilling his guts in order to pin the crime on his supposed friend. Or, they might tell a suspect they already have evidence linking them to the crime, so they might as well come clean and cut a better deal for themselves.

But this time, Solomon went overboard. He preyed on a sick man, who was borderline suicidal and nowhere near being in control of his emotions.

While Littleton was seated, Solomon hovered over him like a bald eagle ready to eat a scared rabbit.

"Ken, before you go, remember if you did it, I am not saying you did, but the polygraph says you are lying, and I never had a bad call on a polygraph," Solomon said. "Ken, Ken, you did it, I know you did it! Give it up. You've been living with this for seventeen years. It's time to be a man, Ken. Do the right thing!"

But instead of cracking, a proverbial light bulb flashed over Littleton's head. He stood to his full six foot three inches, and now he hovered over Solomon, who was maybe five-nine, fat, bald, and sweating like a pig.

The worm was about to turn.

"So this is what it's all about!" Littleton shouted. "This is why you brought me here! It was the same in 1976! To accuse me! To try to make me say I did something I didn't do! But fuck you! I'm getting the fuck out of here, and you can all go fuck yourselves! From now on, you want to talk to me, contact my attorney!"

That said, Ken Littleton stormed out of the police station, and in a few hours, he was safely back in Ottawa, Canada.

"That was the end of the line for him (Jack Solomon) and Ken Littleton," Frank Garr said. "It was also the end of the line for Jack in the Moxley investigation. When Littleton didn't crack, Jack lost all interest, even though his beloved polygraph suggested he (Littleton) did commit the crime. A few days later, Jack began taking his equipment back to the state's attorney's office in Bridgeport. His heart was out of it."

More importantly, Frank Garr could now continue with the Moxley murder investigation without the state attorney's main sleuth, a man who had a preconceived and unshakable notion that Ken Littleton was the killer, impeding the investigation of anyone who wasn't Ken Littleton.

Chapter Forty

The Sutton Report

In late 1992, Len Levitt received a surprise visit from two men at his desk at *New York Newsday*. One was Jim Murphy, a retired FBI agent who ran his own private security firm – Sutton Associates. The other man was Rushton Skakel's attorney and confidant, Tom Sheridan. The two men bestowed Levitt with bombshell information that would change the course of the entire Moxley murder investigation.

Levitt said in his book *Conviction: Solving the Moxley Murder*, "Both men said they sought me out because the Skakels felt my article in the *Greenwich Time and Stamford Advocate* the year before had been fair. They said they had been upset by statements from the Greenwich police and state's attorney Donald Browne that they had refused to cooperate with the investigation. My article had made it clear that Rushton had cooperated – at least during the first few months of the investigation."

Murphy and Sheridan told Levitt that they needed his help in getting the Greenwich police file on the Moxley murder case. Even though the Freedom of Information Act made the files public documents, the Greenwich police had still stubbornly refused to turn over the documents to them. The reason the two men said they needed the documents was because Sheridan, doing the bidding of Rushton Skakel Sr., had hired Murphy with the intention of doing a complete investigation of the Moxley murder case in order to clear Rushton Skakel Sr.'s sons' names.

"You can have mine," Levitt said. "Make a duplicate and return it to me."

Murphy then told Levitt that Jack Solomon was sure that Ken Littleton was the murderer, and that if they could prove that, it would clear both Tommy and Michael Skakel.

"Let me ask you something," Levitt said to Murphy. "What if, after your investigation, you conclude Littleton was not the killer?"

"Before I agreed to this case," Murphy said, "Rushton Skakel assured me that I could pursue any investigation where ever it led."

"What if your investigation brings you back to the Skakels?" Levitt said.

"I was assured that if any Skakel committed the murder – and Rushton Skakel never for a moment believed any of his children did it – the family would publically acknowledge the crime and seek to provide him with medical help," Murphy told Levitt.

Murphy also said, "I feel Rushton Skakel is an honorable man. I feel he's acting for the right reasons. I feel that he is convinced that none of his children had anything to do with the murder, and he needs someone to demonstrate this to the public."

For the next three years, Murphy continued his investigation, aided by former New York City police lieutenant Willie Krebs. But try as they may, they couldn't put a case together against Ken Littleton that would clear Tommy and Michael Skakel. They even floated the zany notion that Littleton was a mass murderer, having killed at least five other girls. The flimsy basis for this theory was that the unsolved murders of these five girls had occurred in Maine, Massachusetts, and Florida at the same time Littleton had resided in those states.

But when Murphy presented his hypothesis to members of Connecticut law enforcement, they demanded facts not theories, and Murphy could not provide them with any.

In 1994, Levitt received a phone call from an unidentified male (Levitt promised he would keep the caller's name secret). The caller said he had information about Murphy's investigation.

"The caller told me that if I would be patient, it would be worth my while," Levitt said.

In early 1995, the unidentified male phoned Levitt again.

"He began by saying that Murphy had sought an analysis by two former FBI colleagues who had run the Bureau's Behavioral Science lab in Washington," Levitt said. "The two, Kenneth Baker and Roger DePew, had studied hundreds of serial killers including the sociopath in the film *Silence of the Lambs*. Now retired from the FBI, they had formed their own consulting company known as the Academy Group of Manassas, Virginia.

"The Academy Group, the caller said, had noted Martha's lack of defense wounds on her arms and hands, and the fact that no screams were heard. This indicated, he said, that Martha did not expect the attack and knew her attacker."

In Levitt's mind, that totally cleared Ken Littleton as the murderer.

Levitt deduced, "Martha didn't know Littleton. Littleton had moved into the Skakel house on the night of the murder. He had never spoken to her, or even seen her before that night."

The caller also told Levitt that Krebs had interviewed Tommy Skakel in the offices of Tommy's attorney, Emanuel Margolis. But before he began his questioning, Krebs had told Tommy that Henry Lee, the state's expert on DNA testing, was doing tests to determine if the killer had left DNA traces at the scene of the crime.

According to Randy James's article, "A Brief History of DNA Testing" in *Time Magazine*:

Since the advent of DNA testing in 1985, biological material (skin, hair, blood and other bodily fluids) has emerged as the most reliable physical evidence at a crime scene, particularly those involving sexual assaults. DNA, or deoxyribonucleic acid, contains the complex genetic blueprint that distinguishes each person. Forensic testing can determine if distinctive patterns in the genetic material found at a crime scene matches the DNA in a potential perpetrator with better than 99% accuracy.

When Martha Moxley was murdered in 1975, DNA testing was not available as a forensic tool. So, when Tommy Skakel absorbed the implications of Krebs's remarks, he changed his story about his actions on the night Martha was murdered.

In 1975, when Tommy was questioned by the Greenwich police, he said he had last seen Martha at about 9:30 pm on the night of her murder. But now he told Krebs that he had returned outside a few minutes later and had spent about 20 minutes cuddling and fondling with Martha. He now said that the last he saw of Martha was not at 9:30 pm, but at 10 pm – the Greenwich police's version of the approximate time of her death, due to the barking dogs (remember, the local coroner said the time of death could have been anytime from 9:30 pm to 5:30 am).

But before Tommy, who was crying and shaking as he spoke to Krebs, could say anything implicating himself in Martha's murder, his attorney, Margolis, ended the interview.

The caller also told Levitt that on August 4, 1992, Krebs had interviewed Michael Skakel at Sheridan's home in Windham, Connecticut. Before the interview began, Krebs told Michael what he had told Tommy about a DNA investigation being underway.

Michael then told Krebs a story straight out of the *Twilight Zone*.

In 1975, when Michael was interviewed by Greenwich police the day after the murder, he said he had went to the Terrien's house at 9:30 pm and had arrived back home at 11 pm. He said he then went straight to bed. But now, almost 20 years later, he told Krebs that he had not gone straight to bed, but he had slinked over to Martha's house, where he climbed a tree directly opposite her second-story bedroom window.

After calling, "Martha, Martha," and getting no response, he masturbated in the tree until he reached a climax.

The caller told Levitt, "When he climbed down, he stopped under a streetlight. He said he could feel someone's presence in the very place her body would be discovered the next day.

He yelled into the darkness, threw something, and then he ran back to his house. Everyone was asleep and all doors were locked. But (instead of knocking) he climbed in through a window and went to bed."

Was Michael Skakel so sure he had left DNA evidence at the scene of the crime that he decided to concoct a screwy story that would explain his DNA near where Martha's body had been found?

Or was he really nutty enough to masturbate while sitting on the branch of a tree outside Martha Moxley's window? (It was discovered later that the tree Michael had described was not opposite Martha's window, but, instead, outside her brother, John's window.)

To write his newspaper article, Levitt needed corroboration of what the caller had said concerning the two Skakels changing their stories about the sequence of events on the night of the murder.

Levitt contacted Murphy, who for reasons Levitt discovered later, would not talk to him. So, he then phoned Sheridan, who had been advising the Skakels since the day Martha's body had been found.

Sheridan invited Levitt to lunch at the New York Athletic Club opposite the south side of Central Park. During lunch, Sheridan dismissed Michael's changed story as being irrelevant, since it occurred after 11 pm, and the time of death, according to the bumbling Greenwich police, was 10 pm.

Then, to Levitt's surprise, the cocky attorney let something slip out of his mouth that, for his client, Tommy Skakel, would have been better left unsaid.

In response to Levitt's question, "Why would he (Tommy) place himself with Martha at precisely the time she was murdered?" Sheridan said, "Oh, so you know about the mutual masturbation?"

"'The WHAT?' I wanted to shout," Levitt said. "'The WHAT?' Poor Sheridan. He had just blurted out something I hadn't known. The caller had merely said Tommy and Martha had spent another twenty minutes together. Did Sheridan mean that during that twenty minutes they had engaged in mutual masturbation?"

Levitt decided to play dumb and give Sheridan the impression he had already known about Tommy and Martha's mutual sexual gratification.

"Okay, let's say Tommy is telling the truth – that Martha was alive when he left her." Levitt said. "Why didn't he tell this to the police?"

"He was afraid of his father," Sheridan said. "Old man Skakel was a nut about sex. He had trashed Michael just for reading *Playboy Magazine*. He would have come down on his children very hard if they had anything to do with sex. And that's also why Michael didn't tell the police about what he had done in the tree."

Rushton Skakel was a lunatic in his own right and an alcoholic to boot. But was fear of their father's punishment the reason both Michael and Tommy Skakel neglected to tell the police for almost 20 years that they had both been engaged in masturbation on the night of the murder: Tommy with Martha and Michael with himself?

Or were they both trying to lay the groundwork if the police confronted them with their DNA at the scene of the crime?

Chapter Forty-One

The Academy Report

In July of 1995, the mysterious caller made a personal appearance at Len Levitt's home. And to back up his new information on the Moxley murder, he bore gifts.

As Levitt reported in *Conviction: Solving the Moxley Murder*, the first was a copy of the Academy Report prepared on October 8, 1993 by Kenneth Baker and Roger DePew of the Academy Group of Manassas, Virginia. This report was based on information provided by investigators Jim Murphy and Willis Krebs. It included examinations of the area where the crime had occurred and interviews with friends of Martha, as well as with Tommy Skakel and his younger brother, Michael.

The report began by describing Martha as "an All-American girl and a flirt who loved the attention of boys and was pretty, popular, confident, and self-assured. The report said she occasionally drank beer, and smoked cigarettes and sometimes marijuana. The autopsy revealed no signs of drugs or alcohol in her system. It also described her as "moralistic and not promiscuous."

The report also noted that, "She was not known to have had sexual relations and that it should be noted that friends felt she was very strong-willed and would have vigorously resisted a physical attack or any attempted to take sexual advantage of her."

After saying that the killer "had acted out of personal rage perhaps because Martha had rejected him sexually," the Academy Report said, "The fact that the offender chose to confront the victim outside, on her driveway, provides several useful clues in understanding his approach, method, and mindset. It's apparent that he knew the victim, knew she would be coming home at around the time frame, and knew she habitually walked up her driveway then across her lawn towards her front door."

The report also quoted witnesses as saying Martha "flirted and participated in teenage physical horseplay" with Thomas outside the Skakel's kitchen door at about 9:30 pm the night of her death. The horseplay was so embarrassing to Martha's friend Helen Ix that the teenager went home, leaving Martha and Thomas alone.

The Academy Group speculated that Martha, whose curfew was between 9:30 pm and 10 pm, walked home at about 9:50 pm and was attacked. The attack began with the offender punching Martha once or twice in the face as she approached the gravel driveway.

After noting the lack of defensive wounds, the report stated that, "Martha, after being punched in the face, most likely rendering her unconscious, was struck in the head with a golf club about 15 times which was obviously 'overkill' because any one of several of the blows would have resulted in death.

"The initial blows to the head were struck with the entire club and were done with 'powerful swings.' These repeated blows to the victim's head provided a 'clear indication of personalized rage, indicating an acquaintance with the victim.'"

The report also said the attack "had taken place at three separate sites; the first was on the gravel driveway leading to Martha's home. The second site, where the most damaging blows were landed, was on her front lawn. The third site was where her body was found under the tree."

The report also speculated that "the killer, after moving the body to under a tree, left for a while, then returned to the body to verify she was dead."

As for the golf club's shaft and handle being removed from the scene of the crime, the report concluded, "He either had a strong proprietary reason for wanting to retain the weapon, or intended to dispose of it in such a way as to prevent it from ever being recovered."

In attempting to profile the murderer, the Academy Report concluded, "The murderer has an explosive temper, a history of fighting, strong sibling rivalry tendencies, behavioral problems at school and at home, under the influence of alcohol or drugs."

The description of the murderer screamed TOMMY SKAKEL! But it also applied in every respect to his younger brother, Michael.

"The caller said I could keep the Academy Group's report for the weekend to study, but that I would have to return it," Levitt said. "That meant he knew I would make a copy. He was, in effect, giving me permission to do so."

The mystery man was not finished supplying Levitt with "goodies."

He then handed him Murphy's sacred Sutton Associates Report, which consisted of two separate documents; one was headed "Thomas Skakel" and the other, "Michael Skakel." Rushton Skakel reportedly paid $750,000 for this report, which took almost three years to compile.

The caller told Levitt he could take notes, but that he could not keep the reports.

The Sutton Report on Tommy Skakel began as such:

No one contests that Tommy Skakel is the last person known to have seen Martha Moxley alive. Partly as a result of this ominous distinction, the second son of Rushton Skakel remains, to this day, a leading suspect, if not the leading suspect, in the investigation of her murder. Those who have labored to establish his innocence have faced as much difficulty as those who have struggled to prove his guilt. As such, Tommy has remained, for better or worse, in a culpable limbo for nearly twenty years.

In addition to collecting and analyzing the findings of other professionals, Sutton Associates has conducted its own extensive investigation into the murder. Tommy Skakel has been among the numerous witnesses and suspects interviewed for this investigation. Sticking largely to the same story he has, to the best of our knowledge, been telling from the outset, Tommy maintains his innocence and professes to have no first-hand knowledge of how Martha Moxley was murdered. The few changes he has made to his story, however, are extremely revelatory. These changes were solicited solely during interviews with Sutton Associates. In conjunction with other circumstantial evidence, they have contributed substantial credence to the possibility of Tommy's guilt and, at the very least, suggest he has willfully deceived authorities, with considerable success, for many years. We will illustrate and explore the significance of these discrepancies.

The Academy Group's profile of the probable offender shares many obvious characteristics with Tommy Skakel (as well as with other leading suspects). Most notably, the Academy Group believes the offender was between 14 and 18 years of age, resided within easy walking distance of the victim's residence, was in the same socioeconomic status as the victim, had regular interaction with the victim, would have exhibited strong sibling rivalry tendencies, would have experienced behavioral problems both at school and at home, and was under the influence of drugs and/or alcohol at the time of this crime.

The report went on to say that Tommy was inconsistent as to when he had last seen Martha Moxley. On the day after the murder, he told the Greenwich police that he had been with Martha until 9:30 pm. But when interviewed by the Sutton Associates, he said, after leaving Martha at 9:30 pm, he had gone back outside with her and stayed until 10 pm.

The report said that when Dorthy Moxley called the Skakel residence at 1:15 am, Julie Skakel went to Tommy's room and asked him when was the last time he had seen Martha. He said he saw her last at 9:30 pm by the back door of his house.

The Sutton Report stated that if Tommy didn't know Martha was dead, why would he not tell his sister Julie the truth about seeing Martha until 10 pm? Or did he know Martha was dead, but that she was not killed at 10 pm?

The report said, "If Tommy knew Martha was dead at 1:15 am, it could mean only one thing. He was involved in her murder."

Len Levitt then started reading book two of the Sutton Report entitled "Michael Skakel."

The Skakel portion of the Sutton Report said, in part:

At the beginning of the official police investigation into the murder of Martha Moxley, Michael Skakel was not a strong suspect. According to some sources, he was ruled out almost immediately due to what was then perceived as an air-tight alibi, substantiated under polygraph by a number of eye-witnesses. Some feel Michael and other suspects were not thoroughly examined at the time, due to a somewhat premature conviction, on the part of local authorities, that Tommy Skakel was the murderer. It was only later when the spotlight of serious scrutiny was placed directly on Michael. His arrest on drunk driving charges in 1978 probably did as much as anything to renew the police's interest.

This got Levitt to thinking.

"So how had Murphy's group come up with the information that Michael's 1978 arrest had 'renewed' the police interest in him?" Levitt said. "Sheridan had represented Michael in his drunken driving arrest. He had also hired Murphy and Krebs. Who else but Sheridan would have suggested that Michael had been a suspect? I was beginning to realize that Sheridan knew more about the Moxley murder than anyone realized.

"My suspicions were confirmed a few pages later. Murphy's Sutton Associates report cited a memo, written on June 6, 1978, after Michael had been sent to Elan, following the drunken driving incident. It said, 'A Tom Sheridan memo of 6/6/78 stated that it was possible Michael Skakel could have committed the murder and doesn't know it, and possibly someone else, i.e. Tommy, could have hidden the body to provide him with an alibi.'"

The Sutton Report continued:

Michael, at the time, was plagued with serious emotional problems, living, by many accounts, a reckless and drug-fueled existence. What gradually emerged, from that point forward, was a portrait of a deeply, and somewhat enigmatically, troubled young man. In this light, and during the course of the Sutton Associates' investigation, serious questions and unresolved issues have been raised about Michael and the murder of Martha Moxley. At the very least, it is fair to say Michael Skakel has, for whatever reason, often acted out in ways certain to arouse suspicion. Reportedly, Michael once even confessed to the murder of Martha Moxley in a therapy session while a patient at the Elan treatment center. He quickly recanted.

Coupled with our extensive knowledge of just how vehemently Michael and Tommy fought with each other, we at least believe Michael had more than ample reason to be extremely upset when Tommy was carrying on with Martha by the side of the house at 9:30 pm.

She turned down an offer to hang out with Michael that night, in order to be with his older brother. It is hard to imagine how such a spectacle would not have made him both increasingly depressed and overly hostile.

The Sutton Report also questioned whether Michael had gone to the Terrien's house at 9:30 pm, which had been his alibi since the day after the murder.

The report stated:

From the time line: 9:15 pm - According to Tommy Skakel, from his interview on 10/7/93, with Willie Krebs, at approximately this time he left the sun porch area and went outside to the side of the house to retrieve a cassette tape from his parent's car. Inside the car, Tommy encountered Martha, his brother Michael, Helen Ix, and Jeffrey Byrne, who were all listening to music. Soon after, he and Martha would move to the area around the shed, off the driveway, and began "making out."

Martha's friends reportedly left shortly after this point because they found Martha's behavior to be embarrassing. Clearly, her activity with Tommy was purposely demonstrative. It seemed likely, as well, that Martha's young friends were disturbed by the inherent awkwardness of watching Martha blatantly and immodestly courting the affection of her ex-boyfriend's (Michael Skakel's) older brother in her ex-boyfriend's presence. We know practically nothing of how Michael reacted to all this, and it is a glaring admission. For certainly he had a reaction, and it may have been extreme.

All this speculation counts for much less if Michael went to the Terrien's and stayed there. There is curious evidence suggesting that this is not exactly what happened.

In an interview under hypnosis, John Skakel was asked where Michael was, while he and Rushton Jr. were at the Terrien's. The interviewer, on repeated occasions, tried to get John to place Michael in the car and then at the Terrien's. John could not. He could only recall that someone else was in the car and that someone else was at the house, but as much as the interviewer persisted, John could not identify that person as Michael.

If Michael did not go to the Terrien's, could he have witnessed Tommy and Martha's sexual encounter? Certainly.

Giving what we know about the highly combative rivalry between these two brothers, and Michael's well-documented psychological problems, there can be no doubt he was extremely upset about what was transpiring. It is not at all unreasonable to assume that he may have wanted to spy on his brother and Martha, to monitor, first hand, any betrayal.

If we accept what Tommy has told us about his sexual encounter with Martha, they were carrying on flagrantly, only 50 feet behind the Skakel residence, in the middle of the rear lawn. Their indiscretion was highly visible, should anyone have been remotely suspicious. Did Michael have reason to be suspicious? Ample reason.

Was Michael someone capable of losing control and acting out in a violent rage of jealousy? We now know the magnitude of certain psychological and emotional problems from which Michael has suffered, and may still suffer, is significant. We know from subsequent incidents that Michael, especially while under the influence of drugs and alcohol, will go to reckless and self-destructive lengths.

Along the lines of speculation, scenarios in which Michael and Tommy could have conspired together have been considered by a number of experts in the case. Given all the information we have at this point, such a scenario seems unlikely, but further investigation and access to pertinent material is recommended.

Needless to say, Michael's cooperation and the continued cooperation of the Skakel family will be required to move forward on this matter.

So, there it was in black and white. The Sutton Report, for which Rushton Skakel had paid hundreds of thousands of dollar to clear Michael's and Tommy's names, had done exactly the opposite. It named them both as suspects; either acting alone, or in concert with each other.

After reading the Sutton Report, Len Levitt said, "When we had first met in 1992, I had asked Murphy what would happen if the investigation led back to the Skakels. Murphy said Rushton has assured him that he would 'back the search for the truth wherever it led and share the information with the Connecticut authorities.'

"Now, as the caller picked up his briefcase, I asked him what Rushton's reaction had been when Murphy presented him with these findings. Recalling Rushton's promise to Murphy, I asked what the Skakel family was now prepared to do. The caller stopped what he was doing and stared at me.

For a moment our eyes met.

'You don't know?' he said. 'After Murphy showed his report to Sheridan, Sheridan fired him.'"

Chapter Forty-Two

New York Newsday *Runs Len Levitt's Updated Article on the Moxley Murder*

Len Levitt, after reading the Sutton Report, knew he had a hell of a story to tell. But could he find a newspaper or even a magazine to publish it?

In July of 1995, the hammer came down, and *New York Newsday* was reduced to a fraction of what it was before.

"*Newsday's* plan was to maintain a scaled-back version of the New York paper by reducing its circulation to 50,000, with the Long Island editors taking full control," Levitt said. "But when I presented my Moxley story to them they showed no interest. For the second time I was sitting atop a story that would break open the Moxley case, with nowhere to publish it."

So, Levitt went back to the same place that had given him the assignment 14 years earlier: *The Stamford Advance and Greenwich Time*.

Ken Bright was still the editor, and at first he seemed interested. Steve Isenberg, the publisher who had flippantly put the kibosh on the story years earlier, had ostensibly, no influence with Bright at the *Stamford Advance and Greenwich Time*. But for some reason, even though Bright seemed enthused at first, he held on to the story for three months without a word of it seeing the light of day. Levitt had no choice but to withdraw the article from the *Stamford Advance and Greenwich Time* and to look for another home for it. Levitt offered to write it on spec for the magazine *The New Yorker*, but was given a thumbs down by the editor.

Did the Kennedy/Skakel cabal have enough clout to kill the story?

Or did the *Stamford Advance and Greenwich Time* and *The New Yorker* just think it was old news and not worthy of the time, black ink, and publication space?

In a last ditch effort to place the story where at least it could be read by a reduced audience, and with the hope of a larger publication picking up on it, Levitt contacted Don Forst, the editor of the diminished *New York Newsday*.

After explaining his problems with Ken Bright, Levitt was pleasantly surprised when Forst said, "Okay, here's what we can do. We'll run it as a local story in what's left of *New York Newsday*."

Forst ran the first part of the four-part story on Sunday, November 26, 1995.

The headline read:

Suspicions of Murder Won't Die

Levitt's article said, in part:

Thomas Skakel, Ethel Kennedy's nephew, was the last person to see Martha Moxley alive and became the prime suspect after police found a golf club in the Skakel house they believed was the murder weapon.

Now, Thomas has admitted to police investigators that he lied to Greenwich police in 1995 about his whereabouts on the night of the murder.

Then, he told police he last saw Martha outside his house at 9:30 pm, and then went inside to write a school report. Witnesses told police the two had been seen "making out," which witnesses described as including pushing each other playfully and flirtatiously.

In 1993, married and the father of two, Thomas told the private investigators that shortly after 9:30 pm, he returned outside to meet Martha, who he says waited for him. They remained together, he says, for an additional 20 minutes in a sexual encounter.

Sure enough, Levitt's article caught the eye of one of the biggest wire services in the world. In just hours, the *Associated Press* scooped up the story, and they ran with it on their national wire. Thousands of newspapers across the country printed the *AP's* heading of Levitt's story, which opened eyes and ruffled feathers all across the continent.

Then, as if by magic, the sea of resistance departed at the *Stamford Advance and*

Greenwich Time.

Joe Pisani, an editor working under Ken Bright, picked up his phone and dialed Levitt's number. He told Levitt that Ken had undergone a change of heart, and since *AP* had already ruptured the dam of opposition, Ken was ready to publish Levitt's article in the *Stamford Advance and Greenwich Time* - a story that he had first commissioned in 1982.

Levitt did a slight rewrite, eliminating backdrop information not essential to the main details of the story and concentrating on Michael Skakel, instead of his brother, Tommy.

The article ran in the *Stamford Advance and Greenwich Time* on Sunday, December 4, 1995, exactly a week after the Skakel bombshell had been dropped, first by *Newsday* and then by the *Associated Press*.

The headline read:

Brothers' Tales/Second Kennedy Kin Admits Lying in Murder Case

The article read, in part:

A second relative of Ethel Kennedy now admits he lied to Greenwich police about his whereabouts the night a teenage neighbor was murdered as she left his Greenwich, Connecticut home.

In 1975, a few days after the murder of Martha Moxley on Halloween Eve, Michael Skakel, then 15, told Greenwich police he had left the victim with his older brother, Thomas, in the Skakel driveway at about 9:19 pm.

Michael said he then drove with two of his older brothers and his cousin, James Terrien, to Terrien's house a few miles away. Michael told police he returned home about 11 pm. and went to sleep.

Now, Michael has admitted to private investigators that he went to the Moxley house around 11:30 pm, and apparently believing Martha was alive, threw stones at a window to awaken her, sources said. He then passed what was later found to be the murder site, where he said he heard noises but saw nothing.

Greenwich police believe Martha was murdered at approximately 9:50 to 10 pm, based on the fact that two neighborhood dogs began barking uncontrollably at that time. If Martha's death occurred then, Michael's admission that he lied would have no significance.

But what if Martha's murder had occurred, like the original coroner's report had said, at anywhere from 9:30 pm to 5 am, a report the Greenwich police was persistent in ignoring? Then, as far as suspects were concerned, it would be "all hands on deck," and two of those hands would certainly belong to Michael Skakel.

Ken Bright's editorial team did have a measure of satisfaction when they eliminated the part of Levitt's article that mentioned that Michael had masturbated in the tree outside the Moxley residence, saying it was not essential to the story.

"I disagreed, to say the least," Levitt said. "But at that point I had to live with it."

At least Levitt could take satisfaction that through his efforts alone, combined with an anonymous source and a little help from certain friends, Martha Moxley's murder was on the lips of every Greenwich resident, and in the minds of two very rich, famous, and influential American families.

In addition, now the state's district attorney's office could not definitively point thumbs down when asked about the possibility of a re-opening the Moxley murder case. Sunlight is the best disinfectant. And the spotlight put on the Moxley murder case caused by Len Levitt's newspaper articles, forced the soldier ants of Connecticut law enforcement to mobilize, and the cockroaches who were involved in Martha Moxley's murder to scatter into the woodwork.

Len Levitt said on the phone to Dorthy Moxley after the *Stamford Advance and Greenwich Time* finally did the right thing, "Well, Mrs. Moxley, it looks like we're back in business."

Chapter Forty-Three

Moxley Murder Case Aired on Unsolved Mysteries

Armed with Len Levitt's December 1995 nationally distributed (by *Associated Press*) articles, Greenwich Detective, Frank Garr, who had not gotten a break in the case for several years, decided he had enough ammunition to again contact every nationally syndicated television show in America and abroad that broadcast these type of explosive stories.

When he had first contacted several television shows months previous to Levitt's article, everyone gave Garr the thumbs down. The reason for the rejections was that the Moxley murder was old news (now more than 20 years old) and without any new evidence, what was the point? Garr was hoping that by televising a show on the Moxley murder, people who had been reticent, or just plain afraid, would now come forward with some new evidence that could nail down a case against either Tommy, or more likely, Michael Skakel.

Levitt's newspaper articles had changed the equation, and when Garr contacted *Unsolved Mysteries*, they admitted that Garr had fresh information that would make an *Unsolved Mysteries* episode on the Moxley murder a prime-time television attraction.

After first sending a film crew to Garr's office in Bridgeport, two months later, *Unsolved Mysteries* was ready to air the show live, and they needed someone familiar with the case to fly out to Burbank, California, to be on call when someone phoned in with a tip.

"I think I should go out there," Garr told his boss, state's attorney Donald Browne, who had been involved with the case from the beginning and had steadfastly refused to file, despite the mounting evidence, any charges against anyone with the last name "Skakel."

Surprisingly, Browne gave Garr the go-ahead.

When Garr arrived at the Burbank studios of *Unsolved Mysteries*, he was surprised at the massive amount of callers who were bombarding the show's operators with phone-in tips. Garr was also shocked that none of the callers were calling in tips that implicated Ken Littleton, or even Tommy Skakel. The avalanche of phone calls concerned one man only: Michael Skakel. And several of those phone calls were from former inhabitants of the Elan School.

Garr explained the callers and the content of their calls as such: "They would say 'This is so and so. I just want you to know I watched the show. Michael Skakel was nuts!' Or 'I was up at Elan with Michael Skakel, and he said he killed a girl with a golf club.'"

The calls were coming in at such a volume, Garr ran like a rabbit from show operator to show operator, sometimes just scribbling down names and phone numbers, and praying to God he didn't miss an important caller because of the sheer volume of the calls.

The most telling phone call was from Phil Lawrence, of Florida, who claimed he had attended a group therapy session at Elan where Michael broke down and said, sobbing, that he had killed Martha Moxley.

"I was there," Lawrence told Garr. "Michael admitted to killing Martha. Michael also had these private meetings with Joe Ricci (Elan's owner) most people didn't have the luxury of having. Ricci was my legal guardian, and I only had one (private meeting).

"And Ricci tape-recorded everything. I guarantee you he has a recording of Michael's confession. I'd bet the moon on it. I bet he taped every conversation he had with Mike because he's not dumb."

"Who is this Ricci?" Garr said. "Is he a psychiatrist or a psychologist?"

"Are you kidding?" Lawrence said. "He's an ex-junkie from New York. He never even went to college."

When Garr got back to his office in Bridgeport, he began the arduous task of contacting all the people who had called in to the *Unsolved Mysteries* television program.

The first person he contacted was former Elan resident Diane Holman, who, after two years of therapy at the Elan school, was now herself a therapist in California. Holman said that one night she was sitting in the Elan dining hall, alone with Michael Skakel. When she asked him why he was at Elan, he replied that he was involved in a "hometown murder." He said he had walked the murdered girl home, and he kissed and made out with her under a tree.

"I think I did it," he told Holman, "But I'm not sure."

Garr then interviewed Anna Goodman, also a resident at Elan at the same time as Michael Skakel. Goodman said that at a therapy session Ricci forced Michael to wear a sign that said, "Ask me why I killed my friend, Martha Moxley."

Eight months after the *Unsolved Mysteries* program aired, the Greenwich police received a phone call from Chuck Seigan of Chicago. Seigan, too, had been a resident at Elan when Michael Skakel was a resident. Garr traveled to Chicago to interview Seigan.

In Chicago, Seigan told Garr that Michael was a "queer teen" with bitter memories.

"Michael would say that his father would sometimes lock him in the closet, and his father would put out cigarette butts out on him on his arms and legs," Seigan said. "There was anger in him when he said it, and disgust and hurt."

Seigan said that eight months after Michael arrived at Elan, he escaped. He was eighteen years old and old enough to sign himself out of the facility. But he bypassed that formality and simply "went over the wall." But a few weeks later, Michael, either by his own volition, or by the mandate of his father, was back at Elan.

Seigan also described to Garr a "general meeting," where he said Michael got his "comeuppance" for escaping.

"The purpose of the general meeting is to humiliate you and to get people really angry at you," Seigan said. "I don't know if it's actually therapeutic, or if it's a way for them to get revenge on a person that splits."

Seigan said that at this general meeting, "Michael was placed in front of his classmates, and the moderator told the other residents, 'Do you have something to say to him?' Literally 50, 60, 70 people ran up to him and began screaming at him.

"At the end of the meeting, the moderator said to the class, concerning Michael, 'Do you know why he's here? He's here because there was a murder in the area of his home, and Michael just doesn't know if he did it or didn't.'"

Seigan said the people at the meeting then started yelling at Michael, "Well, did you do it?"

Michael said that he didn't know.

Seigan said that after that particular group session, the topic of whether Michael had killed Martha Moxley became an everyday discussion.

"Michael would get very nervous," Seigan said. "When the question was asked, 'Did you murder this girl?' he would always come up with the answer, 'I don't know.' That would start the tears. The tears flowed pretty easy for him."

However, when Garr interviewed John Higgins, another resident at Elan at the same time as Michael, Garr was told a different story. Higgins didn't get in touch with Garr. Instead, Seigan had given Garr Higgins's name and phone number, and Garr set up a follow-up meeting with Higgins.

At this meeting, Higgins told Garr that when he asked Michael, "Well, did you do it, or didn't you do it?" Michael had replied, "Yes, I did it."

Higgins then started lamenting as to why Michael had chosen him to confess to.

"I feel like shit, and I'm pissed," Higgins said. "Why did he have to tell me?"

Worried that Higgins might change his story if deposed, when Garr got back to Bridgeport, he phoned Higgins. But this time, Garr taped the conversation.

During this taped conversation, Higgins said, in part, "We got into a conversation about why he was there. He said he didn't know if he murdered someone or not. He told me he remembers being in a garage, having a golf club, being in tall pine trees, and walking up back in his house, and the big dilemma at the time was if he did it or not."

Higgins also said that Michael told him he was sent to Elan, and not his brother, Tommy, because, "Tommy is a cool, calm and collected guy and could deal with whatever might come to the family on this case. And obviously Tom was good at dealing with this and Michael apparently wasn't."

Higgins said that Michael was crying profusely when he was spilling his guts.

"The nut of the conversation was that he had no idea what had happened," Higgins said. "But he had been sent away after this whole thing had occurred because he thinks his father thought he did it, or he doesn't know if he did it and that they were trying to protect him."

Garr was sure Higgins was now not telling him the entire truth. During their first in-person, un-taped meeting, Higgins had said Michael had admitted killing Martha Moxley. Now Higgins was changing his story, saying Michael was unsure if he was the murderer.

So, figuring Higgins was on the verge of losing it, Garr ended the conversation with a promise from Higgins that Garr could speak to him again on the phone in a few days.

When Garr phoned Higgins the second time, he again recorded the conversation.

At first, the frightened Higgins refused to open up. He told Garr, "The fact is that the Skakel family, whether you know it or not, are a very well-connected family."

Sensing Higgins was about to clam up, Garr told him, "I know the Skakels fairly well. My intentions are not to harm you or to cause you problems. My intentions are to work with you and together to get to the bottom of this."

That seemed to calm down Higgins a bit. He then added to what he had told Garr on the previous phone call; information that could break the case wide open.

"Well, Michael was obviously destroyed, and he was just sitting there crying, and he was probably crying for five minutes or so," Higgins said. "I then asked him quietly, 'Did you do it, or didn't you?' He said, 'I did it. I killed her.' He was so sad, I probably gave him a big hug."

When the phone conversation ended, Garr said to himself, "He (Higgins) said, 'I probably gave the guy a big hug!' You don't make up a detail like that. I've got a guy, a credible witness who is going to get on the witness stand and say, 'Michael Skakel told me he killed Martha Moxley!'"

At this point in time, Frank Garr and Len Levitt, on a common mission to expose a killer, became quite friendly; much friendlier than a cop and a newspaper reporter are wont to be.

A few weeks after speaking with Higgins, Garr told Levitt, whom he had come to trust, "Michael did it. I found witnesses. I've got proof. But I can't tell you more than that."

In a detailed memo, Garr also informed state's attorney Donald Browne, who had been given jurisdiction in the re-opening of the Moxley murder case instead of the Greenwich police department, about his new discoveries. But, for some reason, Browne put Garr's memo on his "pay-no-mind list" and took absolutely no action.

The question is – why?

And no one, especially Donald Browne, has ever come up with a satisfactory answer.

Chapter Forty-Four

The Screenplay of the Novel, A Season in Purgatory, *Makes Prime Time Television*

In May of 1996, the mini-series *A Season in Purgatory* was telecast on CBS. It was produced by Aaron Spelling, David Browne, and Buzz Berger.

"The network did teasers for the show every day for a week up until the show aired, saying it was based on an actual crime in Greenwich, Connecticut," Dominick Dunne said. "Newspaper stories talked about the real murder in relation to the mini-series. People were soon discussing the case regularly and openly, but there never seemed to be any progress in solving it."

In December of the same year, Dunne got a call at his New York apartment from Bernice Ellis, a staff worker at Vanity Fair.

"It's about the Moxley case," she said. "I think you better talk to this guy."

Dunne and the unidentified young man met at one of Dunne's New York City haunts, the Patroon, an East 46th Street posh eatery, located on the first floor of a tony townhouse.

According to Dunne, the young man, a fledgling writer, had been asked by the Sutton Associates to put the Sutton Report, paid for by Rushton Skakel, into some sort of readable form. While doing so, this young man became "emotionally involved" in the story and was crushed when Rushton Skakel buried the report and fired the Sutton Associates. As a result, the young man made copies of the Sutton Report, and he gave one to Dunne and said he could keep it (It is not clear if this is the same gentleman who went to Len Levitt's home and showed him the Sutton Report, but did not allow him to keep a copy).

The young man told Dunne the following story, which Dunne repeated in his book *Justice: Crimes Trials and Punishments*:

When the report was presented to Rushton Skakel, it indicated that Tommy had not killed Martha Moxley. Michael, the fourth Skakel son, who had never been a suspect, had in all probability killed her. The report suggested that Tommy may have helped his brother move the body.

Michael and Tommy were very competitive and fought constantly. Michael had a crush on Martha, so Tommy moved in on his territory. That was the way they behaved. Rushton Skakel, a known alcoholic, was personally undone by the findings. He paid the agency, and the report was stashed away, never to see the light of day.

As for the young man, who had given Dunne this telling information, Dunne had the following take:

It was my perception that this young man had developed an enormous sympathy for Martha and her mother, and he was outraged that justice would not be done, that money could make a difference even in the case of murder. Because he was hired several years after the private detectives, no one had thought to have him sign a confidentiality oath. He had read my book and seen me on television, so he secretly appropriated the report and called Vanity Fair.

He was deeply frightened that something bad could happened to him, he said, and he had reason to be. I promised that I would never reveal his name.

Soon after his meeting with the young man, Dunne received a phone call from literary-agent-to-the-stars, Lucianne Goldberg. Goldberg had upped her infamy a notch, when she represented the biography of Linda Tripp, a close confidant of Monica Lewinsky's, a book which, in Dunne's words, "Told the salacious tales of a young lady giving blow jobs in the Oval Office, and had a semen-stained dress that almost changed the course of American history."

Goldberg had recently become the literary agent for the disgraced former Los Angeles detective, Mark Fuhrman, who had pled "no contest" to a charge of perjury that had taken place during the O.J. Simpson trial, for denying he had not, even once in his life, uttered the word "nigger." He was sentenced to three years' probation and fined $200. (Fuhrman's record was later expunged, or stricken from the files related to the criminal charges).

Goldberg had represented Fuhrman in best-selling book, *Murder in Brentwood*, about the O.J. Simpson trial.

While supposedly making idle conversation on the phone, Goldberg let it slip that she was looking for another book where Fuhrman could display, according to Dunne, his "amazing detective skills."

Dunne fell for the bait, and he nearly bit his lip in excitement when he said, "The Moxley case! I have some incredible information that I will give him!"

Dunne rolled out the red carpet for Fuhrman, who, as a gruff Los Angeles cop, seemed not worthy of hanging with the same social set as a blueblood like Dunne. The first thing Dunne did was to invite Fuhrman for lunch to the trendy Four Seasons restaurant at 99 East 52nd Street in New York City.

"People practically fell off their banquettes trying to get a look at him," Dunne said.

Dunne also took Fuhrman to meet Dorthy Moxley, who was so desperate to find and convict her daughter's killer, she would have made a deal with the devil to do so.

Pulling out all stops, Dunne formally presented Fuhrman to New York's elite movers-and-shakers, much in the way an 18-year-old girl is formally presented by her aristocratic parents to her equals in a Debutante Ball.

"I gave a cocktail party for him," Dunne said. "I've always admire cops, and I hate to see the way they are treated on the stand by defense attorneys at murder trials. I invited several of the local cops and their wives, as well as some O.J. junkies among the weekenders who wanted to meet the famous – or infamous – Mark Fuhrman.

"I also called to invite Frank Garr, thinking he would be thrilled that another book on the case was in the works. But he wasn't thrilled at all. He declined to come to the party."

It never dawned on Dunne that an honest, hardworking cop like Frank Garr might not want to be in the company of, and at a party honoring, a disgraced ex-cop like Mark Fuhrman.

Chapter Forty-Five

Skakel Family Friend, Cissy Ix,
Gives Frank Garr Important Information on the Skakels

While Dunne was throwing parties for, and bouquets at, Fuhrman, Garr was hard at work trying to build a case he could present to state's attorney Donald Browne that Browne could not refuse to prosecute.

Using his policeman's instinct, Garr always felt that Cissy Ix was holding back something concerning the Moxley murder. As a result, Garr kept in constant contact with her and her husband, Bob, sometimes even going as far as to visit them in Belle Haven.

"I kept going back because I knew she wasn't giving me everything," Garr told Len Levitt. "She was too intimate with the Skakels not to know more than she was telling me."

After calling to let them know he was coming, and getting their approval, Garr visited Bob and Cissy Ix at their home.

Referring to Len Levitt's bombshell articles, Garr told them, "You know about the change of stories. I can understand why Tommy would lie, but why would Michael humiliate himself, saying something like that, placing himself at the scene of the crime?"

After telling Garr that Rushton Skakel had once found Michael romping in his bedroom, wearing woman's clothes, Cissy Ix went one better.

As was written in Garr's report dated November 20, 1997, "According to Mrs. Ix, Michael told his father that he may have been drinking on the night in question, had blacked out, and may have murdered Martha. Mrs. Ix claims that, due to a confidence she believed she owned Mr. Skakel, she has never revealed this information to anyone."

Garr left the Ix residence knowing he had just found an important piece to the puzzle of solving Martha Moxley's murder; provided to him by someone as close to the Skakels as two coats of paint.

"You can't do much better than that, short of the old man himself telling this to me," Garr told Levitt. "And that wasn't going to happen."

Then, it was Skakel family priest and close advisor, the now-Monsignor Mark Connelly, who decided to communicate to Garr guarded Skakel family secrets. After summoning Garr to the rectory at St. Michael's Church, Monsignor Connelly, who because of his frequent television appearances had a flair for the dramatic, told him that just days before the murder, both Tommy and Michael Skakel had "put a ladder up against Martha's house in order to peep into her window."

"But please don't write this into your official report," the Monsignor said

When Garr asked why not, the Monsignor said, "Michael is so hard to control. He has a horrible temper, and if he found out about me telling you this, he might come here and destroy the rectory."

Then, without much prompting from Garr, Monsignor Connelly said, "After Michael was admitted to Elan, I went to visit him with his father and Tom Sheridan. We spoke to a counselor who told us that Michael had said he was covered with blood on the night of the murder. But when I spoke to Michael later, he denied the conversation with the counselor had ever taken place. He said it was all a lie. I don't know what to believe."

Chapter Forty-Six

State's Attorney, Donald Browne, Retires

In early 1998, someone leaked a report to the press that, in Fuhrman's soon-to-be-released book, *Murder in Greenwich*, he was going to name Michael Skakel as the killer.

Frank Garr hurried over the state's attorney Donald Browne's office, and he pled his case that he had enough evidence for the state to indict Michael Skakel for Martha Moxley's murder.

"We have to move on this," Garr told Browne. "If Fuhrman's book comes out no one will believe we had the information first. We will never convince people that Mark Fuhrman didn't solve out case for us."

"What's he got?" Browne said.

"Nothing I don't already have," Garr said.

Still, Browne refused to issue an indictment.

In March of 1998, Timothy Dumas's book *Greentown* was published by Arcade Publishing Company. When informed of some of the content, Browne got a bad case of indigestion.

Near the end of the book, concerning state's attorney Browne's reluctance to issue indictments in the Moxley murder case, Dumas said, in part, "Some journalists on this story have been wondering – not in print – whether Browne has been 'paid off.' They note that, strategically, he'd be the right man *to* pay off, since he holds the power to keep the case in abeyance.

"Why didn't he convene a grand jury in 1976? He can't remember, but suspects the state lacked a strong enough case. And police were still gathering evidence. What about 1995? He said it was still premature. Yet, he told me, 'I still believe that scientific procedures can and will produce valuable evidence.'

"Legally, Browne is an extremely cautious man. He's convened only two grand juries in 24 years on the job. There are those who are anxious to see him retire for this reason alone; maybe a less cautious prosecutor will spur action for the Moxley case."

Without any advance warning, in April of 1998, state's attorney Donald Browne retired, saying, "I'm stepping down to eliminate any possible 'conflict of interest' perceptions. Whichever way I would have proceeded with the case would have been tarnish by the rumors."

Veteran prosecutor, Jonathan Benedict was immediately tapped to take Browne's place.

Frank Garr wasn't buying Browne's reason for taking a powder.

Garr told Len Levitt, "The real reason he is withdrawing is because he's afraid to make a decision whether or not to go forward with the case. He's using that line as an excuse to bail out."

Levitt then contacted the *Stamford Advance and the Greenwich Time* and told them he had a story they might like to print. The newspaper agreed, but Levitt wanted to be sure that Garr was comfortable with his quote on his feelings about why Browne was resigning.

"You can use the quote," Garr said. "Just attribute it to a law enforcement source."

Levitt then phoned Browne at his home to get the story straight from the horse's mouth.

"I heard you resigned," Levitt said.

And then he paused... waiting for Browne to elaborate.

There was dead silence on the other end of the line.

Was Browne searching for the right words to explain why, for 24 years, he hadn't done a damn thing to prosecute anyone, not even a ham sandwich, in the Moxley murder case?

But Browne wasn't going there. Instead, he did a verbal tap dance, and said, "There's a perception of conflict now. If I proceed to indict now, I'm leaving myself exposed as having done it to avoid the perception I have been paid off. If I don't, then the perception is that I have already been paid off."

John Moxley, Martha's brother, later said, "I think Donald Browne's resignation was a significant milestone, because I don't think he would ever have been as aggressive as Jonathan Benedict has been."

Was Donald Browne paid off by someone in the Skakel/Kennedy cabal to look the other way concerning a possible Skakel involvement in the murder of Martha Moxley?

Or was Browne, conservative by nature – he issued only two indictments in twenty-four years – just following his natural instincts not to prosecute unless he felt he had an airtight case?

Chapter Forty-Seven

Michael Skakel Decides to Write His Autobiography

In December of 1997, the Martha Moxley case went from the sublime to the ridiculous when Michael Skakel decided he wanted to write his autobiography tentatively entitled: *Dead Man Walking: A Kennedy Cousin Comes Clean*. For this project, Skakel enlisted the help of Richard Hoffman, an author, who at the time had a single credit to his resume – *Half the House* – an autobiographical account which was published in 1995 by Harcourt, Brace.

To get the ball rolling and to gauge if there was any interest in a project that at best could be described as "in bad taste," Hoffman, with input from Skakel, wrote a book proposal which was accompanied by a 25-minute audio tape.

On this tape, which was recorded during a weekend at the Skakel family home in Windham, New York, Skakel articulated about the time he found it necessary to masturbate in a tree outside Martha Moxley's window.

"I remember saying, this is crazy," Skakel said on tape. "If they catch me, they're going to think I'm nuts. And a moment of clarity came to my head, and I climbed down from the tree.

"I remember thinking 'Oh my God, if I tell anyone I was there that night, they're gonna say I did it.'"

The book proposal contained a list of the chapters and a synopsis of what each chapter would cover.

Chapter six was described as such:

Chapter 6: 10/30/75: Murder Most Foul

The murder of Greenwich teen Martha Moxley. The character of Halloween and "mischief night." Booze and drugs. The who, what, when, where, and how of that evening's surreal, nightmarish, and ultimately tragic events. Repudiation of various press accounts of that evening, including the account by Mark Fuhrman in his new book, "Murder in Greenwich" which attempts to prove I was the murderer. My relationship with Martha. Why I lied to investigators. Where I really was and what I really did. The investigation's continuing impact on my family. The personal and psychological consequences of that evening include the necessity for ongoing therapy, continuing painful suspicion by the community, estrangement from several of my siblings, and a public vulnerability that has allowed others, particularly the Kennedy family, and now Mark Fuhrman, to cast me as the scapegoat whenever it suits their purposes.

SAMPLE:

Looking back, I'd have to say that my brothers and I were pretty wild, especially when it came to Halloween. Halloween was our favorite holiday of the year, better than Christmas, better than New Year's, better than the Fourth of July. In fact, my brothers and I used to stockpile our Fourth of July fireworks to use on October 30th – Mischief Night – which was the best part of Halloween. Mischief Night meant setting off fireworks, soaping windows, greasing doorknobs, throwing eggs. There was nothing really malicious about it. It was all pranks and laughter. It was sheer fun.

My father was away on a hunting trip that Halloween, in 1975. He'd gone to Gil Wayman's house in Cambridge, New York. Gil had a private 600 acre preserve and my father was among his frequent guests. He'd left on Thursday and wasn't coming back until Sunday, and had left us in the charge of Ken Littleton who had only that week been hired as our live-in tutor. Littleton scared me. He was the football coach at school, a swaggering tough guy who could glare a hole right through you. Humorless and cold, he had a weird quiet way about him that disturbed me.

Probably on my father's instructions, and certainly on my father's tab, Littleton took us all to the Belle Haven Club for dinner that night. When the waiter came around I ordered a rum and tonic. I tried to look nonchalant and waited for Littleton's veto. It never came. About the third drink I began to think that this live-in tutoring might work out nicely. Here I was having just turned 15 years old, ordering rum and tonics and planter's punch with the football coach in this swanky club, and no one batted an eye! I looked around at my brothers Rush, Tommy, and David, my sister Julie and her friend Andrea Shakespeare, my cousin Jimmy Terrien, and Ken Littleton, and I began to form an idea. I would become Littleton's drinking buddy. I would get in good with him, and he would make my life a lot easier by getting the other teachers to lay off me.

After dinner, we went back to the house. We were all drinking my father's booze, hanging around, playing Backgammon, and feeling like – at least trying to act like – grown-ups. This turned out to be pretty boring though so after a while we began to chase each other around, whooping, and giving out "noogies" to each other and knocking things over. Then my cousin Jimmy suggested that we go over to his house to watch a new show, "Monty Python's Flying Circus," that was supposed to be really funny and was going on the air for the first time that night. He also said he had some great pot over at his place.

We had some more to drink, and after a while Martha Moxley, Geoffrey Byrne, Helen Ix, Marjorie Walker, and Jackie Wettenhall came by to see what we were all going to do for mischief. I remember standing in the kitchen drinking with Littleton and telling him that I thought Martha was really pretty. "Yeah, she's hot!" he said. After a while I saw her through the window, standing a little aside from the others, so I went out and asked her if she wanted to hang out and smoke a cigarette in my father's Lincoln.

We called my father's Lincoln the "Lustmobile." After my mother died, my father really went off the deep end trying to impress women with his money and with what he thought was his impeccable taste. He bought the Lincoln and had a sun-roof put in it. He had a machine-shop remove the Lincoln ornament from the front and replace it with a five-thousand dollar Lalique *eagle, and then he had them mount a little light under it. We used to joke around, never within his hearing, that we were going to buy him some fuzzy dice for the rear-view mirror.*

While we sat in the Lincoln, I tried to convince Martha to come to the Terrien's with us. I really liked her. I wanted to kiss her. I wanted her to be my girlfriend, but I was going slow, being careful. The truth is that with Martha I felt a little shy. I thought that maybe if we spent the evening together at my cousin's something romantic might develop between us. Maybe we could hang out there if she wanted. She seemed to like me. I told her there was a new English show that was supposed to be hilarious.

"I can't," she said. "My Mom gave me a curfew. I have to be home by nine."

"Come on! Nine o'clock? That's ridiculous! It's mischief night! Come on, come with us. We'll have a blast!"

"I can't," she said. Then she touched me, on the shoulder. "Tomorrow night, though. OK?"

Tomorrow night, she said. She'd touched me. It was a promise. I nearly swooned with joy.

"We'll go nuts and trash this town," she said.

"Great!" To try to get a kiss then would have ruined everything. Tomorrow night, I thought. Tomorrow night I'll kiss her.

"Hey! Hey, you guys! It's time to go!" My brothers Rush, David, and Johnny and my cousin Jimmy opened the doors. "It's coming on in fifteen minutes, man. Let's go."

Martha got out. I jumped in the back with David and Johnny. Jimmy drove, with Rush riding shotgun. I waved to Martha, my brother Tommy, Helen, Jackie, Marjorie, and Geoffrey at the back door of the house as we pulled away.

We headed over to Terrien's fifteen or twenty miles away. Jimmy always liked to race, to time himself from one place to another. He always had to beat his best time. He was running all the lights, driving like a maniac.

I wished Martha'd come with us. At the Terrien's you never had to worry about anything. My cousins' stepfather was a drunk, and he was always away in New York, living at the New York Athletic Club or shacking up with his latest mistress. My aunt, Georgeanna, was also drunk all the time, and she pretty much kept at her own wing of the house. They had a huge castle-like place. We could do anything. We were basically on our own. I always felt good there. My father couldn't get at me, and my brother Tommy couldn't give me a hard time either; it wasn't his turf. I felt safe there.

It was great. We smoked a lot of pot and drank some more and laughed through the whole Python show. Afterward I wandered off to my older cousin Johnny's room. He was away somewhere. His room was a kid's fantasy, so big it had a balcony, and an oval section with about twenty windows that looked out over a meadow and an orchard. He had a king-size bed with two life-size statues of palace guards, the Beefeaters, on either side. There were three big TV sets stacked on top of one another, and a movie screen that dropped down. In one corner was an old upright honky-tonk piano like the ones I'd seen in Westerns, but the front had been replaced by Plexiglas so you could see the hammers hit the strings. God, I wished I could have brought Martha here, I thought.

I lay on the bed, flanked by the stalwart Beefeaters, thinking of her. I loved this room. I was sleepy with booze and pot. I wanted to fall asleep. I wanted to stay the night, but how would I get back the next day? And the next day would become tomorrow night and I would see Martha. I roused myself.

My brother Rush decided to drive us home. He was really hammered. Johnny, David, and I all rode in the back seat since neither of us trusted him to get us home in one piece. We got out of the Terrien's driveway and on up to Cliffdale Road, about a half mile. Then we turned onto River View Road, but after about 300 yards, Rush pulled over, put the car in park, and fell asleep.

Johnny took the wheel even though he didn't have a license. He managed to get us home.

No one was around. All the lights were out in the house and...I went upstairs. My sister Julie's bedroom door was closed so I figured her friends had gone home. The TV was on in the master bedroom, but nobody was there. I went to the kitchen and got something to eat, then I headed up to bed.

I couldn't settle down. A part of me really wanted to go to sleep but I was keyed up, nervous and horny. After a little while longer, still unable to fall asleep, I kicked off the covers and decided, "Fuck it. I'm going back out."

The tape then delineated the sequence of events Michael Skakel said had happened after he decided to go back outside.

I slipped out of the house and went to spy on a female neighbor, hoping to see her naked.

I changed my mind and headed to Moxley's house to seek a kiss from her. I climbed a tree outside her home, threw rocks at a window, called her name, and fondled myself briefly.

I started home a short time later without seeing Martha, cutting across the family's driveway. I had a feeling there was someone else in the yard.

When I started walking through something in me said, "Don't go in the dark over there."

I remember yelling, "Who's in there? Who's in there?"

Then I went home to bed and was awakened the next morning by Martha's mother, Dorthy Moxley, at the door, asking me whether I knew where her daughter was.

I remember just having a feeling of panic . . . like my worry of what I went to bed with . . . I don't know . . . I just had a feeling of panic.

I hopped on my bike to go looking for Martha Moxley. When I returned, the area around her home was crawling with police. That's when I learned she was dead.

Police later interrogated my older brother, Thomas, who was believed to be the last person seen with Moxley.

You know, the police were at our house every day. You know, they had like dinner with us, and I mean it was just fucking bizarre. And it just kind of left me in shock ever since then, you know.

After shopping the book proposal around for several years, Michael Skakel's and Richard Hoffman's literary representative, the David Vigliano Agency, found no buyers for this vile piece of trash.

Chapter Forty-Eight

A Grand Jury is Convened in the Moxley Murder Case

On June 18, 1998, Connecticut State Attorney Jonathan Benedict did something his predecessor, Donald Browne, was never able to bring himself to do: he convened a grand jury to look into the possibility that Michael Skakel should be indicted for the murder of Martha Moxley. Under a new state law, the grand jury consisted of only one person – Superior Court Judge George Thim. Thim had been appointed by the state's chief court administrator, Judge Aaron Ment.

During the 18 months that Judge Thim presided over the grand jury, over 50 witnesses were called. Also introduced into evidence was Michael Skakel's book proposal and accompanying tape, which Frank Garr had personally obtained from the home of Richard Hoffman after serving him with an out-of-state subpoena at his Cambridge, Massachusetts home.

On August 4, 1998, Ken Littleton was subpoenaed to testify before the grand jury. At first Littleton, on the advice of his counsel, Eugene Riccio, refused to testify, invoking his Fifth Amendment rights. Benedict asked Superior Court Judge John J. Ronan to compel Mr. Littleton to testify, and the judge complied. This move under state law gave Littleton immunity from prosecution for any crime except perjury in the case.

Littleton testified before the grand jury for one-and-a-half hours. Although Attorney Riccio would not discuss what Mr. Littleton said in court, he did tell the *New York Times*, "Ken is much relieved, and he would like to put this situation far, far behind him."

John Moxley, Martha's elder brother, then 39, was both "surprised and hopeful" to hear that Littleton had finally testified before the grand jury.

Moxley said, "When I found out it kind of raised the hair on the back of my neck. Ken was there. He was at ground zero. He was in the Skakel house that night and during the immediate period afterward. He knew what they were talking about. He knew who was in the house. He had a sense of where people were and what they were doing."

John Moxley said that the prosecutor's decision to give Littleton immunity indicated that he believed that Mr. Littleton did not commit the crime.

"I'm assuming that if the police are willing to grant immunity, they knew something we don't know," he said. "We've never gotten this far before. We're cautiously optimistic."

On September 28, 1998, Joseph Ricci, the co-founder and headmaster at Elan School, where Michael Skakel allegedly admitted, in group therapy and person-to-person in private conversations, that he killed Martha Moxley, refused to testify before the grand jury.

In court papers, however, State's Attorney Benedict said, "We has been informed by several former residents of Elan that Joseph Ricci was present and overheard Michael Skakel make admissions as to the murder of Martha Moxley. These admissions were made by Skakel in response to being confronted by Mr. Ricci and other Elan staff members as to Skakel's involvement in the matter."

Michael Skakel's attorney, Mickey Sherman, said that the state's Appellate Court had ruled that Ricci could not be compelled to testify before the grand jury about any incriminating statements Michael Skakel made while in rehabilitation, and under Ricci's care and treatment.

"The Elan program is not a typical Park Avenue psychiatrist," Sherman said. "It is unorthodox, and treatment is made not only when a patient is lying on a psychiatrist's couch, and the state should not be allowed to willy-nilly delve into the private conversations between a patient and a therapist, or his associate."

Outside the courtroom, Ricci told reporters, "At no time did anyone ever say to me Michael Skakel had committed a murder. At no time did I overhear it."

Ricci eventually did testify before the grand jury, but his testimony was sealed. In January of 2001, Ricci passed away from cancer at a hospital in Portland, Maine.

Daniel Greenfield, a psychiatrist specializing in addiction medicine, testified before the grand jury. He said, that patients in residential treatment facilities have an expectation of confidentiality, not only from their psychiatrists, but from staff members and other patients. Greenfield said confidentiality applies to group therapy sessions as well as to more individualized counseling sessions.

Greenfield said there are no communications between patients and lay staff that are not protected by confidentiality in licensed 24-hour treatment facilities, as the Elan school.

"When a person comes into a program like that, that person, that adolescent, should come with the expectation that it all stays there, within the treatment program," Greenfield said. "These are kids, these are adolescents. They say all kind of jerky things."

However, one former Elan School resident, Chuck Seigan, testified before the grand jury that while he was at the rehab center with Skakel, Ricci ran a special meeting that was called to punish Skakel for escaping from the facility after being admitted in 1978 following his involvement in a drunken-driving accident. During that meeting, Seigan said that Ricci confronted Skakel with reasons for his being at Elan School.

"There were many different reasons, but (Ricci) did bring out the fact that there was a murder," Seigan said.

On October 18, 1998, the Skakel family and their attorneys decided to cut off all communications with the grand jury.

According to the *New York Times*, "Rushton Skakel Sr., the father of the two suspects, Thomas and Michael Skakel, so far has refused to appear before a one-man grand jury investigating the murder of Martha Moxley, who lived next door to the Skakels in Greenwich. His lawyer, Richard G. Lubin, said that Mr. Skakel, 74, suffers from mental illnesses. 'Nothing he can say is material,' Mr. Lubin said.

"However Frank Garr, the chief inspector for State's Attorney Jonathan Benedict, said that prosecutors believe Mr. Skakel holds information that is material to their case.

"Emanuel Margolis of Stamford, who represents Thomas Skakel, and Thomas I. Sheridan of Manhattan, who represented Michael Skakel until several months ago, said they had been asked to appear voluntarily next week before the grand jury. Both refused, saying any communication between them and their clients would be privileged."

On January 19, 2000, Connecticut State Prosecutor Johnathan Benedict called a press conference at the Holiday Inn across from the courthouse to announce that the grand jury had decided that there was enough evidence to indict Michael Skakel for the murder of Martha Moxley. However, because Skakel was only 15 years old at the time of the murder, the indictment charged him as a minor. Legal experts said that the state would almost certainly file a motion to have Skakel tried as an adult.

Benedict did exactly that, and Michael Skakel's legal fate was now in the hands of a juvenile court judge in Stamford, who would have to decide if the case should be heard there, or in Connecticut Superior Court, where the penalties for conviction would be much greater than they would be in Juvenile Court.

"If the case is kept in Juvenile Court, the court will probably have little power to punish him," said David Rosen, a lecturer at Yale University and a senior research associate at Yale Law School's Child Studies Center. "The only way to punish him would be through a transfer to the Superior Court. But a transfer may not be a maneuver available to the prosecutor, depending on how the judge interprets the law. Under the law as it stood in 1975, the only thing this guy can be prosecuted for is being a juvenile delinquent. Prosecutors may be walking into a thicket that there is no way out of."

Hugh F. Keefe, a criminal defense lawyer in New Haven, said prosecutors most likely would not have hunted down Mr. Skakel if they did not expect his case to be heard in Superior Court.

"The pressure's going to be on the judge to transfer him out of Juvenile Court and have him tried as an adult," Keefe said. "Mickey Sherman's job is going to be to get the law that applied 25 years ago."

Prosecutor Benedict told the press that because Michael Skakel was a juvenile at the time of the murder, prosecutors are still barred from commenting on any aspect of the case.

"Until those rights are either waived or a court tells us otherwise, it is the obligation of my office to honor those rules," Benedict said.

When asked about the failure of his predecessor, Donald Browne, to seek an indictment during the 25 years after the Moxley murder, Benedict simply said, "I think Donald struggled with the case."

Then, without answering any more questions, Benedict angrily stalked out of the room, followed by a frenzied mob of reporters seeking to know what the next steps in the case might be. But Benedict refused to say another word.

Later that same day, Michael Skakel, now 39, who had been living with his father, Rushton, in Hobe Sound, Florida, decided to voluntarily surrender to the Greenwich police.

Frank Garr, seeing Skakel and his legal team arriving at police headquarters, quickly ducked into the police garage two buildings down from headquarters. With him was Greenwich Police Chief Peter Robbins, who Garr had known since Robbins was a rookie in 1975, the year of the Moxley murder.

When he arrived at police headquarters, Garr approached Michael Skakel, who was with his attorney, Mickey Sherman. At this precise moment, reporters screamed at Skakel, "Did you kill her, Michael? Did you do it?"

Michael Skakel simply smirked.

Garr pulled the arrest warrant from the inner pock of his suit jacket, and he handed it to Skakel, saying, "Mike, I have an arrest warrant charging you with the murder of Martha Moxley. Obviously, you know you don't have to speak to me. You have the right to remain silent."

Skakel simply smirked again.

Within an hour, Skakel had posted a $500,000 bond and was released from police custody. When he exited the police station, he was smiling broadly, like he hadn't a care in the world.

"He's not guilty," Mickey Sherman told the assembled press. "His spirits are good, all things considered. Everyone's been telling him this was going to happen for years."

As Michael Skakel was surrendering to the police in Greenwich, Dorthy Moxley sat beaming next to a painting of Martha in the dining room of her New Jersey home.

"Wild horses couldn't keep me away from the trial," she told the *New York Times*. "When my husband died 12 years ago, we thought there was no hope."

Her son, John Moxley, Martha's elder brother, added, "This will never be behind us, and it will always be part of the fabric of our lives."

Chapter Forty-Nine

Michael Skakel to Be Tried as an Adult

On February 6, 2000, the preliminary hearing began in which Judge Maureen Dennis would decide whether Michael Skakel should be tried as a juvenile, or an adult. The general feeling was that if he was tried as a juvenile, it was a lost cause for the prosecution. The maximum penalty for a 15 year old in the State of Connecticut was incarceration until the age of 21.

In his opening argument, state attorney Jonathan Benedict, who was successful in getting the trial moved to State Superior Court, told the court that he would depend on a mix of physical and circumstantial evidence, and also incriminating statements made by Michael Skakel. Benedict said some of the physical evidence had not yet been publically revealed.

According to Benedict, the evidence included:

Two sections of a bloodied 6-iron golf club, part of a set owned by the Skakel family, that the killer used to beat and later stab Miss Moxley to death. One segment of the club, the handle, was never found.

Sworn testimony from former neighbors and acquaintances of Mr. Skakel. Several former classmates from a school for troubled youths that Mr. Skakel attended more than 20 years ago have told a Connecticut grand jury that they heard Mr. Skakel confess to killing Miss Moxley. Neighbors of Mr. Skakel testified that he told them he had had a sexual relationship with Miss Moxley before her death, according to a retired Greenwich detective.

*A confidential report from 1995 in which Mr. Skakel and his brother Thomas, himself a former suspect in the murder, significantly changed the accounts they gave to Greenwich detectives in 1975 about where they were when the killing is thought to have occurred.

*Nine hours of audiotapes subpoenaed from a writer who helped Michael Skakel create a 38-page memoir over the last few years in which he professes romantic feelings for Miss Moxley, according to people who have read a transcript of the tapes.

Legal experts were mixed as to whether the state had enough evidence to convict.

"I don't think they can prove this case beyond a reasonable doubt; they don't have the evidence," said Alan Dershowitz, a law professor at Harvard University and a well-known defense lawyer.

But Elliot Peters, a former federal prosecutor in New York, noting the origin of the 6-iron used to bludgeon Miss Moxley, disagreed.

"Whoever killed this girl was in this guy's house or backyard," Mr. Peters said. "The fact that the murder occurred in Belle Haven, an exclusive and private neighborhood in Greenwich where the Moxleys and Skakels lived, limits the universe of people who could have done it to a very small number."

On June 21, prosecution witnesses Andy Pugh, a childhood friend of Michael Skakel's, put the first nail in Skakel's proverbial coffin. Pugh testified that years after the Moxley murder Michael Skakel had confided in him that on the night Martha Moxley was killed, he was masturbating in a tree directly above where Martha's body was found the following morning. Pugh also told the court that Michael Skakel had "an infatuation" with Martha Moxley.

The prosecution's final witness was Judith Kallen, an official with the State Department of Children and Families. Kallen may have been the most important witness called by the prosecution, since her testimony dealt with the crux of the hearing: whether Michael

Skakel should be tried as a juvenile, or an adult. If tried as an adult, he was facing 25 years in prison.

Ms. Kallen told the court, "By law, inmates in juvenile detention must be released at age 18. But state officials now use psychologists and other experts to determine whether a juvenile defendant should be tried as an adult, focusing on the child's chances of rehabilitation."

Mickey Sherman in his cross examination, countered Ms. Kallen's statement by saying to the court, "But this case is like no other. The nearly 25-year delay in bringing the case to court has provided state officials 'a crystal ball,' showing all they needed to know about Mr. Skakel's chances of rehabilitation and becoming a productive member of society."

Sherman then said to Ms. Kallen, "Isn't Michael's conduct over the last 25 years sufficient evidence of potential for rehabilitation?"

Ms. Kallen replied, "I do not have that kind of expertise. I have never had to look back at somebody's behavior over a 25-year period."

On June 28, the defense questioned their final three witnesses.

The first two were brought in to contradict the prosecution's contention that Michael Skakel had admitted his guilt while at Elan.

Sarah Peterson, Michael Skakel's former classmate at the Elan School, told the court, "The school's director, Joseph Ricci, once said, to Michael, 'Skakel, you'll never leave here until you admit you killed that girl.'"

Alice Dunn, another one of Michael Skakel's Elan School classmates testified that, "The whole time I knew Michael Skakel there, he said over and over again he wasn't responsible for what happened."

But under cross examination by the prosecution, Ms. Dunn admitted that during a group therapy session called "a general meeting," Michael Skakel changed his story.

"As part of the meeting, Mr. Skakel was put into a boxing ring where a succession of fellow students were sent in to hit him," Ms. Dunn said. "I saw him beaten into submission. Only then, he said over and over again, 'I don't know. I don't know. I don't know.'"

Prosecutor Benedict then read from Ms. Dunn's previous grand jury testimony.

"Ms. Dunn, did you testify before the grand jury that Michael Skakel told you, 'I don't know if I did it; it was either myself or my brother, but I don't know if I did it. I don't remember what happened?'"

"Yes, that was part of my testimony," Ms. Dunn said. "But I never took his comments to be a confession."

The final defense witness was Bernadette Coomaraswamy, a lawyer and state magistrate, who was a juvenile court prosecutor in the 1970s. She was also a close friend of the Skakel family and hardly an impartial witness.

She testified, "I do not believe Mr. Skakel needs further rehabilitation."

Prosecutor Benedict then asked her, "Is your assessment based on the premise that Mr. Skakel is not guilty?"

"No, it is not," she said.

On his final re-direct, Sherman asked his witness, Ms. Coomaraswamy, "Please clarify this for me. Is it your contention that no rehabilitation would be needed even if Mr. Skakel is guilty?

"Yes, that is correct," she said. "Even if he did it."

On August 16, 2000, Judge Maureen Dennis wrote in her 13-page decision that there was "reasonable cause to believe that Mr. Skakel bludgeoned the 15-year-old Martha Moxley to death when they were neighbors in Greenwich, Conn."

Judge Dennis also wrote, "Having considered all of the state's documentary, photographic, and testimonial evidence, as well as the respondent's submissions for purposes of rebuttal, the court finds that there is reasonable cause to believe that the respondent has committed murder.

"From the evidence presented, a reasonable and prudent person of caution could logically infer that Mr. Skakel retrieved the Toney Penna number 6 iron golf club, the instrument used to murder the victim, from his family home and/or the outbuilding thereon and ran through the woods and pine trees near his home to the Moxley property. A person of reasonable caution could further infer and deduct that was at the location where the murder took place and at a time when it occurred. Mr. Skakel has acknowledged to at least two individuals that he was at the scene where the body was found."

As for the former classmates of Michael Skakel's, who said that, while they were at Elan School in the late 1970s, they had heard him confess to killing Miss Moxley, Judge Dennis wrote that she found those witnesses "credible." She also found credible Andy Pugh, a witness who said Mr. Skakel once admitted being at the murder scene on the night of Miss Moxley's death.

"It is also more than mere coincidence," Judge Dennis wrote, "that the respondent made statements concerning his masturbating either on the victim, or in the tree on the Moxley property on the night the victim was murdered."

Judge Dennis then ordered an investigation into whether Mr. Skakel should be tried as an adult in Superior Court. If convicted as an adult, Skakel could face a sentence of life in prison. But if convicted as a juvenile, he would face only a maximum sentence of four years, and he could conceivably get off with no time served at all.

Daniel Weiner, a veteran criminal defense lawyer, who had represented many juvenile clients, told the *New York Times*, "Nothing about this case is normal or usual. Connecticut's juvenile court system has always emphasized rehabilitation and that if Mr. Skakel had been convicted as a teenager, the court's inclination at the time would likely have been to send him to reform school.

"Now, of course, that is not an option. You have a 39-year-old man. How can you send him to bad-boy school? That's preposterous."

Speaking for the prosecution outside the courthouse, Frank Garr said, "I expect a decision shortly that this will eventually be transferred to the adult court. I feel pretty confident at this point."

Miss Moxley's brother, John, speaking for himself and his mother, Dorthy Moxley, said in a television interview on *WTNH*, "We are very pleased that Judge Dennis verified the grand jury findings. But we're a little disappointed that she did not go all the way and recommend the transfer."

Michael Skakel's lawyer, Mickey Sherman, told the press outside the courtroom, "I disagree with the judge's assessment of the witnesses, but I am not surprised by her decision. I always believed this case would be tried, whether by a judge or a jury. I really do trust the system, and I believe that in the end Michael will be exonerated."

On January 31, 2001, Judge Maureen Dennis announced her decision that Michael Skakel must be tried at the Norwalk Superior Court as an adult. The prosecution had wanted the trial to be held in Bridgeport, where its offices were located. The defense had wanted the trial to take place in Stamford, which is adjacent to Greenwich, where they expected to get a more favorable jury.

Norwalk is essentially halfway between the other two Connecticut cities.

Judge Dennis wrote in her decision, "Although the Juvenile Court had the authority to commit a child, who was considered an adjudicated delinquent, to an institution, my decision must be narrowly focus on the availability and suitability of state institutions designed for the care and treatment of children. There are no juvenile facilities that could house Skakel if he was tried as a juvenile. Because the state's Department of Children and Youth Services, which is normally responsible for committing delinquents, prohibited the placement of anyone over the age of 18, I am transferring the case to Superior Court.

"This court further finds that the facilities of the adult criminal division of the Superior Court afford and provide a more effective setting for the disposition of this case. And the institutions to which the adult criminal division of the Superior Court may sentence a defendant are more suitable for the care and treatment of this respondent, should he be found guilty of the murder of Martha Moxley."

Administrative Judge Edward R. Karazin Jr., of the Norwalk/Stamford judicial district, assigned Skakel's case to the presiding criminal judge, John F. Kavanewsky Jr.

Hearing of the Judge Dennis's decision, Michael Skakel again tried to put on a brave front. He told the press, "I'm not bummed in any way. I'm not crestfallen by any means."

Skakel's attorney, Mickey Sherman, tried to put a happy face on the decision, saying, "This is a nice bonus for the defense because it will allow Michael to be tried by a jury of his peers."

Yet, Sherman, a few days later, decided he was not through with trying to stop the trial from taking place.

By telephone from a ski resort in Aspen, Sherman told the *Connecticut Law Tribune* that he would promptly file a new motion to dismiss the case, based on the statute of limitations in effect in 1975, which prohibits a crime, even murder, from being prosecuted after five years.

That motion was promptly denied.

Chapter Fifty

Michael Skakel's Trial for the Murder of Martha Moxley Commences

On May 4, 2002, Michael Skakel's trial for the murder of Martha Moxley finally took place in Norwalk, Connecticut. Judge John F. Kavanewsky Jr. was in charge of the proceedings.

The lead prosecutor, Jonathan C. Benedict, said in his opening statement, "The real truth lay almost under our noses all along.'"

"The state will show you evidence of a concerted effort on the part of the Skakel family, in the guise of cooperating with the investigation, to prevent the discovery of the actual murderer of Martha Moxley, an effort that began the very night of her death and resulted in investigators following the wrong trails for many years.

"Mr. Skakel has been talking of his night of mischief since at least the spring of 1978. Mr. Skakel had confessed sometimes out of apparent feelings of guilt, sometimes out of panic, sometimes as transparent claims made in an effort to further the cover-up."

Benedict also told the jury that, "Miss Moxley was beaten so furiously that the golf club fell apart."

Michael Skakel's attorney, Mickey Sherman, who considered himself a "showman," then took center stage.

Sherman said, "This was a heinous crime. Whoever committed this crime does deserve to rot in hell. But Michael Skakel was innocent then, and he is innocent now.

"The prosecution is going to take you up to Poland Springs, Maine, not for a fresh glass of water, but to hear stories from a hellhole called the Elan School. The case that they have is based loosely on a very shaky house of cards and mostly wild cards and a few jokers as well. You should expect to hear from witnesses suffering from the 'I Love Lucy Syndrome,' who just want to be part of the show.

"Do not be swayed by pity for the victim's family. No matter how much empathy and sympathy that you feel for them, as we all do, this case and the evidence will simply not support a conviction against Michael Skakel."

From the first day of the trial, with the proverbial noose tightening around his neck, Michael Skakel took every opportunity to taunt members of the prosecution, especially Detective Frank Garr, who was the person most responsible for his predicament.

According to Len Levitt in his book *Conviction: Solving the Moxley Murder*, after Michael's old pal and fellow Elan resident, Andy Pugh, told the court Michael had admitted to him, that on the night of Martha's murder, he had masturbated in the tree beneath which Martha's body was found the following day, Michael thrust his face inches from Garr's face, and he spit out the words, "Good coaching! Just wait!"

"Was Michael threatening Frank?" Levitt said. "Was he looking to start a fight in the middle of his trial?

"Frank said nothing. He made no move. Better than anyone he knew Michael was out of control. Michael had taken every opportunity out in the hallway to brush up against Frank, to make sure his elbow struck Frank's arm. Frank disciplined himself never to respond or retaliate, never to get into a confrontation. He had forbidden himself the luxury of even speaking to Michael."

During the recess after Pugh's testimony, Garr told Levitt, "The tension is getting to him. Michael is probably terrified."

A week into the trial, the prosecutors called Matthew Tucciarone to the stand. Tucciarone, a Greenwich barber, had only recently contacted the prosecution and told them he had knowledge of the case that he had not yet revealed. He said a Connecticut state marshal had urged him to get in touch with authorities.

Tucciarone testified that in late 1975, or in the spring of 1976, three young people visited the Golden Touch Hair Salon on Greenwich Avenue in Belle Haven. From photographs, he identified them as Michael Skakel, Skakel's sister, Julie, and an older brother, Rushton Jr.

Tucciarone testified that Michael Skakel was in the barber's chair getting a trim when he said, "I am going to get a gun, and I am going to kill him."

According to Tucciarone, Julie Skakel told Michael, "You can't do that."

Michael Skakel snapped back: "Why not? I've killed before."

Julie Skakel then said, "Shut up, Michael!"

During cross-examination, Skakel's lawyer, Mickey Sherman, interrogated Tucciarone about why he had not contacted the authorities sooner. The barber said he believed Michael Skakel was out of the country and would no longer be a problem in America.

"Weren't you worried that Michael Skakel might kill someone in another country?" Sherman said.

Tucciarone stuck up his nose, and snapped, "That's another country's problem, not ours."

Spectators in the court started snickering, but Judge Kavanewsky put a stop to that by banging down his gavel and shouting, "Order in the court! We'll have no more of that!"

Next, Cissy Ix was called to the stand, and she astounded the prosecutors when she flip-flopped on her grand jury testimony given four years earlier.

It started innocently enough when assistant prosecutor, Susan Gill, asked Mrs. Ix to explain her 1998 statements to the grand jury, in which she said that Rushton Skakel Sr. had told her that his son, Michael, could have killed Martha Moxley while he was drunk.

Mrs. Ix exact statement in 1998 to the grand jury was as follows:

"He (Rushton Sr.) said Michael had come up to him, and said, 'You know, I had a lot to drink that night and I would like to see, I would like to see if, if I could have had so much to drink that I would have forgotten something, and I could have murdered Martha.'"

Mrs. Ix also told the grand jury that Michael Skakel wanted to be administered a truth serum to shake loose the truth from his subconscious memory.

But on the stand four years later, in reply to Ms. Gill, Cissy Ix denied that she ever had such a conversation with Rushton Skakel Sr.

After seeing a transcript of her grand jury testimony, she said, "When I read this I was so flabbergasted because it was my thinking as opposed to Rush's thinking. I was thinking all those things, and I didn't realize when I read it that I had attributed all those things to Rush.

"I assumed something that was really in my heart of hearts and apparently, according to that, I put in Rushton Skakel's mouth what I actually thought."

As soon as the contradictory words came out of Mrs. Ix's mouth, Dorthy Moxley gasped and then fled the courtroom in tears.

She later said concerning the Mrs. Ix betrayal, "I was steaming mad."

Her son, John Moxley, said that Mrs. Ix had perjured herself on the stand.

"What she said was a bunch of bald-face lies," John Moxley said.

Cissy's daughter, Helen Ix-Fitzpatrick, took the stand next, and she also gave testimony that seemed to favor Michael Skakel's innocence.

In question was the instance of the barking dogs, which, according to the accounts of neighbors, occurred between 9:45 pm and 10:15 pm on the night Martha was murdered.

"It is more probable than not that Michael was in a car with relatives at the time that my dog, Zocks, started barking violently in the direction of the spot where Martha's body was found," Ix-Fitzpatrick said. "He was always barking, but not like that. He barked at everything and chased cars. He even barked at us. That night he was barking and barking. He wouldn't come. He would always come when I called to him. He was definitely disturbed by something."

"Are you absolutely sure that Michael Skakel was in the car when the dogs started barking?" Ms. Gill said.

"No, I'm not," Ix-Fitzpatrick said. "Like I said, it is more probable than not that he was in the car when Zocks started barking."

To clarify things in his client's favor, Mickey Sherman then played a tape of Ix-Fitzpatrick's taped interview with the Greenwich police on November 14, 1975, in which she said that Michael Skakel was in the car when she, Martha, Michael Skakel's brother Thomas, and her friend Geoffrey Byrne got out of the Skakel car and remained behind.

Ix-Fitzpatrick said on the tape, "We felt like a third wheel. When we left Martha and Thomas Skakel shortly before 9:30 pm to go home, the two were flirting playfully."

When Gill resumed her interrogation of Ix-Fitzpatrick, she tried a different tactic.

"Isn't it true that you are so close to the Skakel family that you call Rushton Skakel Sr. 'Uncle Rush,'" Gill said.

Ix-Fitzpatrick admitted that statement was true.

The next prosecution witness to take the stand was Andrea Shakespeare-Renna, who was sixteen years old and friendly with both the Skakels and Martha in 1975.

On the stand, Shakespeare-Renna testified that, "Michael Skakel was home and did not leave in the car with the others when I left the Skakel home at about 9:45 pm."

According to Shakespeare-Renna, who had attended dinner with the Skakels at the Belle Haven Club that night, she was playing backgammon with Michael and Thomas when Fitzpatrick and another teenager — whom she later learned was Martha Moxley — entered the house through a door and greeted Julia Skakel, Michael's sister. Renna said that she was certain that Michael and Thomas Skakel were still at home when Rushton Skakel Jr. drove his cousin, Jim Terrien, across town to his house.

In Sherman's cross-examination of Shakespeare-Renna, he tried to attack her memory and her reliability.

Sherman produced documents from 1991 to show that Shakespeare-Renna had told Frank Garr that it had long been her "impression" that Michael was not in the car and that she was not "certain" of the fact, as she had just testified under oath.

Shakespeare-Renna said it was possible that she never mentioned that to investigators before then, and she did not contact anyone in law enforcement after being "shocked" by a claim in one of three books about the case that Michael Skakel claimed he was across town.

"I was stunned. It was counter to what I knew," Shakespeare-Renna said.

On re-direct, Ms. Gill asked Shakespeare-Renna her impression of Michael Skakel's behavior on the day Martha's body was found.

Shakespeare-Renna said, "Michael was all hyper the day after the murder when he told me and Julie Skakel what all the police activity in Belle Haven was about. We asked about the commotion. He said Martha was killed and that he and Thomas were the last to see her that night."

The next witness was Jackie Wetenhall-O'Hara, a good friend of Martha Moxley's.

According to several published reports, "Jackie Wetenhall-O'Hara read from portions of Martha's diary and agreed that the passages for the months before Martha's murder accurately reflected Martha's relationship with Thomas and Michael Skakel. Martha called both brothers 'an ass' in different entries and seemed ambivalent to Thomas Skakel's advances. Wetenhall-O'Hara, whom Michael Skakel liked when they were teenagers, smiled nervously when she identified the now 41-year-old defendant in court.

"Wetenhall-O'Hara confirmed that she had observed Martha and Thomas Skakel flirting on occasions, testimony the prosecution offered to support its theory that Michael and Thomas Skakel were rivals for Martha's affections, and that's why she was killed."

Sherman could do nothing to lessen the impact of Ms. Wetenhall-O'Hara's dramatic reading of Martha's diary. Grasping at straws, Sherman got Wetenhall-O'Hara to agree that there was nothing in the Martha's diary that foretold the tragic and brutal end of her life.

James McKenzie, a lawyer for the Great Lakes Coal and Coke Corporation, which was owned by the Skakel family in 1975, testified next.

According to the *Stamford Advance and the Greenwich Time*, McKenzie said "that he was sent to the Skakel home on the day Miss Moxley's body was found and was asked to 'maintain a little order' until Rushton Skakel Sr. could return from a hunting trip. Of the seven Skakel children, he testified, 'the more difficult child to control was Michael.'"

Next to take the witness stand was the 78-year-old Rushton Skakel Sr., who the defense said was suffering from dementia. Prosecutor Gill called the patriarch of the Skakel family to testify in an effort to prove the prosecution's contention in its opening statement on May 7 that there was a conspiracy to cover up the crime. But she could not get a word of sense to come out of Rushton Skakel's mouth.

On cross-examination, Mickey Sherman asked Rushton Skakel Sr., "What happened on September 11th of last year (the bombing of the World Trade Center and the Pentagon)?"

"It was a very big incident, but I don't remember the details," Rushton Skakel Sr. said.

A smug smile on his face, Sherman simply sat in his seat at the defense table without saying another word.

After Rushton Skakel Sr. was dismissed by the prosecution, he shuffled towards the defense table, where his son, Michael, stood up and gave his dad a big hug.

Next up to bat was Skakel cousin, James Dowdle, now 44 years old. Dowdle testified that Michael Skakel had accompanied him and Rushton Skakel Jr. and others in a car to Dowdle's home in Greenwich at about 9:30 pm on the night of the killing.

Dowdle, who was called Jimmy Terrien at the time (he now took the name of his biological father), testified that after returning from dinner with the Skakels at the Belle Haven Country Club, he, Rushton Skakel Jr., John Skakel, and Michael Skakel jumped into Rushton Skakel Sr.'s Lincoln Continental at about 9:30 pm. According to Dowdle, they drove to Dowdle's home, an estate called Sursum Corda, several miles from Belle Haven, and watched an episode of the television show *Monty Python's Flying Circus*. Dowdle said the show began at about 10 pm, lasted half an hour, and the Skakel boys left a short time after the show ended.

While he perfectly remembered everything that gave Michael Skakel an alibi for 10 pm on the night of the murder, under cross examination from Prosecutor Benedict, Dowdle came up empty on almost everything else that had occurred that night. He did not remember who was with them at dinner at the Belle Haven Country Club. He did not remember who was drinking and how much they drank before they piled into the Lincoln Continental at the Skakel residence.

"It happened so long ago, I just can't remember those kind of details," Dowdle said.

As Dowdle strode from the witness box after his testimony was complete, Michael Skakel rose and turned to greet his cousin. But for some reason, Dowdle approached the defense table, then, without saying a word, he did an about-face, turned his back on Michael Skakel and exited the courtroom.

After his cousin turned his back on him, Michael Skakel had a stunned look on his face.

Rushton Skakel Jr. was the next to testify, and he was also remarkable in only being able to remember certain things from the night on the Moxley murder; all in favor of his brother Michael's defense.

Rushton Jr. testified he was a student at Dartmouth College at the time of the murder. He said that he had only stopped in Greenwich for one night on his way to a homecoming game at Georgetown University in Washington, D.C.

Rushton Jr. testified on the witness stand, "I saw a Monty Python movie while I was at Dartmouth, and it was the funniest thing I'd ever seen. And I was very excited about seeing the television episode."

Following the script first testified to by James Dowdle, Rushton Jr. said that after dinner at the Belle Haven club, he, Jimmy Terrien (Dowdle), John Skakel, and Michael Skakel left the Skakel residence in Rushton Skakel Sr.'s Lincoln Continental at about 9:30 pm.

"We watched the show," Rushton Jr. said. "And we got home about 11:15 pm. I did not see Michael again that night."

Just as Dowdle had testified on the witness stand, Rushton Jr. said he had no recollection of what they had for dinner that night and how much they had been drinking. He also drew a blank about being interviewed several times by police after the Moxley murder.

After winking at his brother Michael from the witness stand, Rushton Jr. told Prosecutor Benedict, "I have no recollection of returning to Greenwich from Dartmouth several days after the murder to be interviewed by the police."

"Well, do you remember that two weeks after the murder you and other members of your family went to the Greenwich Police Department to give statements?" Benedict said.

"I do not," Rushton Jr. said.

"Do you remember telling the Greenwich police in 1976 that your brother Michael was 'going nuts and being obnoxious' the day after the murder?"

"I do not."

John Moxley, Martha's elder brother, was absolutely livid outside the courtroom when he addressed reporters.

"What they specifically recall is their part of the alibi and nothing else," John Moxley said "It's bad acting. Over the years, these guys are forgetting their lines."

Things started going bad for the defense when Judge John F. Kavanewsky Jr. ruled that the jurors could hear the grand jury testimony given by an Elan classmate of Michael Skakel's, Gregory Coleman, who had died the previous year from a drug overdose. Coleman had testified that he had heard Michael Skakel not only confess to Martha Moxley's murder, but he also boasted, "I am going to get away with murder. I am a Kennedy."

The next Elan alumni to take the stand was John Higgins, who was clearly under duress. Between sobs and wiping tears from his eyes, Higgins said, "One night at Elan, Michael told me that he had a hazy recollection of the night Martha Moxley was killed. He said that he remembered that there was a party going on, it was at his house.

"He related that he later was in his garage, and he was running through some woods. He had a golf club in his hand. He looked up, he saw pine trees. The next thing that he remembers is that he woke up in his house.

"Michael was sobbing and crying and through a progression of statements, he said to me that he didn't know whether he did it. He thought he may have done it. He didn't know what happened. Eventually, he came to the point that he did do it. He must have done it. 'I did it.' he said."

After his testimony ended, Dorthy Moxley embraced Higgins as he left the courthouse.

Two more Elan grads took the witness stand after Higgins.

The first was Dorothy Rogers who was still fighting her battle with the bottle. She was brought to the courthouse by marshals from a North Carolina jail where she was serving time for crimes related to her drinking.

Rogers told the jury about a conversation she had with Michael Skakel at an Elan School dance, where she approached him because they were both from Greenwich.

"He said some things that kind of scared me," Rogers said. "He said that he had been drinking the night she was murdered and couldn't remember what he did. He also said his family was scared he might have committed the murder and sent him to Elan to shield him from the police."

Next up was Chuck Seigan, the Elan graduate who had called the Greenwich police after watching the *Unsolved Mysteries* program about the Moxley murder.

After explaining in great detail the horrors endemic at Elan, including physical and verbal thrashings, and "primal scream" sessions, Seigan testified that program director, Joseph Ricci, blurted out at a general meeting that Michael Skakel could have killed someone.

"At smaller group meetings, when Skakel was asked about it, he told the group that he was drunk, stumbling, and in a blackout that night," Seigan said. "He would cry and shake his head, and he said he didn't know if he did it. Other times he would get annoyed."

Larry Zicarelli, the erstwhile Skakel limousine driver, took the stand next.

Zicarelli told the court, "In 1977, Michael Skakel cried all the way on a car trip to New York City to see his psychiatrist. When we got into New York, he said to me he was very sorry, but he had done something very bad, and he had to either kill himself or get out of the country.

Michael then jumped out of the moving car. I went to Rushton Skakel Sr.'s Manhattan office.

"Rushton Sr. told me to have lunch and then to look for Michael at the psychiatrist's office. Without eating lunch, I went straight to the psychiatrist's office, and there was Michael sitting on the sidewalk. We went to have lunch together, but all Michael had was a double scotch on the rocks.

"On the trip back to Greenwich, we were stuck in traffic on the Triborough Bridge. Michael again jumped out of the car and ran to the side of the bridge. Twice, I had to pull Michael off the bridge and into the car. After he quieted down, I asked him what was wrong. He told me if I knew what he had done, I would never talk to him again."

Before the prosecution rested its case, Senior Assistant State's Attorney Christopher Morano introduced the audio tape into evidence after writer Richard Hoffman testified that he began working with Skakel on a book in 1997.

During a long weekend at the Skakel family home in Windham, N.Y., Hoffman had Skakel speak into a tape recorder about his experiences. The tapes were to be used as material for a book about Skakel's life, Hoffman said.

On one tape, Michael Skakel said that after he returned from the Terrien house at about 11:30 pm, "I know a part of me just wanted to go to sleep, and another part of me got horny. I decided to go out. I ran to this (unidentified) lady's house, and you know, I was like spying in her window, and hoping to see her naked.

"Since I was drunk and couldn't get it up, I got a better idea. I said, 'Martha likes me. I'll go, I'll go get a kiss from Martha. I'll be bold tonight.' At the Moxley home I climbed one of the huge cedar trees next to the front door, and called her name and threw rocks and sticks at what I thought was Martha's window. I later learned I was at the wrong window.

"I don't know, I guess I'm a little out of my mind, because I was drunk and high, I pulled my pants down, I masturbated for 30 seconds in the tree, and I went 'This is crazy. If they catch me, they're going to think I'm nuts.'

"Suddenly, I had a moment of clarity. I climbed down the tree, and started to return home, crossing the oval island in the Moxley's circular driveway. It's really dark, and when I started walking through the oval something in me said, 'Don't go in the dark over there.'"

Prosecutor Morano then told the jury, "Martha's body was found the next day under the low-hanging boughs of a large nearby palm tree."

On May 29, 2002, just before the closing arguments, prosecutors sought briefly to allow the jury to consider whether Michael Skakel had committed the crime under extreme emotional disturbance, a legal determination that would sharply reduce any potential prison sentence. But the prosecutors abruptly withdrew the request, saying it raised a thicket of complex legal issues.

"The reason I withdrew the request was to avoid raising an issue that could later be appealed," Prosecutor Benedict said.

Mickey Sherman told reporters outside the courthouse, "Maybe they realized they made a big mistake."

Assistant prosecutor, Christopher Morano, pooh-poohed Sherman's statement to the press.

"Our decision to withdraw the request actually reflected our confidence that the jury would return an unqualified guilty verdict," Morano said.

Chapter Fifty-One

The Closing Arguments

Michael Skakel's defense attorney, Mickey Sherman, was first up to bat for the closing arguments.

Sherman told the jury, "He didn't do it. He didn't do it. He doesn't know who did it. He wasn't there when the crime was committed, and he never confessed. That's the whole case.

"Now, let's talk about the forensic evidence against Michael Skakel."

He paused for a full ten seconds before he said, "Well, that's the end of that discussion."

Then he held up a piece of the murder weapon, a golf club from a set owned by the Skakel family.

"Let's talk about the physical evidence," he said. "There is only one piece of physical evidence. This is it.

"The investigators over the years have shown they will do or say anything to get someone to confess to killing Martha and solving the crime that put the Greenwich Police Department in a bad light for more than a quarter of a century. They didn't show you any evidence. Michael Skakel had some problems, but they never rose to the level Mr. Benedict said. He didn't do it. What do they have to show you that he did? Zilch, that's what they have."

It was prosecutor Benedict's turn and his calm, matter-of-fact speech pattern contrasted with Sherman's verbal bravado.

"Martha Moxley was a pretty, athletic, flirtatious fifteen-year-old kid, one who we learned from her diary, was just as any fifteen-year-old girl just beginning to come into womanhood," Benedict said. "Unfortunately, as we learned from the words of the defendant, from Richard Hoffman, and from Martha's diary, she was drawn into a vortex of the competing hormones of two of the young boys who lived across Walsh Lane."

Benedict then turned his attention to Michael Skakel, who Benedict said, "Started talking about this murder within 24 hours of its occurrence. He has also talked obsessively about the Moxley murder over the years. And he has confessed to several classmates at a school for troubled youths in Maine in the late 1970s."

Benedict then focused his closing remarks on a taped conversation in 1997 between Michael Skakel and Richard Hoffman, the ghostwriter of an autobiography the defendant hoped to publish.

"On this tape, Mr. Skakel admitted being drunk and high on marijuana the night of the killing, and going to the Moxley property, where he said he masturbated in a tree while trying to peep into Miss Moxley's bedroom," Benedict said. "He takes us on this staggering walk down memory lane. In fact, spinning a tale covering all the bases, he took Richard Hoffman right to the crime scene, indeed to the point where rather than spinning a nice tight explanation, he has spun a web in which he has ultimately entrapped himself. He continues to narrate the evening as if it took place in 2001 rather than 27 years ago, despite the fact that he was both drunk and high."

Using an overhead projector to display Michael Skakel's words in big red letters, Benedict then played a recording of the 1997 book interview during which Michael Skakel said he remembered when he got home from the Terrien's house that Andrea Shakespeare-Renna had already left.

Benedict focused on a comment Michael Skakel made in the conversation with Mr. Hoffman about how he stood outside his sister Julie's bedroom that night.

Michael Skakel said, "Her door was closed, and I remember that Andrea had gone home."

"This is where Michael Skakel slipped up," Benedict said. "He could not have known that Andrea had left the Skakel home unless he was home when she left."

As Benedict was delivering his closing argument, Dorthy Moxley and her son, John, sat impassively in their front-row seats next to several relatives. At the end of Mr. Benedict's closing remarks, they and the other Moxley relatives were wiping away tears.

Michael Skakel, sitting at the defense table, looked stressed throughout the closing arguments. After hearing his own words putting himself at the scene of the crime, he put his head in his hands and shook his head, as if to say, "How could I be so stupid?"

While addressing the press outside the courtroom, Mickey Sherman admitted that his client appeared distraught at the end of the closing arguments.

"I'm distraught, too," Mr. Sherman said. "This is a scary proposition to be on trial for murder."

The jury deliberations began on Tuesday morning June 4, 2002.

Chapter Fifty-Two

The Verdict is Announced

Tuesday, June 4th passed by without a verdict, as did Wednesday and Thursday.

The general feeling in the courtroom was that a not guilty verdict would come quickly. But the longer it played out – the longer the jury tossed around the evidence – the more likely they were searching for a way to find Michael Skakel guilty.

On Friday morning, June 7, 2002, at approximately 10:30 am, the jury foreman, Kevin Cambra, announced to the court that all six white men and six white woman of the jury found Michael Skakel – GUILTY AS CHARGED!

As soon as the verdict was announced, about a dozen Skakel family members, who had sat to the right of Michael Skakel in the courtroom, grumbled loudly, and then they angrily stomped out of the courtroom.

As his attorney Mickey Sherman stared at the jury in disbelief, Michael Skakel looked like a broken man. He sat slumped in his chair, shaking his head, and holding back the tears.

Conversely, Dorthy Moxley sat convulsed in tears of happiness, and her son, John, sat next to her, with a tight smile on his face, blinking away his tears.

When Judge John F. Kavanewsky Jr. ordered Michael to stand as each juror's name was called and the guilty verdict confirmed, Michael Skakel's forehead was drenched in sweat, his face was beet red, and he looked like he was about to keel over and topple to the courtroom floor.

Judge Kavanewsky announced that Michael Skakel's bail was immediately revoked and that sentencing would take place on August 28th. The judge then asked the lawyers on both sides if they had anything to add before he dismissed the jury.

None of the lawyers wanted to speak, but Michael Skakel, who never testified in his own defense at the trial, yelled out, "*I'd like to say something.*"

"You will not, sir," the judge snapped back.

The judge then ordered the marshals to cuff Michael Skakel and lead him out of the courtroom.

As Michael Skakel shuffled towards the courtroom exit, his brother, David, tried to reach out and touch him. A marshal rudely pushed him away.

Outside the courtroom, there was both unbridled jubilance and utter disgust.

Dorthy Moxley stood facing a huge contingent of reporters and television crews. She said she had prayed this morning in anticipation of a verdict.

She said, "My prayer started out, 'Dear Lord, again today, like I have been doing for 27 years, I'm praying that I can find justice for Martha.' You know this whole thing was about Martha. This is Martha's day. This is truly Martha's day."

On the courthouse wall, directly behind her, someone had posted a sign: "Justice at Last."

John Moxley described his feelings to the press when he heard hearing the jury say the word "guilty."

"I think my heart stopped beating," Mr. Moxley said. "It was just incredible. I looked at that jury, and I really felt that it was a jury of our peers."

When the press asked John Moxley what message he thought the verdict sent, he simply said, "I think the message is, 'You've got to be responsible for your actions.' But victory doesn't go with this, this is hollow. It doesn't bring Martha back."

Prosecutor Benedict addressed the press along with his crack team of Christopher Morano, Susan Gill, and Frank Garr standing by his side.

He said, "It's nice to say once in a while that justice delayed doesn't have to be justice denied."

A member of the press asked Benedict if there was a seminal moment, or a single event, that was responsible for the case being cracked.

"Yes," Benedict said. "It was Frank Garr's goofy idea in early 1996 for us to present the case on the television program *Unsolved Mysteries*. Almost immediately, calls came in and they all pointed to Michael Skakel as being the murderer."

A juror and two alternate jurors told the press that they were convinced of Michael Skakel's guilt after the prosecution's closing argument on Monday. They said they knew he was guilty because he had willingly made taped statements placing himself at the murder scene. They also said they did not believe his alibi, or the testimony of Skakel family members, including two brothers and a cousin, who testified in support of it.

The jurors noted that Michael Skakel's brothers, Rushton Jr., and John, and their cousin, James Dowdle, all had total memory loss about most events on the night of the murder, yet they still insisted Michael had left the Skakel residence at 9:30 pm.

"He (Michael Skakel) was trying to set up a scenario where he could have been in the tree. I think what he really did was incriminate himself," said Anne Layton, an alternate juror. "And his family were not believable either. This is probably the single biggest thing in their lives as teenagers. There are some things you just remember.

"Plus, I believed Gregory Coleman's grand jury testimony. Just because he was a drug addict and died from a drug overdose doesn't mean he can't give truthful testimony."

When Mickey Sherman addressed the press outside the courtroom, he looked like he had just been beaten up by Mike Tyson.

"We are bitterly disappointed," Sherman said. "There is no way to hide it. This is certainly the most upsetting verdict I have ever had, or will ever have in my life. But I will tell you that as long as there is a breath in my body, this case is not over as far as I'm concerned. I believe in Michael Skakel. He doesn't have a clue who did it. He wasn't there."

Michael Skakel's brother, David, who was only nine when Martha Moxley was murdered, told the press, "For our family, grieving has coincided with accusation. Michael is innocent. I know this because I know Michael, like only a brother does. You may want finality to this tragedy, and our family wants the same, as much as anyone. But truth is more important than closure.

"This trial was a witch hunt. Our family remains more resolute than ever. Twenty-seven years of insinuation and intimidation is enough."

In Greenwich, just 15 miles from the Norwalk courthouse, the general feeling was satisfaction and relief over the guilty verdict.

"I think it's fantastic; it made my day," said Susan Chapman, 40, who knew Rushton Skakel and his family, and whose older sister had attended school with Martha Moxley.

Ms. Chapman said she still remembered the fear and bewilderment that the murder unleashed among the girls in Greenwich after Martha Moxley's body was found.

"We all thought we were going to be murdered the next night," she said. "But as the years passed, and Michael Skakel emerged as a suspect, I was sure that he was the murderer. I think his family was protecting one of their own."

At the swank Belle Haven Country Club, the private club where Michael Skakel had dined with several family members on the night of Martha's murder, Tom and Nancy Shepard said they were pleased with the verdict.

"Everyone thought they would get away with it," said Mr. Shepard, a former publisher of *Look Magazine*. "Many residents felt an antipathy toward the Skakel family. It was not a happy operation over here in Belle Haven."

Peter Robbins, the Greenwich police chief, who was a rookie on the job the night of the Moxley murder, heard the verdict in the police station's coffee room, where about 20 officers were listening to a live television news broadcast.

"We all had smiles on our faces," Chief Robbins said. "We took a lot of abuse throughout the years. Everyone said, 'They're never going to solve it. They don't know how to solve it.' So there's a lot of vindication there."

Chapter Fifty-Three

The Judge Sentences Michael Skakel

On August 28, 2002, Michael Skakel's lawyers made a last ditch effort to prevent him from spending any more time behind bars. They presented Judge John F. Kavanewsky Jr. with legal documents requesting a new trial on the basis that the prosecution withheld crucial evidence from the defense. The judge extended the sentencing to the following day to give himself time to review the legal documents. Still, he allowed family members and friends on both sides to have their say.

Dorthy Moxley, who wore a gold pin shaped like the scales of justice on her lapel, read a statement to the judge describing the things she would never know about her daughter. Mrs. Moxley said that she often imagined her daughter all grown up, with a college degree, a career, and a family.

"I have spent almost 27 years of hell and anguish trying to live what some would think of as a normal life, but stressed to the limit trying to find truth and justice," Mrs. Moxley said. "Michael Skakel sentenced us to life without Martha. I think he should be responsible for his actions, and so it is only fair that he serve a similar sentence."

As Mrs. Moxley spoke in deliberate terms, crocodile tears flowed down both sides of Michael Skakel's face. He would turn the waterworks off and on for the rest of the day; no matter who was speaking.

It was John Moxley's turn to speak next. John, who was only 17 when his sister was murdered, told the judge, "I always will feel a hollowness."

He then described watching his mother crying, and being unable to comfort her because he had mentally shut down. He said that he could never talk about Martha with his father because it was too painful.

Next, it was the Skakel family's turn to address the court.

Ethel Skakel Kennedy did not attend the trial, and she was not present in court for the sentencing.

However, she did send an eight-page handwritten letter which said, in part, "I want to commend Michael for his mental toughness, fortitude, courage, and tenacity in overcoming his difficult upbringing and alcohol addiction and for his sweetness, kindness, good cheer, and love of life. It is with a heavy heart, yet with hope born of the morning sun, I write to ask that your compassion would tip the scales in your decision regarding my nephew, Michael Skakel. I pray that you will season justice with that twice blessed tribute to God, mercy, and let him continue to enrich our lives."

Although he did appear once during the trial, Robert Kennedy Jr. also did not show up in court in a display of support for his cousin at sentencing. He, too, sent a letter to be read in court before sentencing.

The letter said, in part, "I know Michael as well as one person can know another. He helped me get sober in 1983. Michael was a small sensitive child – the runt of the litter with a harsh and occasionally violent alcoholic father who both ignored and abused him. Michael, after a drunken driving accident at 17, was, at his father's behest, kidnapped by four tattooed goons and shipped to reform school, where he was beaten, tortured and brutalized for two years.

"Many people might be poisoned by resentments after such agonizing experiences, Michael has never given in to bitterness. Instead, he has used these episodes to help and heal others."

When it was Michael Skakel's turn to speak, he blurted out disjointed inanities during a 10-minute monologue full of biblical references. In a theatrical display worthy of Orson Wells, Michael Skakel proclaimed his innocence and his faith in God.

Tears streaming down both sides of his flabby rubicund face, he said, "I would love to be able to say I did this crime, so the Moxley family could have rest and peace. But I can't, Your Honor, because to do that would be a lie in front of my God, who I am going to be in front of for eternity. I have to live by his laws, and his laws tell me I cannot bear false witness against anybody or myself. Jesus Christ told people as he walked around the world that he loved them. Should he go to jail for that?

"I stand here today with my life in your hands, and the Good Lord tells me to tell you that in 2000 years this place hasn't changed a bit. But I am also in this court of law and whatever sentence you impose on me, I accept in God's name."

Judge Kavanewsky was unmoved and unimpressed by Michael's Skakel's deity-oriented oration. Instead, he admonished him for failing to accept responsibility for his horrific crime.

"I won't claim to know for certain what prompted or caused the defendant to kill Martha Moxley," Judge Kavanewsky said. "But by the verdict delivered, I do know that for the last 25 years or more, a period well into his adult life, the defendant has been living a lie about his guilt."

The judge then sentenced Michael Skakel to 20-years-to-life in prison.

Outside the courtroom Dorthy and John Moxley stood in a light rain as they answered questions from the press.

When asked how he felt about the sentencing, John Moxley said he felt numb.

"It's too much to take in; it means too much," he said. "I mean, where do we go from here?"

He was then asked what he thought about Michael Skakel's constant sobbing in court.

Using a dismissive gesture with his right hand, John Moxley said, "That's all theater; good method acting. I'm sure they're really tears of fear about spending the rest of his life in jail."

A reporter asked Dorthy Moxley what she had wanted Michael Skakel to say to the judge.

"I'd like to know all the details we don't know," Dorthy said. "I'm positive Mr. Skakel is the one who killed Martha, and I'd really like to hear him say, 'I'm sorry.'"

After saying that she thought the sentence was sufficient, she added, "He has to be punished for what he did to Martha and to other people."

Outside the courthouse, Mickey Sherman stuck to the standard Skakel party line.

"The sentence would be fair if Michael Skakel had committed the crime," Sherman said. "But he didn't. He's totally innocent."

Little did Sherman know that the Skakel/Kennedy cabal would soon do what they did best when things didn't go exactly their way: look for a fall guy to deflect the blame from themselves.

And that fall guy would be Mickey Sherman himself.

Chapter Fifty-Four

Mickey Sherman Gets the Gate

Days after Michael Skakel was sentenced, the Skakels fired Mickey Sherman, blaming his love for the press, courtroom theatrics, but most importantly, his deficiencies, unintentional or otherwise, as a legal technician as the reason. With Bobby Kennedy Jr., as the attack dog, the Skakels maintained that because of the five-year statute of limitations for murder present in Connecticut in 1975, when Martha Moxley was murdered, the case should have never made it into the courtroom.

In a rambling 15,000 word article in *Atlantic Monthly*, RFK Jr., after saying that his cousin Michael Skakel was a cross between John Belushi, John Candy, and Curly from the Three Stooges, said, in part, "Even before the trial began, Sherman failed to make an interlocutory appeal based on Michael's strongest legal argument—that the court no longer had jurisdiction to hear a case against anyone who was accused of a murder that took place in 1975, because at the time the statute of limitations for murder was five years.

"Sherman says that he thought the right time for such an appeal was 'after the final judgment.' The whole point of an interlocutory appeal, however, as Hope Seeley, the lawyer in charge of Michael's appeal, recently explained, is not to have to wait for a final judgment—or endure the expense and emotion of a lengthy trial. An early victory in such an appeal would have deprived Sherman of the nationally publicized trial he expected would boost his career.

"By the time Sherman's behavior became worrisome to the Skakels, it was too late to change lawyers. Julie Skakel told me:

'We'd already paid Mickey a million dollars, and at that point it was too much.' The family had originally been persuaded, they said, by Sherman's charm and confidence, and especially by his frequent assurances before the trial that he was in control, and there was no chance Michael would be convicted."

Over the next 10 years, several appeals were rejected. But, in 2013, the Skakel/Kennedy cabal finally struck pay dirt. And again, it was Mickey Sherman who took the brunt of the blame for Michael Skakel's conviction.

The October 23, 2013 headline in the *New York Times* read:

Skakel Gets New Trial in '75 Killing of Teenager in Connecticut

The story read as follows:

A Connecticut judge on Wednesday ordered a new trial for Michael Skakel, a nephew of Ethel Kennedy who was convicted in 2002 of bludgeoning a neighbor with a golf club in 1975, saying his original lawyer had not represented him effectively.

The decision was another turn in a high-profile case that drew television crews and celebrity crime writers like Dominick Dunne. Judge Thomas A. Bishop set aside the murder conviction of Mr. Skakel, 53, who was sentenced to 20 years to life for killing the neighbor, Martha Moxley, when they were both teenagers in Greenwich.

The 136-page decision amounted to a review of the trial and an attack on the way Michael Sherman, the lawyer who represented Mr. Skakel before he was convicted, had handled his defense.

Judge Thomas A. Bishop said Mr. Sherman had been "in a myriad of ways ineffective" as Mr. Skakel's lawyer.

"The defense of a serious felony prosecution requires attention to detail, an investigation and a coherent plan of defense" that is capably executed, the judge wrote.

"Trial counsel's failures in each of these areas of representation were significant and, ultimately, fatal to a constitutionally adequate defense. As a consequence of trial counsel's failures as stated, the state procured a judgment of conviction that lacks reliability."

Then, Judge Bishop stated that there was just as much evidence that Tommy Skakel had killed Martha Moxley as there was for Michael Skakel being the killer.

Judge Bishop wrote:

Mr. Sherman had failed to argue that a brother of Mr. Skakel's, Thomas Skakel, who had fallen under suspicion at one point during the long investigation, could have killed Ms. Moxley; that he had not called a witness who could have supported Mr. Skakel's alibi; that he had not adequately contested one man's claim that Mr. Skakel had confessed the murder to him, even though there were witnesses available to challenge the claim; and that he had presented a weak closing argument without mentioning the concept of reasonable doubt, among other problems.

Robert Kennedy Jr. was all too eager to pile on Sherman.

"Mickey got distracted by the glitter and the glare," Kennedy Jr. said. "He was not lifting up every rock, and if he had, Michael Skakel would not be in prison for the last 10 years, and Mickey knows that."

What didn't help Sherman's reputation was that he was behind paying his federal taxes, with debts to the Internal Revenue Service that topped $1 million. In 2010, he was charged and pleaded guilty to "willfully failing to pay his federal income taxes." Documents in the tax case described Sherman as an, "inveterate spender, one who friends and family said in letters of support could be all too openhanded with gifts."

Sherman's license to practice law was suspended for a year, and he was sentenced to a year and a day in prison, spending about half of that at a minimum-security camp and a few months at a halfway house.

While replying to Robert Kennedy Jr.'s accusations, Sherman waxed philosophical.

"They pay people like me to win," Sherman said. "So, I don't blame them."

Judge Olson, in his decision to award Michael Skakel a new trial, did not approve bail for Michael Skakel, saying the question as to whether to grant bail belonged with the criminal court in Stamford, where Michael Skakel will be retried if the state decided to go forward with another prosecution.

On November 20, 2013, Skakel and his umpteenth attorney, Hubert Santos, appeared before Judge Gary White of Connecticut Superior Court in Stamford to request that Skakel be released on bail.

The prosecutors did not object to the setting of bail, just the amount. Santos suggested $500,000 as being fair; John Smirga, the lawyer for the state, recommended $2 million as proper bail. Among the factors he wanted the judge to consider were the brutality of the murder, and Skakel's resources, character, and mental condition.

Mr. Santos scoffed at the notion that his client would flee, even if he wanted to.

"His is the most recognized face in America," he said. "So he's not going anywhere."

Considering, that in 2013, Barack Obama was the President of the United States, Santos's statement boarded on the absurd.

Santos then lobbed a grenade at the prosecution team who had orchestrated Skakel's conviction in 2002.

"If the prosecution had found a homeless guy at a train station who claimed that Mr. Skakel confessed to the murder," Santos said. "He would have been on the stand in a New York minute."

After carefully considering both sides of the argument, Judge White set Skakel's bail at $1.2 million. He ordered him not to leave the state without permission, and to always wear a tracking device strapped to his ankle. Plus, he was ordered to have no contact with the Moxley family.

Skakel's brother, John, provided the bank checks to cover the bail.

At a news conference outside the courthouse, Dorthy Moxley, standing next to her son, John, expressed displeasure at the decision.

"We knew this day would come, so I wasn't completely destroyed," Mrs. Moxley said.

The forgotten man, until recently, Tommy Skakel, who was thrown under the bus in order to get a new trial for his brother, told the *New York Times*, "It's difficult to see how there could be any victory in this."

For whatever reason, the hearing as to whether Michael Skakel will face a new trial, or not, did not start until February 23, 2016. The crux of the matter before the court was whether Michael Skakel, because of the inadequacies of his attorney, Mickey Sherman, was deprived of his constitutional right to a fair trial.

Again, Skakel's lawyer, Hubert Santos, argued that maybe the wrong Skakel brother had been tried for murder.

"The weight of the evidence is that Tommy Skakel killed Martha Moxley," Santos told the six Connecticut Supreme Court justices hearing the case. "That's what Greenwich police believed for 10 years. Evidence that was presented during the 2013 petition for a new trial leads to the inescapable conclusion that the probable killer was Tommy Skakel, not Michael Skakel. Now, my client doesn't really want me to say that. It's his brother."

If it were true that Michael Skakel didn't want Santos to implicate his brother, Tommy, then all Michael had to do was tell his lawyer, Santos, whom his family was paying handsomely, to keep his yap shut and not to point the finger at someone else in the Skakel family. The truth is Michael and Tommy never got along, and, in fact, some people said they hated each other.

A longtime Greenwich resident who grew up with Michael and Tommy Skakel, said, "Cain and Able had nothing on those two. They were always fighting."

The general feeling in Greenwich is that if Michael Skakel had to pin Martha Moxley's murder on someone to save his own skin, his brother, Tommy, would be near the top of his list.

Susan E. Gill, who was part of the original prosecution team that successfully prosecuted Skakel in 2002, vehemently disagreed with Santo's assessment.

"This was far from a slipshod defense," Ms. Gill told the court. "This was a well-planned, well-thought-out defense. Mr. Sherman pulled in a lot of resources and presented a coherent defense."

Then, she added, "The state had no reason to believe Thomas Skakel was the murderer."

As for Tommy Skakel, he was nowhere to be found. Members of the press, and even Michael Skakel's lawyers, tried to contact Tommy by phone, email, and texting, but were not successful.

As he was leaving the court, Michael Skakel refused to speak to the press, but Robert Kennedy Jr. was all too happy to accommodate them.

"My cousin, Michael Skakel, is innocent," Kennedy Jr. said. "He's my cousin and I know he didn't kill Martha Moxley. He didn't get a fair trial, and he's not guilty."

Outside the courtroom, a weary Dorthy Moxley, now 83 years old, told the press, "I am sure Michael is the young man who swung the golf club. There's no doubt in my mind about that. I'll just be glad when it's over. I want him back in jail."

Chapter Fifty-Five

Where Do We Go From Here?

We now await the six Connecticut judges' decision as to whether or not Michael Skakel goes back to jail to finish out his sentence for his 2002 conviction for the murder of Martha Moxley. If the judges rule in Skakel's favor, then the state of Connecticut said they will retry Skakel at the cost of tens of millions of dollars to the Connecticut taxpayers. In that case, partly because of Skakel's bevy of high-priced attorneys, the prosecution will be working at a great disadvantage.

In the first Moxley murder trial, Prosecutor Benedict was brilliant in his presentation of his case in court; especially so in his closing arguments where he ultimately convinced the jury of Skakel's guilt. However, the prosecution shot their wad in the first trial, and unless new evidence comes to light 41 years after Martha's murder, they are stuck with presenting basically the same game plan in the second trial.

Knowing the prosecution's playbook in advance helps the defense formulate a new strategy in proving to the jury that Michael Skakel is not, beyond a reasonable doubt, guilty of the murder of Martha Moxley.

The only reason Michael Skakel is now a free man awaiting the six judges' decision is because of the Skakel family's unlimited cash resources. After Michael Skakel's conviction, the Skakels, digging deep into their piggy banks, hired the best attorneys money can buy. Hubert Santos, one of those attorneys, was able to convince the gullible Judge Thomas A. Bishop that if Mickey Sherman had done his job properly and turned the spotlight on Tommy Skakel as being Martha's killer, the 2002 jury, because of reasonable doubt, would not have been able to find Michael Skakel guilty of the murder of Martha Moxley.

My best guess is that the six Connecticut judges will ultimately rule in Skakel's favor. In the second trial, the prosecution, its hands tied because of no new evidence, will not be successful. Michael Skakel will walk out of court a free man, with no strings attached, while thumbing his nose at a court system that is tilted in favor of those with deep pockets.

Sadly, this has been the case since God found Cain guilty of the murder of his brother, Abel.

Now if Cain had the Skakel's money...

The End

Addendum

The headline on the June 5, 2016 *Greenwich Time* blared:

Skakel attorney does not anticipate Supreme Court decision until end of year

The story read, in part:

Attorneys for Michael Skakel are not expecting a decision soon from the highest court in Connecticut on whether he received an adequate legal defense when he was convicted in 2002 of killing Martha Moxley in Greenwich.

The decision by the state Supreme Court, which heard arguments in February, still could take months, said Skakel's attorney Stephan Seeger.

"There were some fairly beefy briefs, and of course, it's a large case. I expect the court will take some time before it responds. It wouldn't surprise me if it came at the end of the year, sometime in that time frame," said Seeger.

"We're waiting. And we prepare as much as we can for the trial," said Seeger. "We anticipate being in court in the near future, following up on some motions, in advance of that trial," said Seeger.

It seems that the gears that spin the wheels of justice for Martha Moxley, her mother, Dorthy, and her brother, John, are slowly grinding to a halt.

The Connecticut Supreme Court was given the case in October of 2013, but, for some inexplicable reason, they didn't begin the hearings until February 2016.

Now, the six judges, who will decide this case, are being besieged by, as attorney Seeger said, "fairly beefy briefs," from the Skakel legal team that will delay the judge's decision until, at best, the end of 2016, and in all likelihood into the year 2017.

This is another example that if you have enough money to pay an unlimited amount of expensive lawyers, and those lawyer use every trick in the book to delay legal proceedings, you could extend those proceedings almost indefinitely.

Or, in other words, "Money talks."

So sad, but so very true.

Mobspeak: One Man's Opinion

An aging knock-around street guy from New York with alleged mob connections, whom we'll call Nunzio, was recently overheard saying:

"So this happened in 1975, right? I don't care if it happened in 1975, or 1925, or 2025. But I'll tell you one thing for sure. If this had happened in a neighborhood controlled by good people, someone would have snatched this Skakel punk, and the cops would have found him butt-naked on Forty-Second Street and Times Square with a Ben Hogan driver blasted up his ass – club head first.

"Screw the Greenwich cops! No one in any of our neighborhoods ever said, 'Call the cops.' We handled things like this ourselves. And this is the way scumbags who put their hands on women are dealt with; especially someone who beats to death a poor defenseless 15-year-old girl. Fuhgeddaboudit!"

Re: RFK Jr.'s Book.

Just prior to the publication of this book, Robert Kennedy Jr.'s tome *Framed: Why Michael Skakel Spent Over a Decade in Prison For a Murder He Didn't Commit* went on sale to mixed reviews. I will not comment on the contents of his book except to say that RFK Jr. and I see eye to eye on virtually nothing concerning Michael Skakel's guilt in the Moxley murder.

However, people who rail against even the thought of RFK Jr. writing his book, in my opinion, are way off base.

I grew up in a tight-knit Italian-American family. My mother's family (she was the youngest of twelve children) grew up in Manhattan's Little Italy on the Lower East Side of Manhattan, and my father's family (he was the eldest of five children) grew up in an Italian-American section of Brooklyn – Bensonhurst.

If someone in my family was accused of committing a horrendous crime, and this relative told me they were totally innocent and were being railroaded, of course, I would do everything in my power to help them out; maybe even write a book trying to prove their innocence, if I believed that to be the case.

That's what people in tight-knit families, like mine and the Kennedys/Skakels do – circle the wagons when one of us is under fire for a specious crime, yes, even murder. Hell, especially murder.

I don't blame Robert Kennedy Jr. one bit for writing his book. My feeling is that he firmly believes his blood-cousin, Michael Skakel, is not guilty of the murder of Martha Moxley, and he is doing his best to clear his cousin's name and to make sure Skakel doesn't go back to prison.

I think RFK Jr. is dead wrong in his conviction that his cousin is innocent, but I applaud him for going to bat for one of his own.

Too many people abandon their blood in their time of need.

RFK Jr., who proved himself to be a stand-up guy, is not one of them.

Postscript

It all started for me around the year 2000 at a "yard sale" in Sarasota, Fl.

After living amongst the tenements on the Lower East Side of Manhattan in New York City for 48 years, a yard sale was an oddity to me. But my wife figured she could pick up a valuable item or two for almost nothing, so we stopped at a yard sale which took place in someone's driveway.

As my wife picked through the clothes, figurines, and appliances that were lined up on two long picnic tables, I fingered through a box of paperback books that was laying on the concrete floor. The one that caught my eye was a book featuring a pretty blond girl on the cover. Next to her face in red lettering was written, "WHO KILLED MARTHA MOXLEY?"

The title of the book was *Murder in Greenwich*, and was written by Mark Fuhrman. I knew Fuhrman's name from the infamous O.J. Simpson trial, but I didn't know he had become an author. (Unbeknownst to me, Fuhrman had also written a previous book on the Simpson trial called *Murder in Brentwood*.)

I paid 50 cents for the book, took it home, and put it on a huge shelf of books that I planned to read sometime before I perished.

Fast forward to November 2014 – 14 years later.

I don't know why, but I picked up *Murder in Greenwich* and started reading it. At this point in time, I didn't know that anyone in the Kennedy family was involved, and I thought a Skakel was a form of foreign currency. When I finished *Murder in Greenwich* the takeaway was that Fuhrman predicted that

Michael Skakel, then 15 years old, was the killer of 15-year-old Martha Moxley in Greenwich, Connecticut on October 30, 1975.

Before I sat down and started my research for *The Mysterious Murder of Martha Moxley: Did the Political and Financial Power of the Kennedy/Skakel Families Trump the Truth?*, I knew nothing about the case except what I had read in Fuhrman's book, in which the time period had ended in 1998.

On January 2, 2015, I began my research in earnest and continued it for one full year. On January 2, 2016, while still immersed in my research, I started writing this book in earnest.

I started this project with no preconceived notions. With 40 years of journalistic experience in my back pocket and more than 45 published books in the bank, I did my research by reading more than a dozen books on the subject of either the Moxley murder, or the Kennedy family's connection to the Skakels; in particular those concerning Ethel Skakel Kennedy, who married the former United States Attorney General, Robert F. Kennedy. I also pored over more than 200 magazine and newspaper articles available on the internet; especially the *Samford Advocate and Greenwich Times*, and *the New York Times*.

And like Nero Wolfe, I never left the comfort of my home.

I have not spoken to anyone connected with this case: none of the Moxleys, Skakels, or Kennedys and none of the detectives or law enforcement agencies involved. The only contact I had with anyone involved in the Moxley murder case was via several emails with journalist Len Levitt, who wrote: *Conviction: Solving the Moxley Murder* in 2006.

Still, all the quotes I needed and all the facts that are pertinent to this case were already available in print in one form or another. But it takes someone with decades of investigative journalism experience to piece together all the facts into a coherent and plausible narrative. Without tooting my horn too loud, I have that experience.

After researching the Moxley murder case, and while writing the first draft, I changed my opinion on certain things several times. In fact, after I finished the first draft, I threw it out (deleted it in computer terms), and started from scratch from a different perspective.

This book is my absolute honest opinion of what transpired in the Martha Moxley murder case.

Opinions are like noses; everybody has one. But I back mine up with facts, not other people's opinions.

And more importantly, unlike other books which have recently been written by people connected to the case in one way or another, I have no horse in this race. I let the chips fall where they may, and stated my conclusions, with no emotions involved.

Of course, I feel compassion for the Moxley family. They, along with their daughter, Martha, are the real victims here. No matter what anyone with a vested interest in this case may say.

Martha Moxley (1960 – 1975) – may she rest in peace.

* * * * *

I want to especially credit and thank Len Levitt, whose book, *Conviction: Solving the Moxley Murder* was instrumental in helping me lay out the sequence of events that eventually led to the 2002 conviction of Michael Skakel. I firmly believe that, without Levitt's book, I would have had difficulty making sense of a complicated and convoluted situation, in which certain newspapers refused to print pertinent news, certain investigators refused, despite the evidence, to change their mind as to who was and who was not the killer. And most importantly, certain prosecutors refused to prosecute when all available evidence screamed for a prosecution.

I also believe that without Levitt's dogged investigative journalism covering the Moxley murder case, which spanned almost two decades, there would have been scant chance, if any, that Michael Skakel would have ever been arrested, let alone convicted of the murder of Martha Moxley.

Chalk one up for the good guys.

A brief note from the author:

I hope you enjoyed reading "The Mysterious Murder of Martha Moxley" as much as I enjoyed writing it. If you want to be added to my email list, email me at **jbruno999@aol.com**.

I would also appreciate it if you wrote a short review on Amazon.com. My author's page, which has all my 36 books listed, is at:

http://www.amazon.com/Joe-Bruno/e/B0047OPD9S/ref=ntt_athr_dp_pel_pop_1

All reviews, positive and negative, will be greatly appreciated.

Bibliography

Buckley, William. *The Syracuse Post Standard.* September 29, 1966.

Idaho Statesman. September 26, 1966.

Connecticut Law Tribune, February 2001.

Dumas, Timothy. *Greentown.* Arcade Publishing 1998.

Dunne, Dominick. A Season in Purgatory. Crown Publishers. 1993.

Dunne, Dominick. *Justice.* Crown Publishers. 2001.

Fuhrman, Mark. *Murder in Greenwich.* Harper Collins. 1999.

Greenwich Times, Various Articles.

Levitt, Leonard. NYPD Confidential. 1993.

Levitt, Leonard. *Conviction: Solving the Moxley Murder.* ReganBooks. 2006.

Leamer, Laurence (2011-02-22). *The Kennedy Men: 1901-1963* (Kindle Locations 5312-5313). HarperCollins. Kindle Edition.

Leamer, Laurence. *The Kennedy Women.* Villard Books. 1994.

Leslie Yager. *Norwalk Patch.* December 23, 2013.

Police Chief Magazine. March 2016.

The Post Standard. William F. Buckley. September 29, 1966.

New York Herald-Tribune. Red Smith. September 29 1966.

Oppenheimer, Jerry. *RFK Jr.* St. Martin's Press. 2015.

Oppenheimer, Jerry. *The Other Mrs. Kennedy.* St. Martin's Press. 1994.

Scott, Gini Graham. *Homicide by the Rich and Famous: A Century of Prominent Killers.* Greenwood Publishing Group. 2005

The New York Times. Various editions.

UnsolvedMysteries.com

Printed in Great Britain
by Amazon